# ZOO●●

# ZO●● 10

# 09 / 2001

Book cover:
(front)
Farrokh Madon/Ng Tian It
at Saatchi & Saatchi, Singapore
Changi Airport *Movie Theatre*

(back)
J. Walter Thompson, Melbourne:
Australian Red Cross *Camouflage*

Inside front:
Blue Source
Fatboy Slim *Sunset (Bird of Prey)*

Marcelo Krasilcic
For *Dazed & Confused*
May 2001
Courtesy: Marcelo Krasilcic;
h.a.1, London

Inside back:
Jens Passoth
Courtesy: Photography Now,
Berlin

**ZOO**
245 Old Marylebone Road
London NW1 5QT
UK

t [44 20] 7258 6900
f [44 20] 7258 6901

www.zooworld.net

**Publisher & Editorial Director**
Will Gompertz
will.gompertz@zooworld.net
**Editor**
Eliza Williams
eliza.williams@zooworld.net
**Advertising Editor**
Becky Fryer
becky.fryer@zooworld.net
**Architecture Editor**
Steve Hare
steve.hare@zooworld.net

**Art + Photography Editor**
Eliza Williams
eliza.williams@zooworld.net
**Design Editor**
Liz Brown
liz.brown@zooworld.net
**Moving Image Editor**
Katrina Dodd
katrina.dodd@zooworld.net
**Design + Art Direction**
James Goggin/Practise
james@practise.co.uk
Louise Jennings/Burnt
louise@burnt.net
**Production Director**
Liz Brown
liz.brown@zooworld.net
**Production Assistant**
Emma Tilley
emma.tilley@zooworld.net
**Publisher**
Sibylle Koehler
sibylle.koehler@zooworld.net

**Business Development**
Rachel Macrae
rachel.macrae@zooworld.net
**Publishing Assistant**
Tanya Cilliers
tanya.cilliers@zooworld.net
**Group Publisher**
James Booth-Clibborn
james.boothclibborn@zooworld.net
**Commercial Director**
Alex West
alex.west@zooworld.net
**DVD Video Compression/**
**DVD Authoring**
Metropolis, London
dvd@metropolis-group.co.uk
**DVD Duplication**
Technicolor, Cwmbran, Wales
**Printed by**
The Friary Press
sales@friary.co.uk
**Paper**
Courtesy of Sappi

# INTRODUCTION:

Berlin continues to adapt triumphantly to huge architectural and cultural changes and developments, and in this issue our lead feature looks at the excellent creative work that is being produced in these changing times, including work by designers, artists, photographers, film-makers, architects and advertising agencies (p. 16).

In exclusive artwork features produced for this edition of ZOO, advertising agency KesselsKramer addresses the issue of the Euro (p. 68); while Dutch fashion photographer Edel Verzijl returns to the school gym (albeit a more glamorous one than most of us would remember on p. 56); and graphic designer Ben Drury shouts 'Oi London!' (p. 48).

Our showcase contains the usual collection of outstanding creative work, including in-depth features on Italian painter Margherita Manzelli (p. 88); the recent Swedish 'Bo01 City of Tomorrow' architecture exhibition (p. 130); a series of work by photographer Martina Hoogland Ivanow (p. 206); the work of creative communication agency Blue Source (p. 232); three directors from Aardman, the acclaimed animation company (p. 284); Åbäke, the London-based design group (p. 160); four creative advertising teams in Australasia (p. 338); and Magnum Photos' recent exploration of the XVIII district in Paris (p. 354). Blue Source and Aardman's work is also profiled in detail on the ZOO DVD, which provides unique access to moving-image work by artists, designers, and architects; as well as over an hour of commercials and pop promos.

Finally, we unfortunately have to say a sad goodbye to James Goggin. James has been ZOO's art director and designer for this year, and was instrumental in developing ZOO's new look, but is moving to New Zealand to continue his design work there.

# CONTENTS ZOO 10

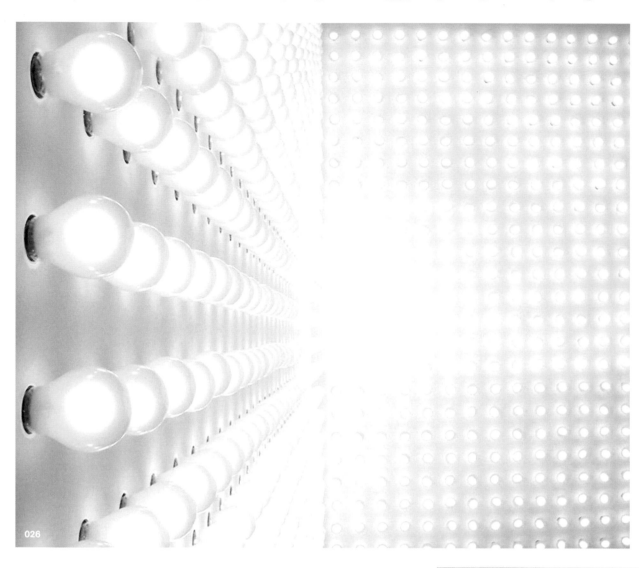

026

161

136

→

# CONTENTS ZOO 10

→

180

223

114

338

237

137

226

# CONTENTS ZOO 10

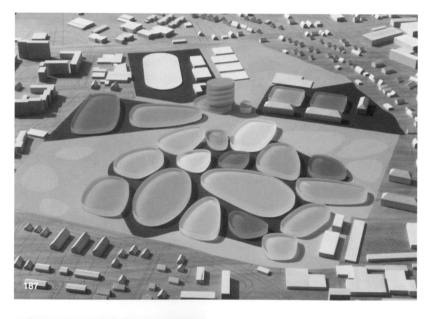

www.youwontbelievewhatthiscando.com

**Introducing Painter 7.** Overflowing with creative tools, it will seamlessly take your work to places you have only dreamed of. Adobe® Photoshop® compatible, Painter 7 is one in a line of innovative procreate™ products designed for creative professionals. Take yourself to the website above for a peek at the possibilities.

procreate™

www.adobe.co.uk

## Adobe GoLive.
### Plays well on the web. Plays well with others.

It's the ultimate head rush. Develop your ideas from concept to final production with Adobe® GoLive™ software. GoLive uses the familiar Adobe interface, so you can design and deliver finished sites in no time. What's more, it works seamlessly with programs you already know, like Adobe Photoshop,® Illustrator,® and LiveMotion.™ With our new 360Code™ feature, your source code stays tight, clean and unaltered. And of course, GoLive is available for both Windows® and Macintosh® platforms. Now that's hardcore. See for yourself at **www.adobe.co.uk**

Inspiration becomes reality.™     Adobe

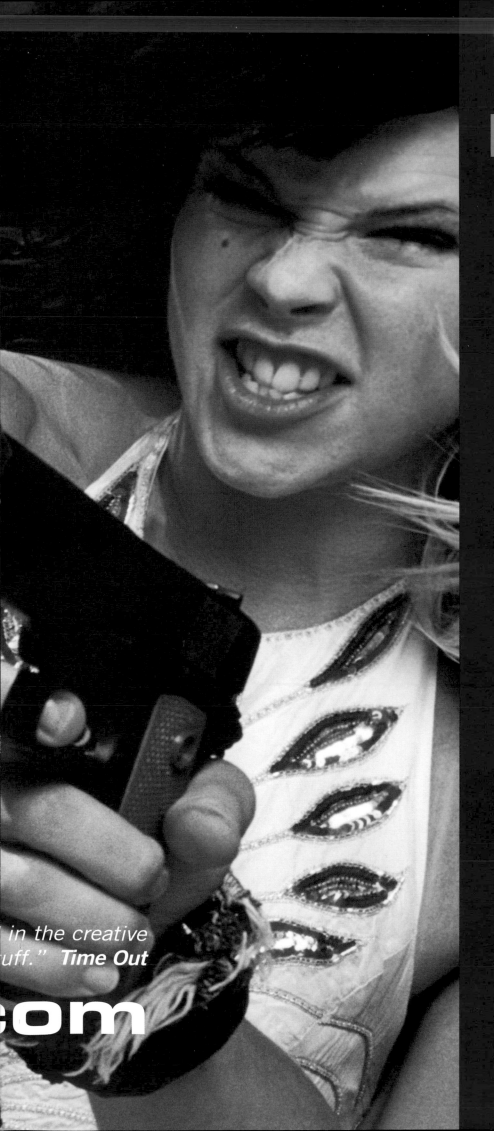

**Metropolis Presents:**

Creative Magic for DVD

5.1 Surround Mix-to-Picture Studio
5.1 Surround Audio Mastering Studio
Award-winning Producers
Creative Services and Direction
Audio & Video Encoding
DVD Authoring & Emulation
(DVD-Video, DVD-Audio and DVD-ROM)
DVD-R & DLT Output

*Metropolis DVD - where technical excellence is driven by creative innovation*
The Power House, 70 Chiswick High Road, London W4 1SY
Telephone, 020 8742 1111. Fax, 020 8742 3777

**BERLIN:** AIMAQ–RAPP–STOLL
SCHOLZ & FRIENDS/TBWA B
/ARCHIMATION/ZVI HECKEF
GEWERS KUHN & KUHN/SAU
BRAUN ARCHITECKTEN/PHIL
GREBERT/NORMAN HAFEZI/
/WERNER AISSLINGER/MOC
BERTA FISCHER/CHRISTIAN
ALLAMODA/THOMAS KIESEW
CARSTEN HOLLER/DANIEL P
/CHRISTOPH KELLER/JENS
LES SCHLIESSER/MANFRED

/MELLE, PUFE, W,H,S/
RLIN/TOCHTER + SOHNE
/DANIEL LIBESKIND/
RBRUCH HUTTON/MARK
STOLZL/JOHANNES
ORK UNSTABLE MEDIA OST
U/METADESIGN/SHIFT!/
ANKOWSKI/BETTINA
TTER/ANTON HENNING/
LUMM/SABINE HORNIG
ASSOTH/KAI SCHIEMENZ/
ERNICE/PATRICK VOIGT

# BERLIN

**David Linderman**

Creative Partner

fork unstable media ost, Berlin

My first visit to Berlin was in 1991. East Berlin was still a grey wasteland of sooty empty blocks, and, like a lot of Americans, I acknowledged nearly every evidence of military engagement left in the streets and broken façades in a brief verbal confirmation of awe. It was darkly inspiring to stumble into a Hinterhof that looked like a set for *Saving Private Ryan*. The grandeur of really-old-economy competed for attention next to bludgeoned prefab highrises, Red Army trophies, and monuments to forgotten heroes. Today, crystal corporate palaces are erupting from post-Wall emptiness and in that grey wasteland continues a couple of centuries of Darwinistic city planning.

The story of post-Wall Berlin starts out something like a neo-praxis Utopia of illegal clubs, occupied housing and Generation-X entrepreneuralism, an anarchic orgy founded on optimism and ingenuity and a whole lot of room — not on money or inspired government. The story is probably not that far-fetched but it seems more and more historical and not nearly as Marxist nowadays.

Since the War, Berlin has never had a booming economy and surprisingly, the New Berlin is, at least for now, actually getting smaller. Even after moving the German capital to the former island city, nearly every year since 1993 there has been a small but steady decrease in population. Berlin-Mitte, one of the most talked about neighbourhoods in town, had nearly three per cent fewer residents between 1999 and 2000. As Eastern flats are renovated to Western standards complete with adjusted rent (still nearly half that of other German cities), unemployment hovers around 12 per cent. In some Eastern neighbourhoods it's as high as 17 per cent.

So where's the boom? Evidently more in the media and the hearts of us newbies than here at home. Until recently, Berlin hasn't been taken seriously and first and foremost by fellow Germans for that very reason. Money *fehlt*.

That's changing. It's hard not to be proud of Berlin. After nearly eight years of living in Germany in three other cities, my previous homes impressed me more with their rock-steady Deutschness and outright provinciality than their ability to attract and inspire youth culture (or to have much of one to begin with). A large part of the city image comes from an active do-it-yourself community of compulsive location-scouters, club owners and economically challenged artists, musicians and designers turning industrial ghettos into hip sensations on a shoestring budget. Moving from space to space in an obsessive drive to outdo their last location, avoid state attention or simply find a cheap rent, they leave behind them a trail of freelance collectives, startup agencies and real-estate speculation. For a lot of disillusioned big-city refugees, it's hard to believe that you can still find spacious flats on the East side for $400 a month. In fact, nowadays it might be the only way that a lot of people can afford to start their own business, create a studio or meet a lot of others doing exactly that.

The most inspiring reunification of East and West comes from these young locals bonded through nightlife and a traditional lack of interest in the rest of Germany. As a lot of Ur-Berliner are moving out, a lot of newbies are moving East. Berlin epitomises unfettered speculation divorced from long-term cultural significance not because of some masterplan or an inspired democracy but explicitly the lack of both. The city is an East-meets-West love story in a rough urban frontier shaped by a burgeoning youth culture. Yet, as the city tries to cash-in on this very hype, it is more or less ignoring the needs of the real movers and shakers behind the dark paradise in a stubborn German sensitivity for the way-things-should-be, not the way they happen naturally.

Like any growing business, a little *Ordnung muss sein*. The city, it seems, would like to clean up before the real party starts, clamping down on the less-than-legal demonstrations formerly known as parties, occupied housing and the most popular city hubs. To cover almost a decade of mismanagement and no-plan, the city sells property and the cultural landmarks on it to developers. After a few years of gestation, what was formerly a throbbing nightlife becomes empty office space and a hermetically still restaurant/café/bar for tourists. If they come.

Despite clear signs of gentrification, the symptoms are for now confined to a few small hubs of slickness surrounded by blocks and blocks of what in other cities might be deemed ruins — if you want to judge a book by its cover.

Maybe the kids are right. Small agencies, studios and artists that made a name for themselves and the city did it through a lot of perseverance and ingenuity together with some healthy nights of release. Now approaching a similar coolness that grunge and slackers gave Seattle, Berlin is seeing the bigger fish move in to get a piece of the action. Still, it's the local culture behind Berlin's attractiveness and this preserves the charm of the city's history by reoccupying old fortresses once filled by factories, simultaneously planting seeds for new neighbourhoods and attracting more young people doing the same. In turn, this produces more babies, hair salons and chic new restaurants. It's a vicious cycle with hopefully no end. A wet dream for politicians and investors if they wouldn't keep waking up.

New York, London and Paris may have become part of our collective memory through film, TV, music, and magazines, but Berlin is a metropolitan experiment in continuum and if you're already here you probably have a interest in shaping it, because you still can. It is a mixed marriage between old-Eastern socialism and new-economy come-late speculation; on its way from a beautifully broken yet insignificant urban Moloch to becoming perhaps synonymous with a new Germany; a 1968-generation of politicians and a modest quality of living. If you believe the hype.

Aimaq-Rapp-Stolle

01
**Title** *Website*
**Client** Heineken
**Agency** Aimaq-Rapp-Stolle;
Baudhaus New Media

02
**Title** *Mirror*
**Client** Heineken
**Production** Hope & Glory, Berlin
**Director** Stephan Hadjah

03
**Title** *Battle of
the Neighbourhoods*
**Client** Nike
**Illustration** Sinead Madden

04
**Title** *What's next*
**Client** *IQ* magazine

**Film Delux** ↘ ●   **Markenfilm** ↘ ●

**01, 02**
**Title** *Frisbee; Subway*
**Client** Stella Musicals
**Agency** Jung von Matt, Hamburg
**Production** Film Delux, Berlin
**Director** Stephan Hadjam

**03**
**Title** *Hotel*
**Client** e-Sixt
**Agency** Jung von Matt, Hamburg
**Production** Markenfilm, Berlin
**Director** Marc Schölermann

**Melle, Pufe, W,H,S:**

**Client** youwant.com
**Illustration** Ute Kuehn

SECOND-HAND-CENTER

## Scholz & Friends

**01**
**Title** *Strong Locks*
**Client** Bicycles AG

**02**
**Title** *ON-Computing*
**Client** Apple Service

**04**
**Title** *Attention Doorframe*
**Client** Riccardo Cartillone

01

02

## Töchter + Söhne

01
**Client** Kilroy Travels

02, 03
**Title** Avant-garde poster
**Client** Self-Promotion

03

## Archimation

**Project** Lehrter Bahnhof,
Berlin proposals
**Architect** von Gerkan, Marg und
Partner, Berlin
**Visualisation** © Archimation,
Berlin; for Tishman
Speyer Properties

**Project** Museum of Contemporary
Art + Moving Image Centre,
Sydney
**Architect** sauerbruch hutton
architects, Berlin/London
**Visualisation**
© Archimation, Berlin

## Zvi Hecker

**Project** Museum of Modern Art,
Bolzano, Italy; competition
entry

## Daniel Libeskind

**Project** Imperial War, Museum,
Manchester (01); Summer
Pavilion; Serpentine Gallery,
London (02); *Tristan und Isolde*,
Saarbrücken (03)
**Photography** Chris Duisberg (01);
Frank Knight (02); Torsten
Seidel (03)

## Gewers Kühn & Kühn
Architects

**Preliminary design** Becker Gewers
Kühn & Kühn
**Project** Ostbahnhof: Railway Station
of the Future, Berlin (01);
DaimlerChrysler Aerospace – MTU
Maintenance Customer and Training
Centre, Berlin-Brandenburg (02)
**Client** Deutsche Bahn AG,
WestProject & Consult (02)

**Grüntuch Ernst
Architekten BDA Projects**

**Project** Office and flats building
at the Hackescher Markt in
Berlin
**Photography** © Mads Mogensen,
Soprabolzano, Italy

**Project** Office building on the
harbour edge in Neumühlen,
Hamburg
**Photography** © Jörg Hempel,
Aachen, Germany; © Christian
Gahl, Berlin

**Project** Architectur and Design
School in Wismar, Germany
**Photography** © Christoph Gebler,
Hamburg

## sauerbruch hutton architects

**01, 02**
**Project** Experimental Factory,
Magdeburg
**Photography** © Gerrit Engel,
Munich

**03**
**Project** Zumtobel Staff
Showroom, Berlin
**Photography** © Bitter + Bredt
Fotografie, Berlin

## Barkow Leibinger
## Architekten

**01, 02, 03**
**Project** Biosphere and Flower
Pavilion, Potsdam, Germany

**04**
**Project** HAAS-Laser Factory,
Schramberg, Germany
**All photography** © Margherita
Spiluttini, Vienna

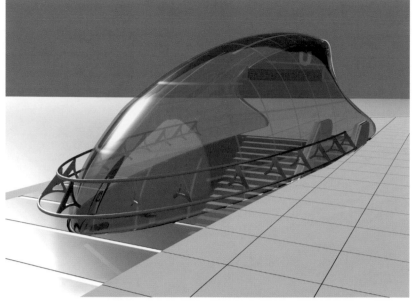

## Mark Braun Architeckten

**Project** Urbanliving; Concept study of combined loft/car project
**CAD render** Bünck + Fehse, Berlin

**Project** Subway Stations, Vienna; Europe-wide competition
**Architect** Mark Braun Architekten BDA RIBA, Berlin in joint venture with Novotny Mähner Assoziierte, Berlin
**CAD render** Novotny Mähner Assoziierte, Berlin

## Raumlabor

**Project** Moritzplatz, Berlin
Three sequences of public space
scene 3: innercityforestliving

**Zoran Bihac**

*Links 2-3-4* promo for Rammstein
**Production** Flaming Star, Stuttgart; Trigger Happy Productions, Berlin
**Record company** Motor Music, Hamburg

**Philip Stölzl, Johannes Grebert**

*Rock 'n' Roll Übermensch* promo for Die Ärzte
**Production** Department M, Berlin
**Record company** Hot Action Records, Germany

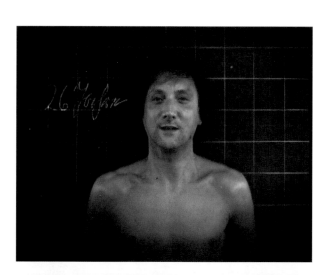
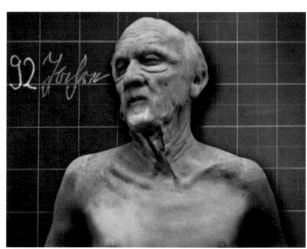

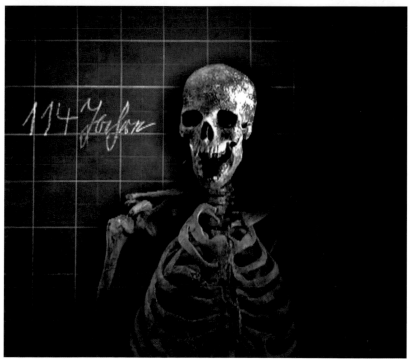

**Philip Stölzl, Johannes Grebert**

*Nimm Mich Mit* promo for Marius Müller-Westernhagen
**Production** Department M, Berlin
**Record company** WEA

Matthias Freier

*Sag Mir Wo* promo for Clueso
**Production** Trigger Happy
Productions, Berlin
**Record company** Four Music
Productions, Stuttgart

Norman Hafezi

*Lost and Blown Away* promo for
Novastar
**Production** Department M, Berlin
**Record company** Warner Music
Benelux

fork unstable media ost

→

**01**
**Designer** David Linderman
**Title** *Seriously* spread for *032*
magazine
**Date** September 2000

**02**
**Designer** Christopher Stoll,
David Linderman, Farid Rivas,
Jeremy Abbett, Leo Lass
**Title** 4rk propaganda:
Stickerwar III
**Date** November 2000

**03**
**Designer** David Linderman,
Leo Lass
**Title** 4rk de Verano
**Date** August 2000

**04**
**Designer** David Linderman, Farid
Rivas, Heimo Wenzel, Klaus
Voltmer, Leo Lass
**Title** Künstlerhaus Vienna video
installation
**Date** June 2001

Marcus Bauer

*Rhapszódia in Fish Minor* short film

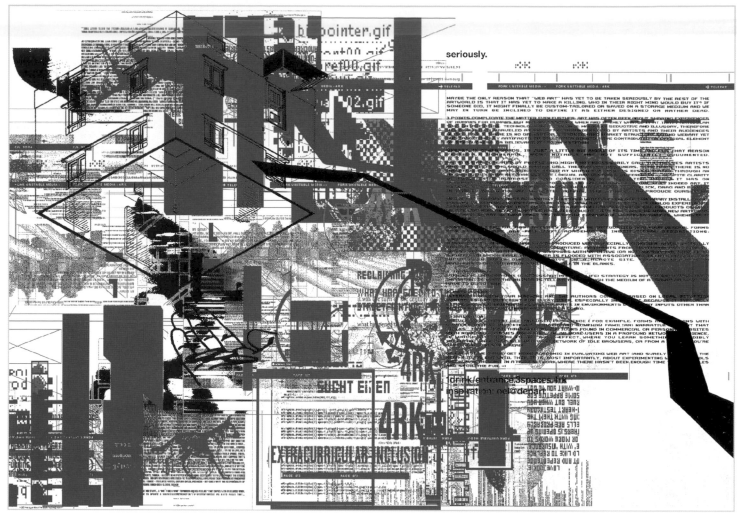

01

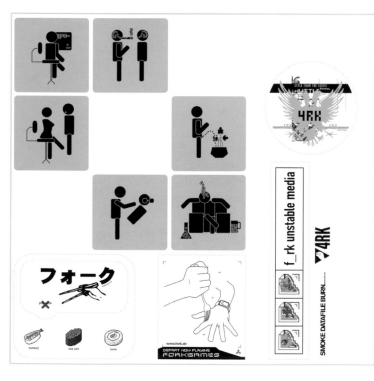

02

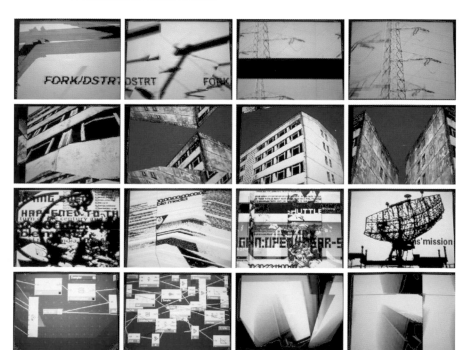

MetaDesign

**Designer** MetaDesign
**Title** Stylepark
**Date** March 2001

01

Shift!

01
**Designers** Anja Lutz, CX Huth at
Shift!
**Title** Videoproject,
Lichtbildvortrag
**Date** 2001

02
**Title** Berlin (collaborative
design experiment)
**Designers** Anja Lutz, Dorothee
Mahnkopf, Rik Bas Backer,
Martijn Oostra, Lawrence
Thompson, Neil Gardiner, Lewis
Berman, Richard Cleall-Harding,
Peter Green at Shift!
**Date** 1998

02

italienische nacht

11. – 13.05. › 20h

Italienische Nacht › 400ASA | von › Ödön von Horváth | Regie › Samuel Schwarz | Bühnenbild › Chantal Wuhrmann | Dramaturgie › Lukas Bärfuss |
Kostüme › Esther Schmid, Nic Tellein | Licht › Matthias Keller | Musik › Frank Heierli
mit › Fabian Krüger, Werner Schöni, Wanda Vyslouzilova, Catriona Güggenbühl, Grazia Pergoletti, Ted Gaier, Kaspar Weiss, Ingo Heise,
Fabienne Hadorn, Philipp Stengele, Verena Weiss, Jo Stone, Daniela Mitidieri und Gäste
sophiensæle › Sophienstraße 18 | Berlin-Mitte | Kartentelefon 030 283 52 66

von ödön von horváth

400ASA › SOPHIENSÆLE

PRO HELVETIA    tip    die tageszeitung    RADIO multikulti

## Ständige Vertretung

**Designers** Ständige Vertregung
**Title** Italian Night (one of a
series of posters for the
sophiensæle theatre Berlin)
**Date** May 2001

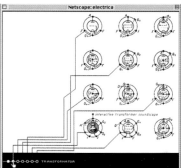

## skop

**Designers** Gundula Markeffsky,
Peter Mühlfriedel, Leonard
Chaumann at skop
**Title** Electrica — a journey into
electric sound
**Date** September 1999

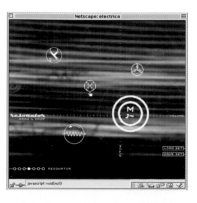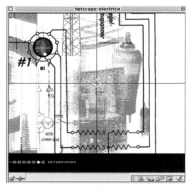

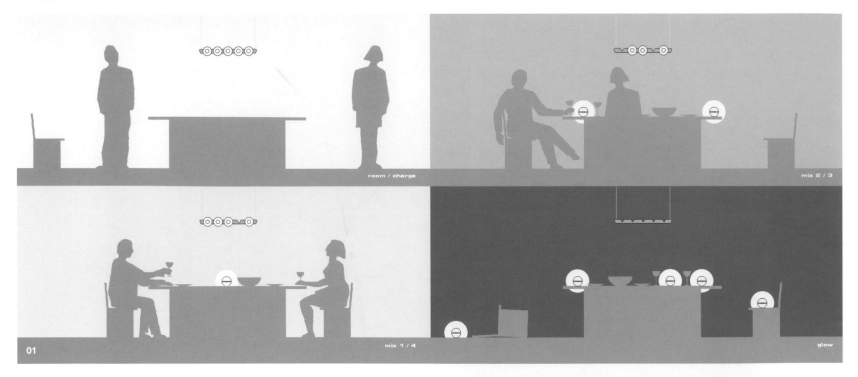

## Werner Aisslinger

**03**
**Title** Gel lounge chair for Cappellini
**Date** January 2001

## Designbüro...Adam und Harborth

**01**
**Title** take-away lights
**Date** January 2001

**02**
**Title** Ern carpet pictograms
**Date** October 2000

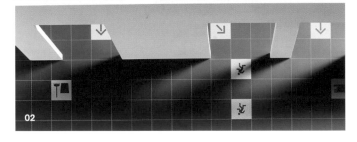

## Stefan Thiel

**04**
*Kobe*
2000-01
Cut-out drawing
100 x 100 cm
**Courtesy** griedervonputtkamer Galerie, Berlin

*Self-portrait*
2001
Wall painting
**Photograph** © Menga von Sprecher, Zurich
**Courtesy** Galerie Zürcher, Paris

## Moccu

**Title** www.moccu.com
**Designers** Heiko Freier, Christoph Petersen, Jens Schmidt, Thomas Walter, Björn Zaske
**Date** January 2001

## Andreas Siekman

*Zoom*
1999
Felt-tip, acrylic, watercolour
on paper
**Courtesy** Galerie Barbara
Weiss, Berlin

## Berta Fischer

2001
Installation: Galerie Giti
Nourbakhsch, Berlin
**Courtesy** Galerie Giti
Nourbakhsch, Berlin

## Mathilde ter Heijne

**01**
*Ne me quitte pas,* 2000
Sound installation
Doll, clothes, CD-player, radio
**Courtesy** Arndt & Partner, Berlin

## Katharina Schmidt

**02**
*Diamanten-Tapete,* 2000
Dimensions variable
*Er liebt mich nicht, er liebt mich... (12)*
2000
Oil on canvas, 170 x 140 cm
**Courtesy** Galerie M + R Fricke,
Berlin

## Christian Jankowski

**03**
*The Matrix Effect* , 2000,
Janine Antoni
C-Print, 47 x 55.8 cm
**Courtesy** Galerie M + R Fricke,
Berlin

## Henrik Oleson

**04**
*Homosexual Rights around the World*
2000
Publication, A4 booklet,
1500 copies
*Authority / Shoe, 2000*
Size 41 shoe
Installation: Klosterfelde,
Berlin (2000)
**Courtesy** Klosterfelde

## (e) Twin Gabriel

*Lemonade From Africa*
1996
Installation: Neuer
Berliner Kunstverein
**Courtesy** Galerie Barbara
Thumm, Berlin

## Heike Baranowsky

*Parallax*
1999
Video, double projection
700 x 280 cm
**Courtesy** Galerie Barbara
Weiss, Berlin

01

02

03

04

**Albrecht Schäfer**

*Berlin Alexanderplatz*
*Scenario 1.1*
2001
Lambda colour print, plexiglas
115 x 160 cm
**Courtesy** Galerie Kamm, Berlin

**Ulrike Feser**

*Tourist (Auto)*
2001
Lambda Print
30 x 45 cm, framed 52 x 62 cm
**Courtesy** Galerie Kamm, Berlin

**Andrej Glusgold**

**Courtesy** Photography Now, Berlin

**Bettina Allamoda**

*ready to wear colonial*
2001
Installation: Galerie Barbara Thumm, Berlin
**Courtesy** Galerie Barbara Thumm

**Thomas Kiesewetter**

**Courtesy** Galerie Neu, Berlin

**Anton Henning**

*Interieur No 85*
2001
Oil on canvas
189 x 220 cm
**Photograph** Jörg von Bruchhausen
**Courtesy** Galerie
Wohnmaschine, Berlin

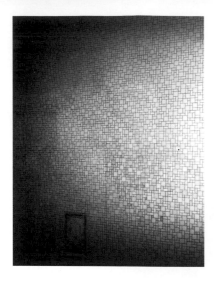

**Birgit Meixner**

*Manuel*
2001

**Robert Lucander**

*Ich hatte nichts davon, mich an die
Geschichte von jemand anderen
anzuhängen*
2001
Coloured pencil, acrylic on wood
120 x 170 cm
**Courtesy** Contemporary Fine
Arts, Berlin
**Photograph** Jochen Littkemann,
Berlin

**Paschutan Buzari**

From *Moderne Ultramoderne* series
2001

## Carsten Höller

**01**
*Lightwall*
2001
**Courtesy** Schipper + Krome,
Berlin

## Christiane Haid

**02**
**Courtesy** Photography Now, Berlin

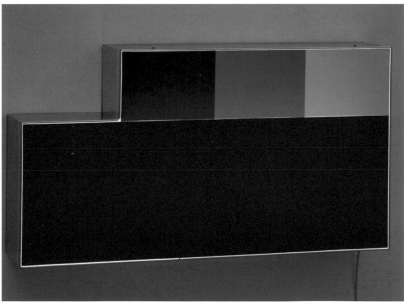

## Daniel Pflumm

*Untitled*
2000
Lightbox
85.5 x 45 x 15 cm
Edition of 5
**Courtesy** Galerie Neu, Berlin

## Christian Flamm

*Untitled*
2001
Papercut
55 x 70 cm
**Courtesy** Galerie Neu, Berlin

## Sabine Hornig

*Window*
Photograph
**Courtesy** Galerie Barbara
Thumm, Berlin

## Ronald Dick

**Courtesy** Photography Now, Berlin

## Erik Göngrich

Plastic bags filled with foam,
used in:
*Sitting Abroad,* Berlin, 2000
*Representation of...,* Berlin, 1999
*Interface Rue de Chevaleret*, Paris,
1999
**Courtesy** Erik Göngrich

## Erik Schmidt

*Timecode XIV*
2001
Gloss drawing pen on
fashion magazine
30 x 23 cm
**Courtesy** carlier | gebauer,
Berlin

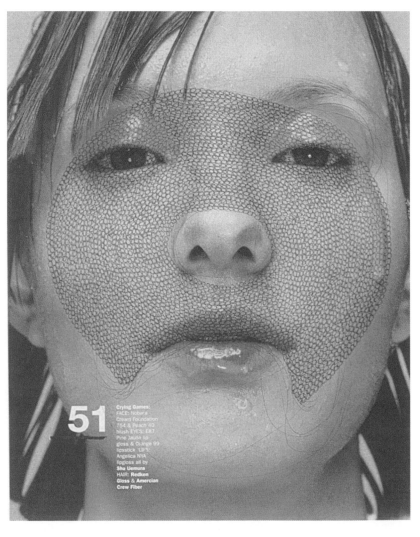

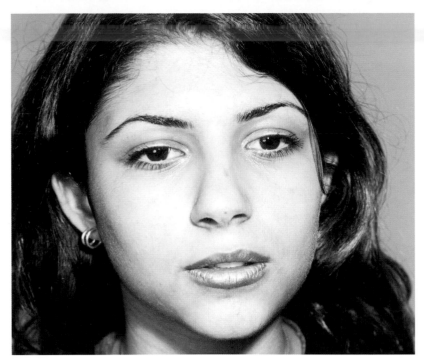

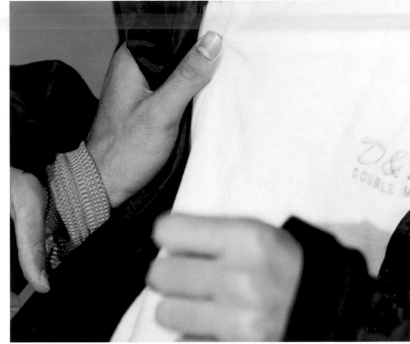

**Sabine Schründer**

*sevda*
Images from a slide-installation
**Courtesy** Sabine Schründer;
Photography Now, Berlin

**Christoph Keller**

*Bahnhof Friedrichstrasse*
**Courtesy** Schipper + Krome,
Berlin

**Florian Zeyfang**

*DV MEANS DZIGA VERTOV*
*(L.A.nd version)*
2001
**Courtesy** Florian Zeyfang

**Florian Merkel**

*Venus*
1998
131 x 100 cm
**Courtesy** Galerie
Wohnmaschine, Berlin

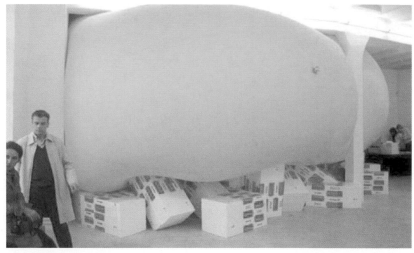

## Hans Hemmert

*O.T. (gelbe Skulptur passend zu*
*Galerieraum und 39 Styroporblöcken)*
2000
Latex balloon
3.6 x 9 x 6 m
Exhibition: Galerie Rehbehn,
Cologne
**Courtesy** carlier | gebauer,
Berlin

## Heiko Laschitzki

**Courtesy** Photography Now, Berlin

## Jens Passoth

**Courtesy** Photography Now, Berlin

## Kai Schiemenz

*vacuum games 2*
2001
Silkscreen on Paper
110 x 66 cm
**Courtesy** Koch und
Kesslau, Berlin

## Les Schliesser

Film still from *Gap Stories II*
2001
Installation: griedervonputtkamer Galerie, Berlin
**Courtesy** griedervonputtkamer Galerie

## Katharina Wulff

*Situation*
2000
Oil on canvas
50 x 70 cm
**Courtesy** Galerie Neu, Berlin

**M Joo**

**Courtesy** Photography Now, Berlin

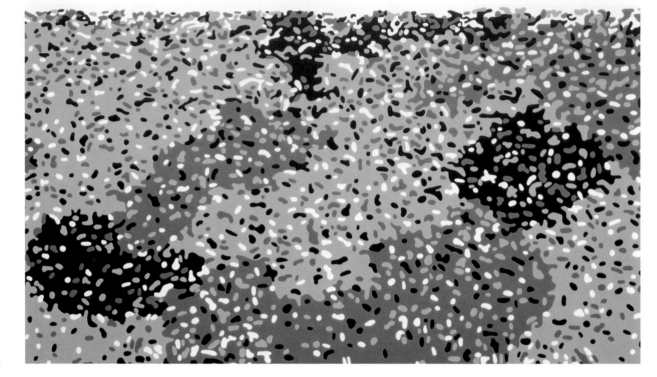

**Matten Vogel**

*Sicher ist Sicher, trendy
version* (Detail)
2000
Acrylic on canvas
130 x 120 cm
**Photograph** Lutz Bertram
**Courtesy** Kuckei + Kuckei, Berlin

**Manfred Pernice**

*Untitled,* 2000
Painted wood
140 x 70 x 70 cm
**Courtesy** Galerie Neu, Berlin

**Nikolaus Geyer**

**Courtesy** Photography Now, Berlin

## Peter Pommerer

*Die Pest der Phantasmen*
2000
Wall drawing
Exhibition: Galerie Gebauer,
Berlin (2000)
**Courtesy**
carlier | gebauer, Berlin

## Nora Bibel

*Cemja*
**Courtesy** Nora Bibel; Photography
now, Berlin

## Oliver van den Berg and Victor Kégli

*Dose*
2000
Tarpaulin, steel
180 x 200 cm
**Photograph** Oliver van
den Berg, Berlin
**Courtesy** Kuckei +
Kuckei, Berlin

## Patrick Voigt

**Courtesy** Photography Now, Berlin

# BEN DRURY: EXPERIMENTS W

H 3D TYPOGRAPHY

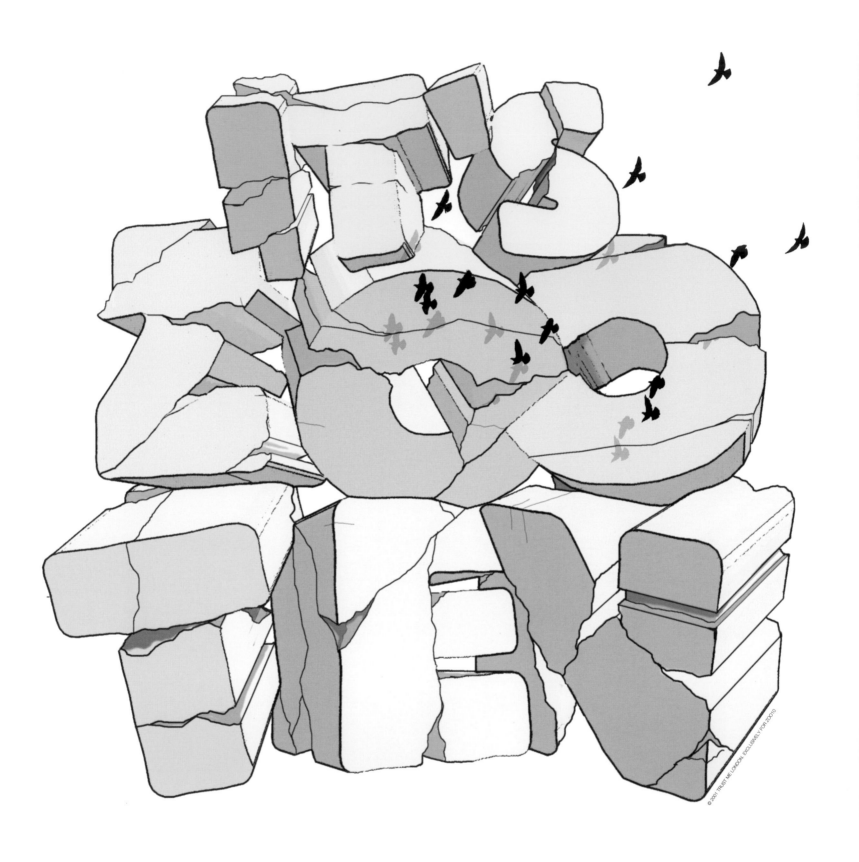

URAGE

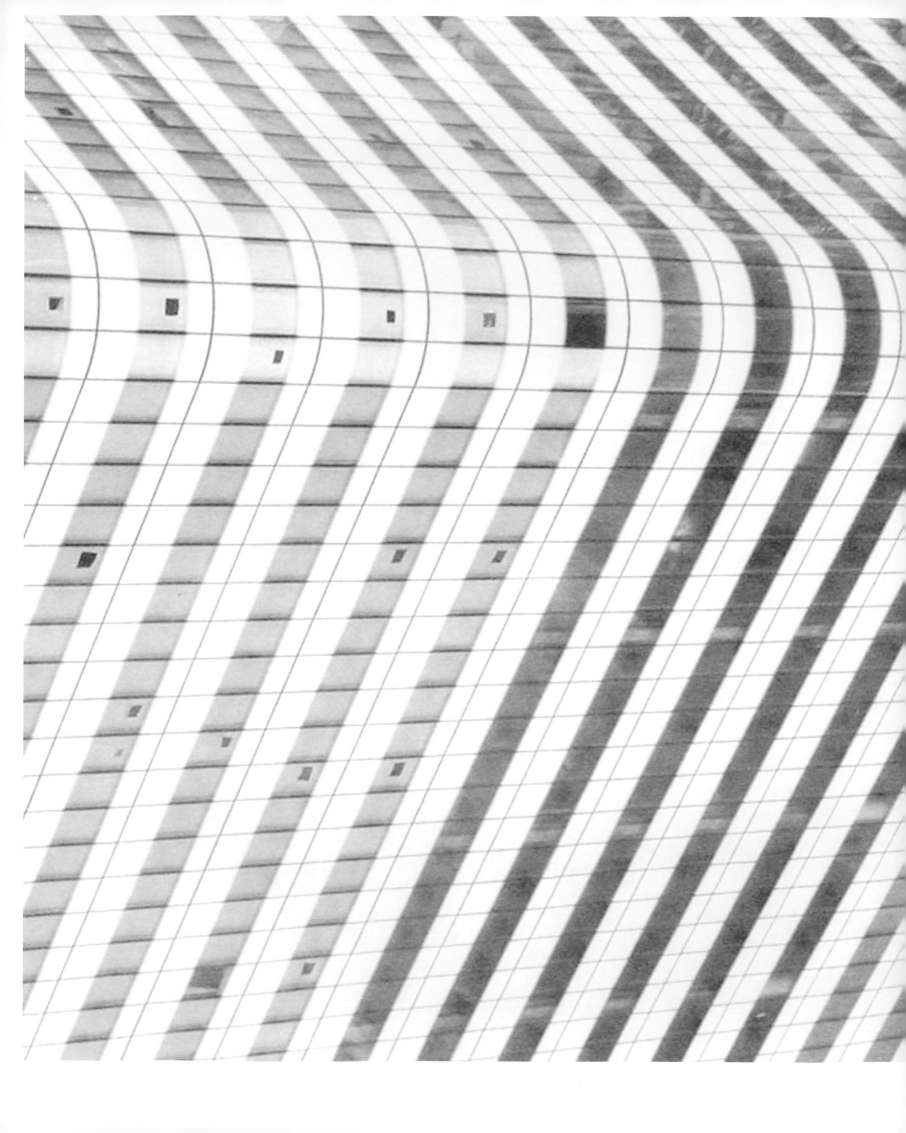

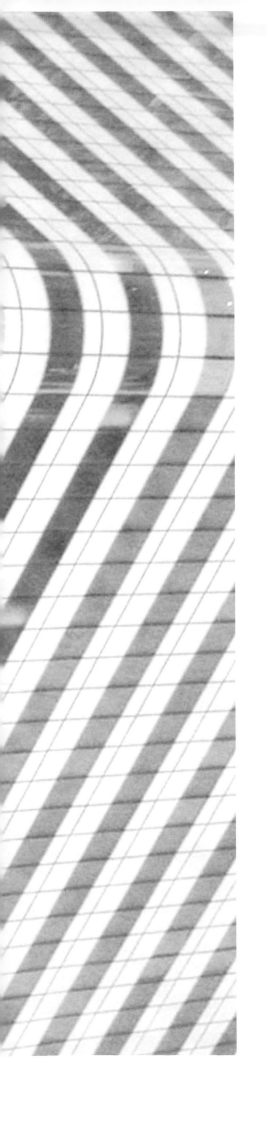

EDEL VERZIJL: PHOTOGRAPH
NEL EUROPE AND USA IMAGE

# FEATURE REPRESENTATION
# COURTESY NEL

02

04

05

07

08

**01** Elena wears vintage pullover and black pleated skirt from Episode, black twillsilk jacket from Ann Demeulemeester.

Caroline wears vintage stretch lace body and red cotton aerobic singlet from Waterloopleinmarket, jeans by Levi's Red.

Benjamin wears black trousers by Ato.

Rahel wears black with lace-embroidered blouse by Gilles Rosier and knickers from Hema. Roos wears black combishort by Keita Maruyama.

Lene wears stretch lace top with batwing sleeves by 0.918, medal from Waterloopleinmarket and slip from Hema.

Veza wears vintage sleeveless pullover from Episode, skirt by Cacharel and cut-off netstockings by Analik.

**02** Benjamin wears off-white vintage net-singlet from Episode and striped trousers by So by Alexander van Slobbe.

Veza wears blue stretch lace top by 0.918 and medals from Waterloopleinmarket.

Roos wears vintage yellow pullover from Episode, blue painted colbert by Levi's Red and yellow leather shorts by Analik.

David wears embroidered vest and striped trousers by So by Alexander van Slobbe.

Cheryl wears vintage sweatshirt by Puma from Waterloopleinmarket and white cotton shorts by Moon Young Hee.

**03** Lene wears yellow sweatshirt with cut sleeves by Antik Batik and tulle skirt with embroidered paillettes by Marjan Pejoski.

**04** Roos wears white cotton dress with printed ship on the front by Cosmic Wonder.

Caroline wears vintage net-sin-glet from Waterloo-pleinmarket, denim skirt by Levi's Red and black jacket by Martine Sitbon.

Benjamin wears red-and-white pullover by Martine Sitbon, pied de poule 3/4-trousers by Only for Men Xavier Delcour and boots by Ato.

Cheryl wears black lace body by Gaspard Yukievich and jogging trousers by Oscar Suleyman.

Rahel wears red bathing suit by Ronald van der Kemp, vintage striped blouse and stockings.

**05** Veza wears pink dress by Missoni and rosette by Annemie Verbeke.

Roos wears (as before) vintage yellow pullover from Episode, blue printed colbert by Levi's Red and yellow leather

shorts by Analik.

David wears T-shirt by Vivienne Westwood and trousers by So by Alexander van Slobbe.

**06** Caroline wears Mickey Mouse printed blouse with batwing sleeves by Marjan Pejoski, fringes by Joannis Guis and vintage leggings from Waterloopleinmarket.

Rahel wears vintage bathing suit and belt from Episode.

Cheryl wears satin printed top by Christophe Lemaire and vintage pleated skirt from Laura Dols.

David wears flowered-covered trousers by Jean Colonna.

Veza wears vintage flowered blouse from Laura Dols and flesh-coloured leather shorts by Analik.

Roos wears striped lurex blouse by Gilles Rosier, knickers from Hema and vintage belt from Episode.

Benjamin wears striped shirt with white collar by Levi's Red, shorts by Moritz Rogosky, boots by Ato and belt from Laura Dols.

**07** Veza wears vintage sleeveless pullover from Episode and white cotton shorts by Moon Young Hee.

Benjamin wears pale pink turtle neck by Moritz Rogosky, jeans

by Levi's Red and Juventus scarf from Episode.

Caroline wears black-and-white top and belt by Ann Demeulemeester and vintage ski leggings from Episode.

Lene wears (as before) yellow sweatshirt with cut sleeves by Antik Batik and tulle skirt with paillettes by Marjan Pejoski.

Rahel wears black-and-white striped blouse by Christophe Lemaire, black trousers by Gilles Rosier and vintage NL-front from Waterloopleinmarket.

Roos wears transparent top with leather by Isabelle Ballu.

**08** Roos wears paisley blouse by Antik Batik.

Caroline wears vintage body with lace from Episode.

Rahel wears flesh bodysuit by Analik.

**09** Elena wears vintage sleeveless pullover from Episode, soccer shirt stylist's own, and green suede shorts by Gilles Rosier.

KESSELSKRAMER: A CREATIV

EUROPEAN AFFAIRS FOLLOWI

THE EURO IN 2002

INTERPRETATION OF
G THE INTRODUCTION OF

- - - - - Counting the Days - - - - - - - - - - - - - - - -
- - - - - - - - - - - - - - - - - - - - - - - - - - - - - -

On January 1, 2002, the Euro will be in full circulation. The former national currencies of 12 countries must then be exchanged before February 28, or they will become totally worthless. The following is the story of eight individuals and their race against time - - - - - - - - - - -
- - - - - - - - - - - - - - - - - - - - - - - - - - - - -
- - - - - - - - - - - - - - - - - by KesselsKramer

Pretty Boy Dacio - - - - - - - - - - - - - - - - -
Release Date: January 2003 - - - - - - - - - - -
- - - - - - - - - - - - - - - - - - - - - - - - - - -

Archibaldo Dacio was popular with female bank tellers. In just three hours, he managed to smooth-talk two Portuguese banks out of 3,000,000 escudos. The authorities tracked him down after learning that he'd left his phone number with a customer during one of the hold-ups. It's rumored that he stashed the money in his mother's house, where he was living until the arrest - - -

**Wilma "Jimbo" van Marle** - - - - - - - - - - -
- - - - - - - - - - - - **Release Date: May 2005** - -
- - - - - - - - - - - - - - - - - - - - - - - - - - - - - -

Secretly living her life as a man, bank robber Wilma van Marle managed to avoid the Dutch authorities for over 3 years before her televised capture in 1995. It's estimated that Wilma robbed the homes of two wealthy furniture designers for over 5,500,000 guilders. However, only 3,000,000 of it was recovered. A reliable source stated that it was rolled up in a sock somewhere. This has yet to be confirmed - - - - - - - - - - - - - - - - - -

01049  A

Star

Voor

Geldig

*) Behou

Station

# Adalwolfa "She Wolf" Papadopoulou

- - - - - - - - - - - - - - - - - - - - - - - -

Release Date: March 2008 - - - - - - - - - - - -

- - - - - - - - - - - - - - - - - - - - - - - -

87 year-old Papadopoulou was given her nickname by an arresting officer who described her to the Austrian press as "a wolf in granny's clothing". She confessed to robbing more than 432 young boys of their lunch money after luring them into her kitchen for Weihnachtsbaeckerei and milk. When investigators asked her where she was hiding the estimated 500,000 shillings, she said she couldn't remember - - - - - -

# The Joyful Brothers - - - - - - - - - - - - - - - - - - - -

Release Date: March 2010

- - - - - - - - - - - - - - - - - - - - - - - - - - - - - - - - -

Gwen and Coty Alaire ("joyful" in French) were among France's most violent criminals. In 1997, they robbed a coach full of German tourists at gunpoint for more than 450,000 francs. According to the other 16 people in the getaway car, the money is hidden in someone's ear

- - - - - - - - - - - - - - - - - - - - - - - - - - - - - - - - -

# The Pocket Billiard - - - - - - - - - - - - - - - - - -

Release Date: December 2004

- - - - - - - - - - - - - - - - - - - - - - - - - - - - -

If you ask an Italian who Giusaffa Zohanbaptista is, the chances are they will say they didn't know. They'd be lying. As the owner of 14 Best American Pizza franchises in Sicily, Zohanbaptista is no stranger. Yet he was able to run his money-laundering racket with little suspicion for six years. The police now suspect that over 20,000,000 lire were baked into the crusts and distributed to Zohanbaptista's "pizza posse", who were disguised as stoned university students. The nickname "Pocket Billiard" is still a mystery - - - - - - - - - - - - - - - - - - - - -

Gotthard "Kid" La Mode - - - - - - - - - - - - - -
Release Date: August 2004 - - - - - - - - - - - -

Computer whiz-kid Gotthard La Mode operated from his family's Luxembourg cottage to swindle cash from more than 14,500 impotent men. His virtual company, Faux Her Pleasure, grossed more than 400,000,000 francs in 2000 until a neighbor became suspicious of all the catnip he was borrowing, and turned him in. According to a "shower mate", the money is rumored to be behind one of the boy-band posters in his closet - - - - - - - -

Mother Lemon Drop - - - - - - - - - - - - - - - - -
- - - - - Release Date: April 2002

Mother Adalia had a weakness for super-sour candy and church donations (she stole 50,000,000 pesetas worth). Some say that one addiction fueled the other. Together, they were the lethal combination that got her 20 years in Valdemoro prison. To this day, she swears that she is innocent, blaming low church attendance on the empty donation boxes. God only knows where she's really hiding the money - - - - - - - - - - -

01

# MARGHERITA MANZELLI

"There are no particular stories behind my work. While I make one painting I usually come up with the following one. This results in a group of works, even if I don't consider them to be a series. Each work is autonomous and stands alone. It is linked to the others only because of the time frame in which they're done. Each work attempts to get as close as possible to an image I have in my head."

Margherita Manzelli was born in Ravenna in 1968, and now lives and works in Milan. This feature shows a range of her work including her oil paintings, which she is more well-known for, and also a series of her watercolour 'faces', which are quite different to her other works – "the quickness makes it easier for one face to lead to another so that a group of 'faces' are structured more as a series. But I don't think it is important. It's a mechanism that's structured within the technique. When the 'faces' are in a 'pack' in order to justify themselves, I'm dissatisfied. I like it more when they're together in order to contradict themselves. Some are victims, others are bitches. The beautiful ones stay alone.

I never use watercolour. I only use it to do the 'faces' which is the only thing I can think of doing with watercolour; at least for the moment. Sometimes it feels very strange to me that I can't even imagine that I made those watercolours. I look at them as one looks at the work made by somebody else. The person who made that work looks like a fast type and I'm not fast."

Margherita's work has been shown internationally, including exhibitions at the ICA in London and the Walker Art Center in Minneapolis. When commenting on her inspirations and influences, she says "I find this kind of question very difficult. I like many things and I don't mean specifically related to the art world. I'm not fixated on anything in particular. I don't have a particular leaning towards painting, and work which feels close to mine I am usually not interested in. When my work is juxtaposed with the work of someone that is thought to be close to mine, I'm usually irritated but I'm not exactly sure why."

Margherita is represented by greengrassi in London and Studio Guenzani in Milan.

02

01
*Untitled*
2001
Pencil and watercolour on paper
56.5 x 76.3 cm

02
*The City Loves You*
1999
Oil on linen
150 x 220 cm

01

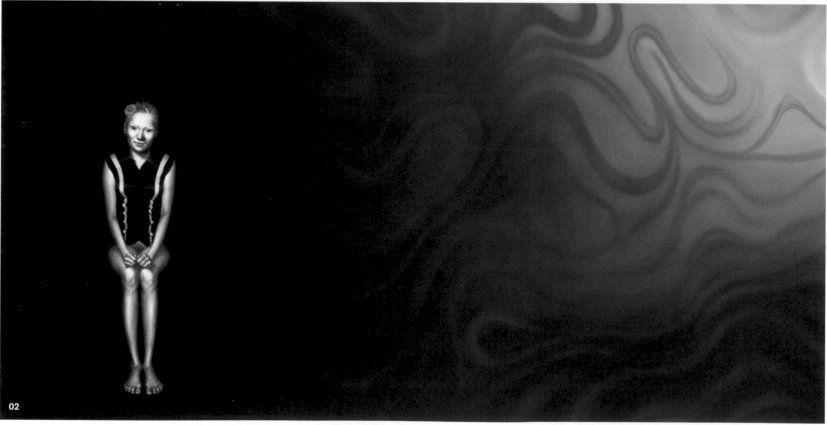

02

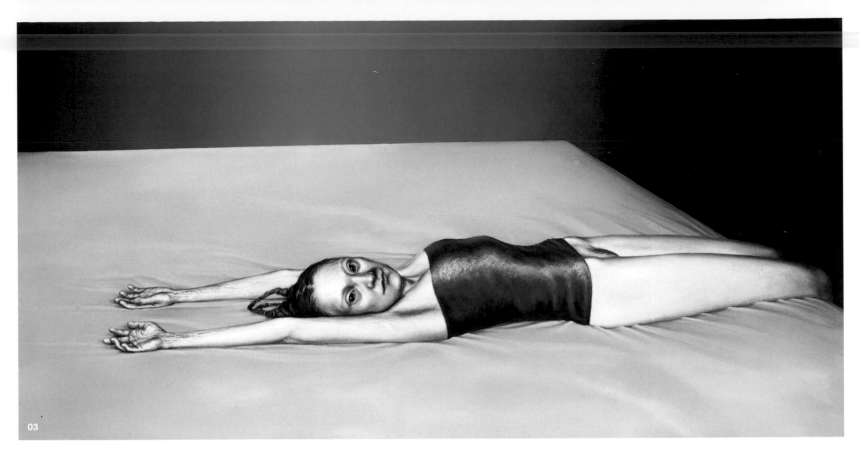
03

04

**01**
Programma Disciplina Maestro
(t. m. h. S)
2000
Oil on linen
190 x 400 cm

**02**
*Binaural*
2000
Oil on linen
180 x 370 cm

**03**
*T.S.S*
1999
Oil on linen
90 x 212 cm

**04**
*Nottem*
2000
Oil on linen
250 x 200 cm

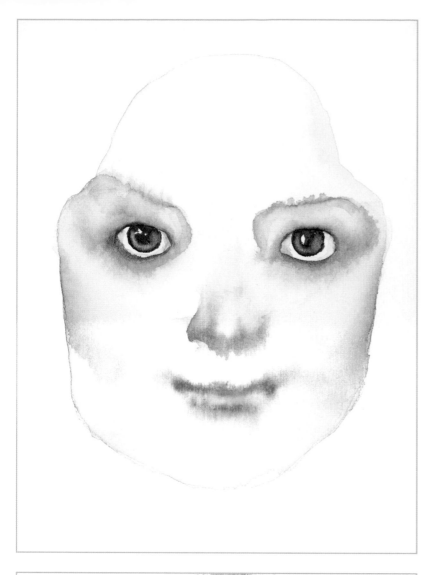
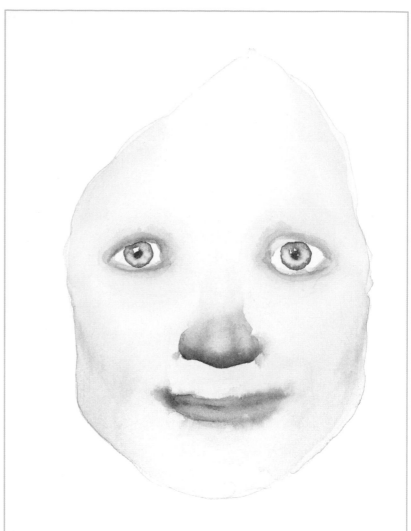
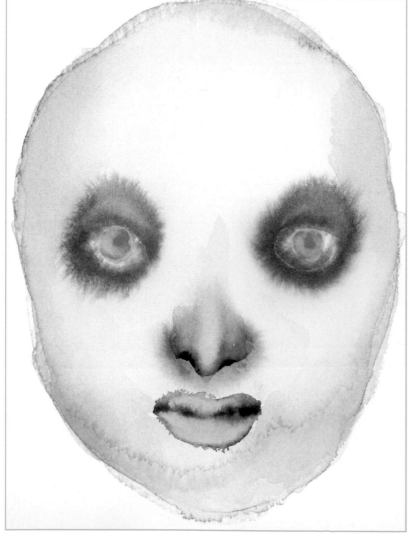
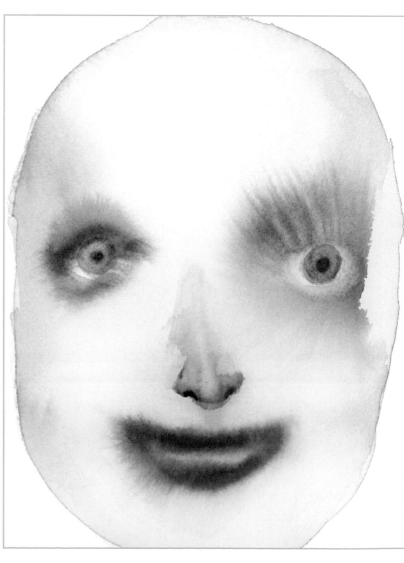

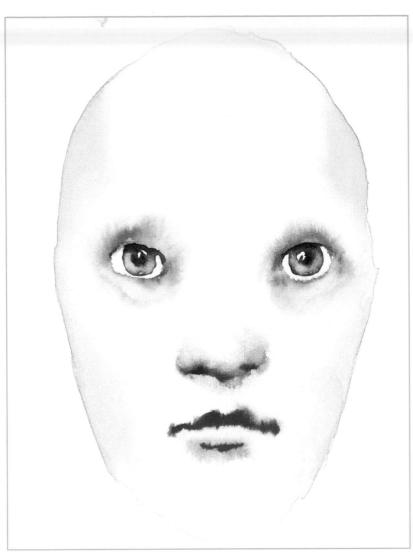

*Faces*
2001

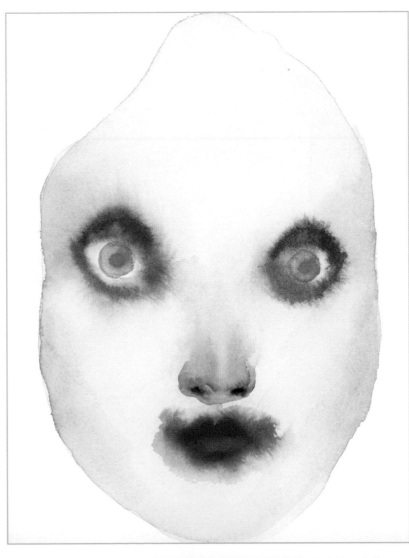

*Smaller Splash*
2000

# Luis Sanchis

**Place of birth** Valencia, Spain
**Place of residence** New York
**Representation** Art + Commerce,
New York
**Courtesy** Luis Sanchis; A+C
Anthology, New York

*Gentleman in Rome*

## Bianca Pilet

**Courtesy** Bianca Pilet

**Description of work** "*Two Models and Two Men in the Street* was from a fashion story made for the *Independent Magazine* at the Hyères Festival in France. *Gentleman in Rome* was a lucky shot on the streets of Rome.

**Materials used** "I use different kinds of 6 x 7 cameras and an automatic 6 x 4.5, as I like the quality of the format. And I work on colournegative, and keep control of the printing. I spend most time on finding the right location and the best people/models, that is really important for my photos.

**Creative inspiration** "Elsie's Sunday dinner, because it keeps me going." Bianca Pilet

*Two Models and Two Men in the Street*

## Max Vadukul

**Representation** Art Partner,
New York
**Courtesy** Art Partner

Max Vadukul was born in Nairobi, Kenya, and is of British nationality. He is firstly known as a fashion photographer working for Condé Nast for 15 years, and is only the second photographer in the 100-year history of *The New Yorker* to have a contract as a photo-journalist. Vadukul has just released his first book, called *MAX*, showcasing his many years in the photographic industry. He is now returning his focus to editorial and fashion (which is one of his passions) with work for many major magazines including *i-D, Numero* and all the Condé Nast international publications.

*Defo#1*

Shirley Manson for *Gear* magazine

Angelina Jolie for *Premiere*

Slipknot for *Rolling Stone*

## Frank W. Ockenfels 3

**Representation**
Art + Commerce, New York
**Courtesy** Frank W. Ockenfels;
Art + Commerce, New York

Frank W. Ockenfels 3 is renowned for his portrait photographs. His portraits of such diverse personalities as Drew Barrymore, Jerry Seinfeld, Hillary Clinton, Kurt Cobain, Tom Waits, Spike Lee, and Martin Scorcese have appeared in leading magazines

throughout the world. Ockenfels's work is seen frequently in *Rolling Stone, Time, Entertainment Weekly, Us, Premiere, Esquire, New York Magazine,* and *Spin.* His work (including collaborations with artist Robert Longo) has appeared in galleries and museums in New York, Los Angeles and Berlin.

**Creative inspiration** "Robert Frank, for his constant ability in seeing anew; Francis Bacon, for his insanity and for questioning his own talent; and Joseph Beuys, just because!" Frank W. Ockenfels 3

*Journal / Everclear*

*Journal / David Bowie*

*Journal / Berlin 99*

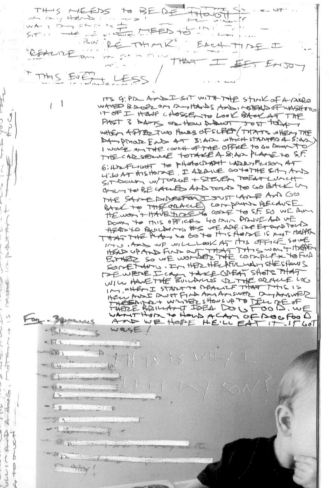

*Journal / Question?*

Rosa 2
Model: Rosa
Make-up: Mo Karadag
Hair: I. L. Hem

## Anna Tiedink

**Date of birth** 1970
**Place of birth** Zutphen, Netherlands
**Place of residence** Amsterdam
**Representation** NEL Europe and USA
**Courtesy** NEL

**Recent exhibitions** PANL Awards, Amsterdam (2001) > *Not Tom Dick and Harry*, Fries Museum, Leeuwarden, Netherlands (2001) > Gallery Speak For, Tokyo (2000) > *The Spiritual Side of Beauty (Part II)*, Galleria Marelle Arte Contemporanea, Milan (2000) > *We Mortals, 25 Portraits about Death by 25 Photographers*, Nieuwe Kerk Amsterdam (1999) > *Backlight, 10 Visions on Fashion*, Paraplufabriek Nijmegen, Netherlands (1999) > Milk Studios, New York (1999) > PANL Awards, Amsterdam (1998)

"The theme for this work (which is part of a series) is very simple – bronze. The make-up artist came up with the bronze theme, I just let him surprise me. As I was doing the make-up I thought of the lighting.

"I always shoot on 8 x 10 Polaroid because I like the colour and softness of it. Because you develop the image right away, it gives me the opportunity to play with colour and cropping because you can see immediately how it fits together.

"I am influenced by many people and many things, but for the last year I have been simplifying my images. Going back to my roots." Anna Tiedink

Anna Tiedink's work has featured in several publications including *Elle, Marie Claire, Stern, i-D, style&thefamilytunes, Depeche Mode* and *Squeeze*.

*Malgosia out of focus*
2001
Unpublished image for *Mummy*
*Dearest* story for Citizen K
**Styling** Laurent Dombrowicz
**Model** Malgosia
**Make-up** Carole Lasnier
**Hair** Seb Bascle

# Wendelien Daan

**Date of birth** 1965
**Place of birth** Eindhoven, Netherlands
**Place of residence** Amsterdam
**Representation** NEL Europe and USA
**Courtesy** Wendelien Daan; NEL

**Recent exhibitions** Dutch Touch, Galleria Del Cortile, Rome (2001) > E-Werk, Berlin (2001) > Intern Fashion Photography Festival, Tokyo, Kobe and Fukuoka, Japan (2000) > Gallery Speak For, Tokyo (2000) > *Tegenlicht,* Paraplufabriek, Nijmegen, Netherlands (1999) > *Masterminds of Mode,* Intern Fashion Photography Festival, Tokyo, Kobe and Fukuoka, Japan (1999) > Milk Studios, New York (1999) > *Raw Skin,* NFI,

Rotterdam, (1998) > Gallery 2 1/2 x 4 1/2, Amsterdam, (1996)

"I shoot on 4 x 5 chrome, for realistic, hyper-sharp images like I see with my own eyes.

"I am very inspired by science-fiction film, romantic/classical art and fairy tales, as well as daily life." Wendelien Daan

## Axel Hoedt

**Date of birth** 1966
**Place of birth** Freiburg, Germany
**Place of residence** London
**Representation** klosslondon.com,
**Courtesy** Axel Hoedt

**Description of work** Axel Hoedt's work has been shown in *i-D*, *Independent on Sunday*, and *Tank*, and he also exhibited at the 2001 Hyères Festival in France.

**Materials used** "4 x 5 camera, and negs, as it gives the possibility to work as I want and results in a more conscious process."
Axel Hoedt

## Leila Méndez

**Date of birth** 1973
**Place of birth** Buenos Aires
**Place of residence** Barcelona
**Courtesy** Leila Méndez

Leila Méndez's work has been published in *Big*, *Wallpaper*, *Track*, *Self Service*, *Alternative Press*, *El País Semanal*, *Marie Claire*, *La Vanguardia*, *Rolling Stone*, *Neo2*, *Elle* and *Time* magazine, amongst others, and she has worked with clients including Levi's, Warner and Virgin.

**Description of work** *Evolutive*: "This is reportage done in the USA as a personal project. I wanted to create a kind of odd and weird feeling from American lifestyle scenes. The whole report will be released as a monographic in *Evolutive* magazine."

*Disco2000*: "These portraits have been published in *Disco2000* magazine. They are not from the same shoot but are related to each other. It was a fashion shoot but the people are not models, they are people selected owing to their attitude, helping the picture to become more real and strong. It's fashion achieved through a journalistic viewpoint."

*Amaya Arzuaga*: "These are pictures from the Autumn-Winter 2001 catalogue for the designer Amaya Arzuaga. All the images

were planned and taken backstage, to create a different way to see the product, more dynamic and cheeky."

**Materials used** "I work 50-50 in small and large format, but my favourite is 35 mm. This lightness gives you the freedom and capacity to have a dialogue with the person in a natural way, without scaring them. The more simple and minimal the set, the more comfortable the subject.

"My working method varies depending on whether it's commercial or personal work. However, in both cases I like to control carefully all the pre-production phase. At the shoot, I like to work loose and explore the unexpected random events that can happen, to give a chance for improvisation."

**Creative inspiration** "I feel a deep respect for people such as Richard Avedon, Irving Penn, or Helmut Newton. In my opinion, the strength that leads in an Avedon portrait is above the millions of trends that pass through fashion photography.

"However, I think there's a lot of new talent making new stuff and giving fresh and strong ideas. Film-makers such as David Lynch, who has a disturbing photographic eye, gives me a lot of inspiration. The main thing is to not repeat formulas and not follow strictly the photographic trends because they change all the time."
Leila Méndez

**01**
*Disco2000*

**02**
*Evolutive*

**03**
*Amaya Arzuaga*

All images:
*Four Days in LA: The Versace Pictures*
2000
C-prints
121.9 x 160 cm

Steven Miesel

**Place of residence** New York
**Representation** Art + Commerce,
New York
**Courtesy** © Steven Miesel; Jay
Jopling/White Cube, London

For *Dazed & Confused*
May 2001

## Marcelo Krasilcic

**Place of birth** Brazil
**Place of residence** New York
**Representation** h.a.l, London
**Courtesy** Marcelo Krasilcic; h.a.l

Marcelo Krasilcic graduated from New York University with a bachelor of fine arts degree in photography and since then has developed a multi-faceted career with projects that involve and often blend the notion of art, fashion, portrait and architectural photography.

Marcelo's work has been shown in galleries such as the Museum of Modern Art in São Paulo and Vienna, Kunstforeningen in Denmark, Parco Gallery in Japan, Fotogalleriet in Norway and White Columns Gallery in New York. His photographs have appeared in several magazines including *Purple*, *Spin*, *Harper's Bazaar*, *Made in USA*, *Self Service*, *Art Forum*, *Details*, *Big* and *Vogue Hommes International*.

**Description of work** "This was a shoot about a boy who wanted to be a hero but he doesn't know how and feels disillusioned and frustrated.

"[My work develops] usually from an emotion I am experiencing. Then I bring it to a rational level and try to convey that emotion."

**Creative inspiration** "My yoga teachers, ex-lovers, designers like Bless, Susan Cianciolo and Viktor & Rolf, trees, my parents, most people I work with, because of their passion and devotion." Marcelo Krasilcic

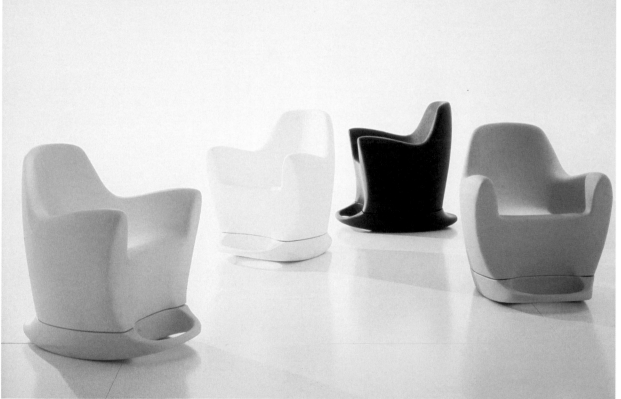

## Claudio Dondoli: Flip; Miss Flip

**Designer** Claudio Dondoli
at Archirivolto
**Nationality** Italian
**Country of residence** Italy
**Date of birth** 1954
**Title** Flip, Miss Flip
**Date** April 2001 at the Milan
Furniture Fair

"We wanted to create a piece of furniture that could be used equally indoors and out-doors. And it had to be comfortable and coloured – to make life beautiful!"
Claudio Dondoli

Flip, the rocking chair, and Miss Flip, the armchair, are in polyethylene made with an innovative printing system for plastic materials. It is this very resistant material, which is also easily recycled, that makes both designs suitable for both indoor and outdoor environments. The design took

approximately two years' work, since all ergonomic and technological criteria were assessed precisely.

Flip and Miss Flip are available in six different colours: white, yellow, prune, light grey, blue, and dark blue. The rocking chair is obtained by adding a support to the base of Miss Flip.

Flip's dimensions are: 76 cm (width); 89 cm (depth); 90 cm (backrest height). Miss Flip's dimensions are: 76 cm (width); 72 cm (depth); 83 cm (back rest height).

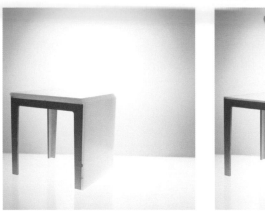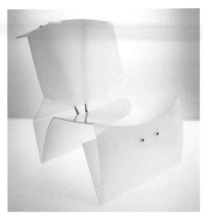

## Moorhead & Moorhead: Polypropylene Chair Low; Polypropylene Stool/Table

**Designers** Granger Moorhead, Robert Moorhead
**Nationality** American
**Country of residence** USA
**Date of birth** 1969, 1972
**Title** Polypropylene Chair Low, Polypropylene Stool/Table
**Date** In production May 2001
**Major awards** Honourable Mention in Furniture, 47th Annual Design Review, *I.D.* Magazine, USA, July/August 2001 (Polypropylene Chair Low)

"Both pieces are a result of exploring the 'living hinge' property of polypropylene.

"Polypropylene Chair Low is a sheet of plastic folded along integral hinges and held in place by a pair of stainless-steel rods. Its dimensions are: 71.2 cm (height); 55.9 cm (width); 68.6 cm (depth).

"Polypropylene Stool/Table is a sheet of plastic mounted on a plywood base that unfolds along integral hinges to provide a self-supporting leaf. The materials used are polypropylene, and birch plywood. The dimensions are: 45.7 cm (height); 45.7 cm (width, closed); 91.4 cm (width, open); 38 cm (depth)." Robert Moorhead

01

02

## Job Smeets: BE chair; BE sofa

**Designer** Job Smeets
**Nationality** Dutch
**Country of residence** Netherlands
**Date of birth** 1969
**Title** BE chair (02), BE sofa (01)
**Date** April 2000, at the
Milan Furniture Fair

Following the Curved Furniture (1998-2000) and Modular Furniture (2000), the BE Furniture has been developed in 2001. While the Curved series discusses the classics and Modular Furniture is about 'sculpting', BE Furniture asks itself how long it remains furniture and when it becomes an object. Be Furniture is bent like a paper clip but 'filled' where comfort is needed.

## Konstantin Grcic: Chaos chair

**Designer** Konstantin Grcic
**Nationality** German
**Country of residence** Germany
**Date of birth** 1965
**Title** Chaos chair for ClassiCon
**Date** April 2001 at the
Milan Furniture Fair

"When I designed Chaos I consciously wanted to break with the convention of correct and formal seating. The chair – which is my first project in upholstery – avoids imposing any particular posture. Instead it invites us to do what we do anyway: to perch, to fidget, to turn, or shift. The chair's volume is extremely narrow in profile, but its opulent front/rear elevation offers all the comfort for cool, relaxed sitting (even two people can sit next to each other...). Chaos can become a platform for activity, or an island for retreat. I imagined it for all those situations where a chair needs to offer more than just something to sit on." Konstantin Grcic

Chaos is made using injected polyurethane foam with a frame of steel tubing with rubber webbing. The visible floor tubing is chromed steel; the cover is in fabric (removeable) or leather. The dimensions are: 90 cm (width); 52 cm (depth); 74 cm (height).

01

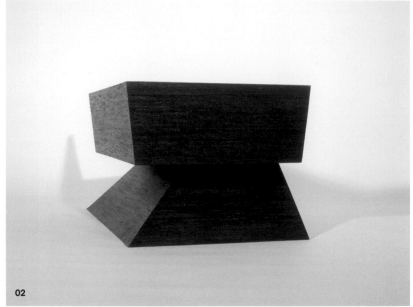

02

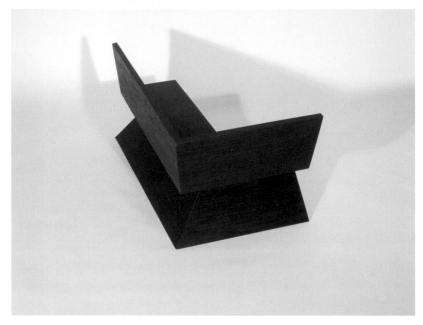

## alias_gampermartino: Sit Around bench; Come Together sofa

**Designer** Martin Gamper at alias_gampermartino
**Nationality** Italian
**Country of residence** UK
**Date of birth** 1971
**Title** Sit Around bench (02), Come Together sofa (01)
**Date** Design completed April 2001; in production April 2001
**Major awards** USP Awards 2001 (given by the Cultural Institute in Vienna; the prize was to spend four months in Paris on an artist-in-residence programme)

"This design proposal engages two problematic entities: furniture and corners in a mutual, beneficial amalgamation, where every piece of furniture interacts with the specific properties of the corner, and the furniture therefore evokes the meaning of space and behaviour to us." Martin Gamper

Come Together sofa's dimensions are: 210 cm (length); 160 cm (width); 120 cm (depth). It is made using leather, cardboard tube, foam, MDF, buttons, and a mirror.

Sit Around bench's dimensions are: 53 cm (width); 60 cm (depth); 95 cm (length). It is made in solid wood.

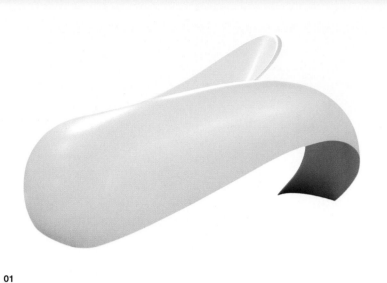

01

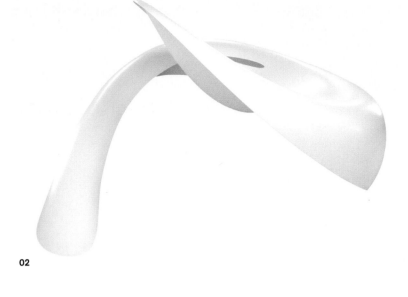

02

03

04

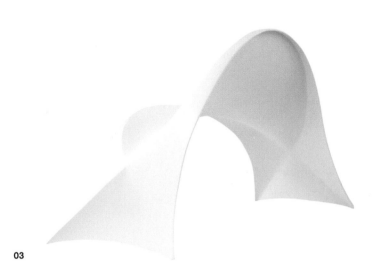

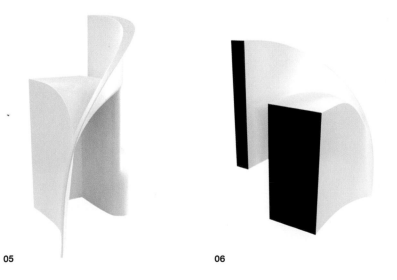

05                    06

## Jérôme Olivet: Bionics collection

**Designer** Jérôme Olivet
**Nationality** French
**Country of residence** France
**Date of birth** 1971
**Title** Bionics collection
**Date** First shown April 2001 at the Salone Satellite, Milan
**Major awards** Salone Satellite 2001, Milan

"The genesis of a new world requires a return to oneself. Objects become witnesses to this intimate rebuilding. This is a concept based on the spiral. It gives movement to space, slow and infinite. As a result of this kinetic design, architecture takes us on a personal voyage at the end of which, knowledge deepens.

"The chair Cosmos (01, 02) plunges us into the womb. We live a perpetual rebirth there. The chair Fragment (03, 04) breaks up the light. It becomes furtive in its surroundings and secretly disappears. The chair Hyperspace (05, 06) has two black rectangles in levitation and a tree structure of form with lines on the back. A voluptuous movement extends around us. A new dimension appears.

"The Bionics collection is the proof that today, design can increase the senses and refine the human emotions to rebuild a new society." Jérôme Olivet

All pieces are in fibreglass.

## Christophe Pillet: Beach table

Satyendra Pakhale: Bell Horse chair

**Designer** Christophe Pillet
**Nationality** French
**Country of residence** France
**Date of birth** 1959
**Title** Beach Table
**Date** April 2001

"The project is a simple table and is based on the techniques and image of the surf board." Christophe Pillet

The dimension are: 160 cm (length); 45 cm (width); 50 cm (height). It is constructed in foam and fibreglass with serigraphy print.

**Designer** Satyendra Pakhale
**Title** Bell Horse chair
**Date** April 2001

## Cappellini Collection 2001

**Producer** Cappellini
**Country of residence** Italy
**Title** Cappellini Collection 2001
**Date** Projects unveiled at the Milan Furniture Fair April 2001

All projects shown over these four pages are part of Cappellini's 2001 collection, which was shown at the Milan Furniture Fair this year.

01

## Ronan & Erwan Bouroullec: Glide; Tavolo & Tavolino; Brick

**Designers** Ronan Bouroullec, Erwan Bouroullec
**Nationality** French
**Country of residence** France
**Date of birth** 1971, 1976
**Title** Glide (03), Tavolo & Tavolino (01), Brick (02)
**Date** April 2001

Tavolo & Tavolino, Brick: "Corian is a material resistant and flexible enough to make supports like table legs, but which also provides a suitable finish for the vase. It is a one-material monochromic object."
Glide: "This large sofa unit is smaller than a long chair plus a sofa plus a shelving unit, yet it combines all these elements." Ronan & Erwan Bouroullec

02

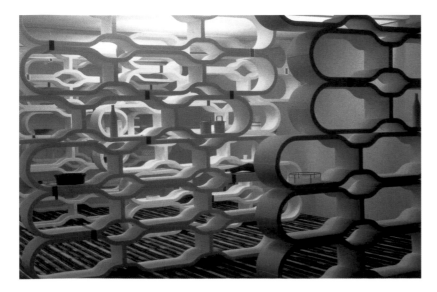

03

01

## Marcel Wanders: Stone chair; Fish Net chair

**Designer** Marcel Wanders
**Nationality** Dutch
**Country of residence** Netherlands
**Date of birth** 1963
**Title** Fish Net chair, Stone chair
**Date** April 2001

The Fish Net chair is a continuation of the Knotted chair, with its transparency and detailed quality. In opposition to the Knotted chair the Fish Net chair is designed to be industrially manufactured. It is constructed from a two-dimensionally knotted net or better, pipe, which could be knotted by a machine. Because of the low production numbers, it is currently knotted by hand. Its dimensions are: 67 cm (height); 38 cm (seat height); 81 cm (width); 77 cm (depth).

The materials used are aramide, carbon, and epoxy.

Stone chair is polyester covered with silicone and pebbles. Its dimensions are: 68 cm (height); 32 cm (sitting height); 78 cm (width); 82 cm (depth).

**01**
Stone chair

**02**
Fish Net chair

02

## Fabio Novembre: Org

**Designer** Fabio Novembre
**Nationality** Italian
**Country of residence** Italy
**Date of birth** 1966
**Title** Org
**Date** April 2001

"I just wanted to design a table by rethinking what's under it. In my mind it was like a floating organism with its feet-roots and you had to interact with them, let them mix and confuse with your own legs.

"The glass top is provided with stainless steel holders in which to screw the legs. The legs, either soft or structural, have the same dimensions and covering. The hard ones are in steel, the soft ones in cord for climbing. The construction system allows various dimensions." Fabio Novembre

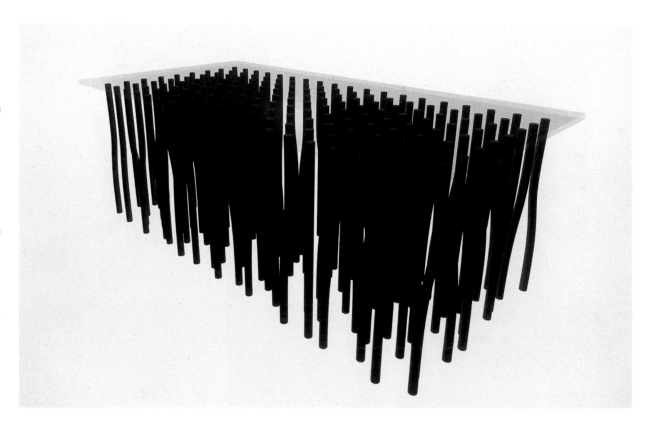

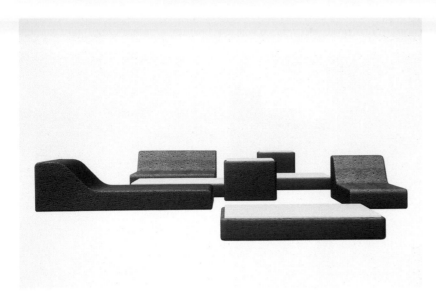

## Piero Lissoni: Progetto Tufo

**Designers** Patricia Urquiola, Shane Schneck, Piero Lissoni at Lissoni Studio
**Nationality** Spanish, American, Italian
**Country of residence** Italy
**Title** Progetto Tufo
**Date** April 2001

"The brief for Tufo was presented by a masonry company outside Rome, which was looking for ideas to use an 'out of fashion' stone (tufo). We conceived of the project as an outdoor 'lounge landscape'. The proportions were based on a 80cm² module that then allowed us to determine the individual pieces: a chaise-longue, a double chaise, pouf, bench, and low table. The result was very 'modern-Flintstone'." Lissoni Studio

The dimensions of the chaise longue are: 160 cm (width); 160 cm (depth); 20 cm (height). The double chaise measures: 80 cm (width); 160 cm (depth); 20 cm (height). The low table measures 80 cm (width); 80 cm (depth); 20 cm (height). The pouf measures 40 cm (width); 40 cm (depth); 40 cm (height). The bench measures 40 cm (width); 160 cm (depth); 40 cm (height).

## For Use: 005

**Designers** Sven Jonke, Christoph Katzler, Nikola Radeljkovic
**Nationality** Croatian, Austrian, Croatian
**Country of residence** Austria
**Date of birth** 1973, 1968, 1971
**Title** April 2001

"The brief was to make a plastic chair and barstool with a low backrest – as low as possible. Out of this concept we tried to get a different but still rather classical shape, playing with lines and proportions." For Use

## Claessons Koivisto Rune: Pebbles

**Designers** Claessons Koivisto Rune
**Country of residence** Sweden
**Title** Pebbles
**Title** April 2001

## büro für form: Rocker; Stonehenge

**Designers** Benjamin Hopf,
Constantin Wortmann at
büro für form
**Nationality** German
**Country of residence** Germany
**Date of birth** 1971, 1970
**Title** Rocker rocking chair and
Stonehenge chaise-longue
**Date** April 2001 at the Milan
Furniture Fair

"We designed both pieces for our exhibition at this year's Salone Satellite at the Milan Furniture Fair. You can't believe how comfortable Rocker is: it is made in upholstered, moulded wood, covered with dark brown leather. While sitting on this chair you can easily change your position by rocking back and forth.

"Stonehenge is a comfortable chaise-longue. The inspiration was the famous Stonehenge in Britain... three elliptic elements, arranged like big stones, incidentally put together. Stonehenge is foam-moulded."
Benjamin Hopf, Constantin Wortmann

 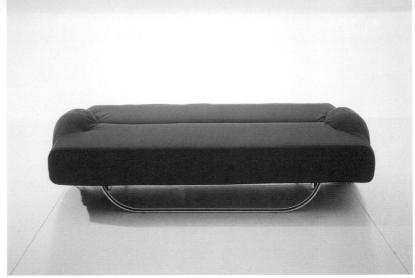

## Denis Santachiara: Bongo

**Designer** Denis Santachiara
**Nationality** Italian
**Country of residence** Italy
**Date of birth** 1950
**Title** Bongo for Styling srl
**Date** April 2001 at the Milan
Furniture Fair

"The Bongo sofa bed was conceived as an expression of design that communicates because of its transformational qualities more than its static qualities."
Denis Santachiara

Bongo is a one-piece sofa that turns into a bed, thanks to a system integrated into the rubber. The frame is in aluminum-varnished metal, the upholstering is in differentiated-density expanded polyurethane covered by fabric. Furthermore, in order to increase Bongo's uses, the handles on top can be used to hold a large service container for newspapers, flowers and objects.

Bongo's dimensions are: as a sofa: 228 cm (width); 103 cm (depth); 88 cm (backrest height); as a bed: 228 cm (length); 123 cm (width); 43 cm (height).

## Monica Förster: Load light

**Designer** Monica Förster
for David Design
**Nationality** Swedish
**Country of residence** Sweden
**Date of birth** 1966
**Title** Load light
**Date** First shown April 2001
at the Milan Furniture Fair

"Load is an opal portable lamp with a round soft shape; it can be used cordless anywhere, just like your mobile phone.

"Load glows for five hours once charged. A red light will tell you when it is time to recharge, and a green light will tell you when it's ready to be portable again.

"Load can both be on or off during charging, which takes between two and four hours.

"Load is made of rotation-moulded ethyl vinyl acetate, which feels nice and soft in your hand. I chose a soft plastic in order to give a nice soft feeling when touched and also to make Load more resistant to damage. The combination of soft material and the organic shape makes the lamp shockproof." Monica Förster

## Plan A: Streol chair

**Designer** Anette Hermann at Plan A
**Nationality** Danish
**Country of residence** Denmark
**Date of birth** 1970
**Title** Streol chair
**Date** April 2001
**Photography** Erik Brahl

"The idea was to create interactivity between a chair and its user. The user of the Streol is the creator of a chair. Streol can also be used for storing things, by placing them between the rubber sheets. When not in use Streol is placed up against a wall." Anette Hermann

Its dimensions are 200 cm (height); 60 cm (width); 2.5 cm (depth). It is made up of a stainless-steel frame and natural rubber: metal for a stable construction and rubber for flexibility and experience.

## Marcel Wanders: B.L.O. light

**Designer** Marcel Wanders
**Nationality** Dutch
**Country of residence** Netherlands
**Date of birth** 1963
**Title** B.L.O. for Flos
**Date** First shown April 2001

The lamp can be switched on and off by blowing through dedicated electronics.

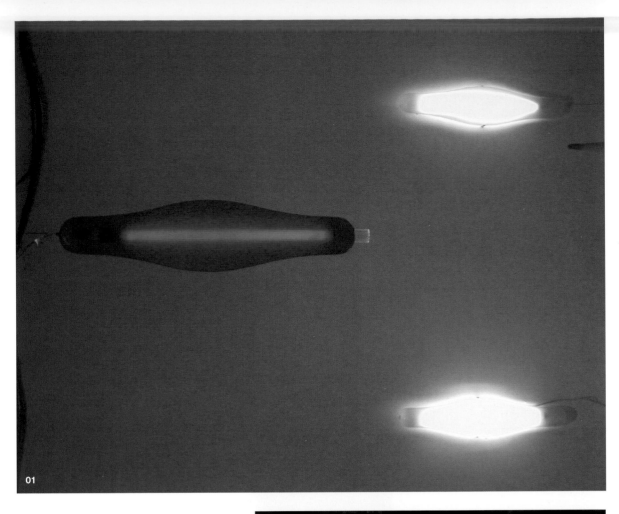

01

## Harry & Camila Creators of Signs: Okkio; Geldrop

**Designers** Harry & Camila
**Nationality** Dutch, Chilean
**Country of residence** Italy
**Title** Okkio standing lamp (02),
Geldrop light (01)
**Date** First shown April 2001 at
the Milan Furniture Fair; first
shown May 2001

"The inspiration for the design [of Okkio] was science-fiction movies; the music of groups like, among others, Air and Daft Punk; sculpture; and making a futuristic piece of functional sculpture/totem, silently waiting when not in use but which also demands full attention to the well-defined outer lines from which it is difficult to tell when it was made or designed."
Harry & Camila

Okkio was designed for Idée and Sputnik, Japan. Its dimensions are: 180 cm (height, standing); 49 cm (width); 53 cm (height, table); 36 cm (width). It is rotation-moulded polypropylene; the body of the lamp is translucent; the head transparent (non-coloured or coloured versions).

"The idea [for Geldrop] was to make a soft, nice-to-touch light object whose shape represents the liquidity, softness and transparency of the material. The inspiration was Mother Nature, water, cocoons, etc."
Harry & Camila

Geldrop was designed for Idée, Japan. It has a silicon body; the inner tube is acrylic. Its dimensions are: 80 cm (length).

02

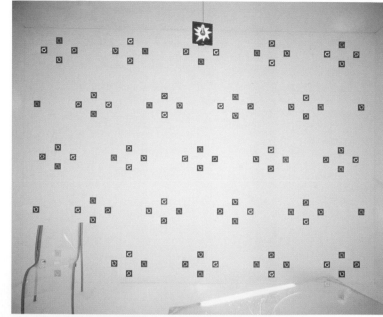

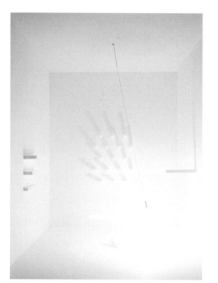

## Ingo Maurer: Spazio Krizia 2001 installations; Hi, Bruce

**Designer** Ingo Maurer
**Nationality** German
**Country of residence** Germany
**Title** Spazio Krizia 2001
installations; Hi, Bruce
**Date** April 2001

"The exhibition at Spazio Krizia, Milan, consisted of one-of-a-kind pieces in three rooms. The theme, of course, is light. New expressions and new techniques result in new aesthetics. One room shows what might be the first illuminated wallpaper. Based on

LED techniques, a light pattern covers the wall in different colours. By using a dimmer, different light intensities and moods can be created; a water-mattress becomes a lighting element. My intention is to inspire people to think more about light and what could be done with it. Wallpaper becomes a light source. We continue working on this idea. In the second room, a cube is suspended from the ceiling; a bare light bulb swings from left to right, casting shadows on the wall. Nothing stands still, everything is moving. The atmosphere is quiet and meditative: a play with light, shadow and movement. The third room is static and peaceful. It is a light pattern of straight lines, based on the ancient Chinese oracle

*I Ching.* Again, a clear water-mattress slowly changes its colour. From the ceiling hangs Dangle Dee, a limited edition. Rays of light come from a non-existent light bulb.

"Hi, Bruce is a neon chandelier made of ready-made license-plate lights: a neon cloud of blue, red, magenta, and green. I am fascinated by Las Vegas aesthetics – I could have called it just as well Going to Las Vegas. To the license plates I added aluminium reflectors instead of numbers and letters, to give a more poetic expression. The piece itself is static, but from different angles one has different impressions: light and movement in a static piece. The total diameter is 160 cm."
Ingo Maurer

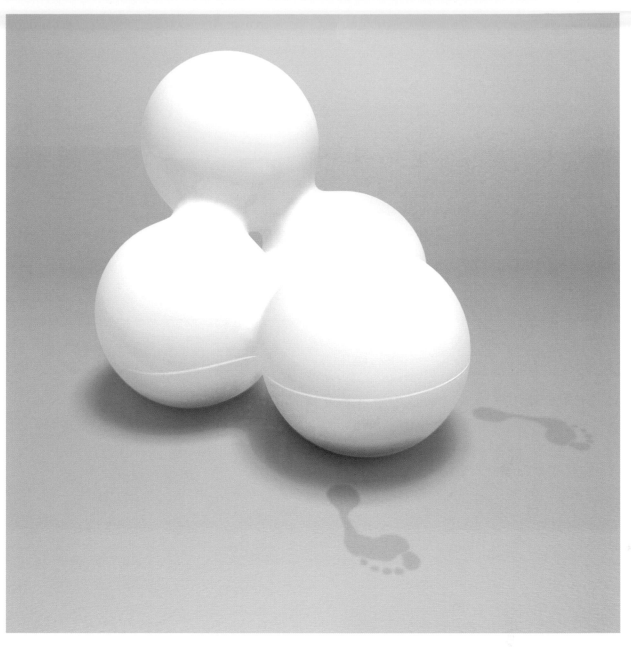

## Inflate: Kintama; Strip light

**Designer** Nick Crosbie at Inflate
**Nationality** British
**Country of residence** UK
**Date of birth** 1971
**Title** Kintama, Strip light
**Date** Both May 2001

"Developed in collaboration with the architectural practice Ushida Findlay, Kintama (Japanese for 'golden balls') was designed for Ushida's client Claydon Heeley. The Kintama packs flat and inflates to give a soft cushioned seat that can be stacked into multiple configurations or used singularly." Nick Crosbie

Kintama's dimensions are: 180 cm (width); 180 cm (depth); 180 cm (height). It is constructed using rotational-moulded soft pvc.

"Strip light was an in-house project to develop a product that would enhance standard fluorescent strip lights. The light shades are currently in situ in the Inflate design studio and plans for mass production are in the pipeline, following the enthusiasm expressed by studio visitors!" Nick Crosbie

Strip light's approximate dimensions are: 400 cm (length); 50 cm (width); 25 cm (depth). It is constructed in pvc.

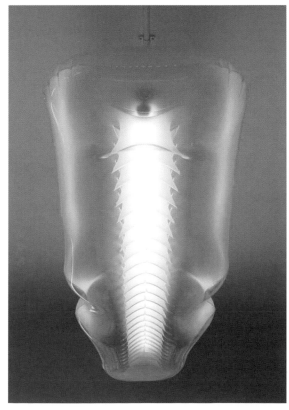

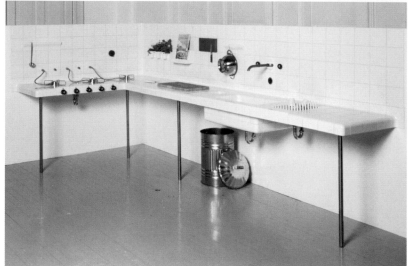 

## Droog Design: Tile Kitchen; Handy Burner

**Designers** Arnout Visser (Tile Kitchen), Erik Jan Kwakkel (Tile Kitchen), Peter van der Jagt (Tile Kitchen, Handy Burner) for Droog
**Nationality** Dutch
**Country of residence** Netherlands
**Title** Tile Kitchen, Handy Burner
**Date** First shown April 2001 at the Milan Furniture Fair

"A collection of construction tiles gives complete freedom to create a one-of-a-kind kitchen made to fit into any space. The function tiles are used on request. You can also use the tiles for other areas, like bathrooms, swimming pools or even the outside of a building. We are now also working to contribute new function tiles for outside and inside. The industrial-made tiles are perfect for creating a personal environment. The tiles are fitted in a grid of 15 x 15 cm, and you can build as many as you like...." Arnout Visser

## Linge Hansen: Cubic house

**Designer** Linge Hansen
**Nationality** Danish
**Country of residence** Denmark
**Date of birth** 1968
**Title** Cubic house
**Date** First shown May 2001 at the Scandinavian Furniture Fair; design completed September 2000
**Major awards** Association of Danish Designers Award

"From the beginning the idea was to create an allotment garden house. However, the house can actually fulfill several needs: a guesthouse; a contemplative workplace as an annexe to your main domicile, or as a weekend cottage. The cubic wooden house stands in a corner of a low plateau that is four times the area of the house. The design was inspired by the idea of the square and the rectangle. This is reflected also in the strict character of the spartan, simple and functional furniture. The house is fully equipped with a multi-purpose bed that also serves as a sofa and storage device. The mobile kitchen allows you to cook on the terrace. The house has two expressions – open and closed. The blinds in front of the glass entrance can be angled to provide a shaded cover. The entrance can be opened so that there is no division between inside and out; the window blinds unhook and serve as tables. In the diagonals of the upper two corners of the cube are firstly a space for the cylinder-formed steel tank collecting water for the outdoor shower; and secondly a skylight positioned to direct a shaft of light across the internal wall. The house needs no power. The ecological toilet is placed in a separate building next to the main house. The fridge is placed below ground inside the house to keep a constant temperature also during the summer. The cubic house measures: 3 m x 3 m x 3 m. The materials used are concrete, wood, steel, and glass. The foundations of the house are concrete. The house is made in wood, and the roof is of steel. The colours are discreet, to give the house a light expression. To add contrast the surfaces vary between smooth and rough, and matt and glossy. The furniture is made in birch veneer with details of black mdf." Linge Hansen

01

## Karim Rashid: Orgy; Sloop; Pleasurescape; Plob

**Designer** Karim Rashid
**Nationality** Canadian
**Country of residence** USA
**Date of birth** 1960
**Title** Orgy sofa/bed (01), Sloop chair (02), Plob interactive environment (03, 04), Pleasurescape environment (05)
**Date** May 2001 (Orgy); April 2001 at the Milan Furniture Fair (Sloop); shown from February 2001 to August 2001 (Pleasurescape); April/May 2001 (Plob)

"Orgy is an upholstered couch for three people to converse and engage with each other. The partially enclosed sofa and (removeable) ottoman come together to form a flat surface large enough for a guest bed or casual play pen. The inspiration centred around thoughts of meeting, casualness, engaging, multi-use, soft,

organic, menage, converse, sleep, work, relax, play, contain, social, oval, and centred.

"Sloop is part of a series of furniture called Klear Karim for an exhibition in Tokyo for Idée, Japan, at the Milan Fair, April 2001. It is a one-piece inch-thick acrylic chair. A perpetual loop created on one mould – the chair's ribbon-like qualities – communicates the flow of plastic, the flow of immateriality, and the organomic organic quality to meet the needs of human comfort, both physically and psychologically. Remember, beauty is more phsycological than physical.

"Pleasurescape was shown at Rice Gallery, Houston, TX, USA; Deitch Projects, New York; and SFMOMA's *010101* show in San Francisco. Pleasurescape is constructed in fibreglass RFP with automotive lacquer. Pleasurescape sets a stage for a non-stop amorphous plastic scape that denotes a world with no boundaries. The space extends itself via plastic organic modules of repetition – a continuum of surface based on a conventional Cartesian grid of the gallery floor. Pleasurescape is a metaphor for a continuous world, a neutral

landscape, and an undulating surface that is reconfigurable and sizeable ad infinitum. The entire 400 square feet of repeated forms are made from three modules and can be assembled together in various arrangements. Inevitably our entire physical landscape will merge and connect. Furniture and space merge.

"Object and environment, city and town, water and ground, highway to highway, being to being. Pleasurenation is part of the Pleasurenation – a place and time for solitude, The cocoon as communal. A world that I am developing.

"Plob is a plastic blob. A plob is the state between liquid plastic and solid material object. Plob was shown at Capp St. Gallery, San Francisco. Plob is made using rotationally moulded polypropylene, a computer, software, 280 pieces, 280 coloured lights, motion sensors, and 12 tracks of original music by Karim Rashid and Yujin Morisawa. Lights and diverse synchronised sounds are activated through human motion in the Plob." Karim Rashid

Plob's dimensions are: 365 cm (width); 731 cm (length); 304 cm (height).

03

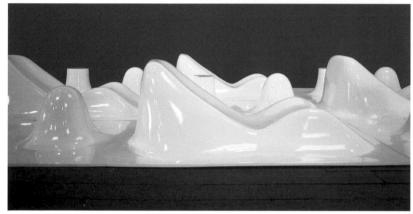

05

02

04

Image © Dalgaard/Edvars

# BoO1 CITY OF TOMORROW

*BoO1 City of Tomorrow*
European Housing Fair and Exhibition, Malmö, Sweden

Following an initiative from Sweden, the EU's Housing Ministers decided in 1996 to give their support to a European Housing Exhibition with an ecological theme. The idea developed into *BoO1 City of Tomorrow*, which took place between 11 May and 9 September 2001, on a reclaimed industrial estate by the sea, and within walking distance of the city centre and Ribersborg beach, with views of Öresund bridge and Copenhagen.

The *City of Tomorrow* has been one of Europe's largest housing exhibitions ever – a world-class spectacle and an ecological spearhead for the new millennium. The target was one million visitors. *BoO1 City of Tomorrow* consists of two parts – a permanent housing area, and exhibition site. The whole expanse covers about 30 hectares. Here about 800 new apartments are being built on the water's edge, with quay promenades, marina and parks – with Santiago Calatrava's Turning Tower planned as a focal point for the whole new complex.

The theme of *BoO1* is stated as: "The city of tomorrow in an ecologically sustainable information and welfare community. Beauty and  stimulation are keywords in the new society with human beings at its centre."
www.bo01.com

## Kim Dalgaard & Tue Trærup Madsen

**Project** 'Trähus 2001' (Timberhouse 2001)
**Architect** Kim Dalgaard & Tue Trærup Madsen Arkitekter
M.A.A., Copenhagen
**Creative team** Tue Trærup Madsen & Kim Dalgaard;
Assisting architect; Anna Müller
**Main contractor** Skanska, Sweden

"The project was awarded first prize in a 1999 international competition for the experimental development of multi-storey apartment housing in wood construction. The demands of the site, a small block in the new neighbourhood of the Bo01 expo, are urban and very complex, with a park at one side and the intimate scale of a small town on the other sides. The project, which contains terraced houses, one- and two-storey flats, shop facilities and a garage, offers a rich and varied environment for the everyday life of the inhabitants – and also for the neighbours and passers-by. The architects have admirably managed to master the complexity of the program and the process, and also the challenge of the technical research in wood and its experimental use in the construction, in the elevations and other finished surfaces and in the detailing. Their solution is clearly urban, rich and elegantly articulated within a distinct whole – this applies also to the interiors. The project is experimental and rational in nature. It reflects the orderliness and the living nature of wood. It is offering a beautiful example of sustainable housing." Professor Klas Tham, Bo01 Exhibition Architect

## Erskine Tovatt

**Project** Housing block
**Architect** Erskine Tovatt Arkitektkontor AB, Drottningholm, Sweden
**Creative team** Ralph Erskine; Beth Götesson, Magnus Andersson, Janne Liedström, Jörgen Trollmo
**Interior decorator** Fabrizia Sollevi, Sollevi Arkitektstudio
**Client** NCC Boende

"The site of the project is located at the corner of the waterfront and the road leading to the Turning Torso. Given this position, the building has been shaped with a taller, glazed part accentuating the corner, an accentuation that is even more pronounced by windows and bay windows. Another factor that contributes to this effect is the height of the boundary between the lower, darker white-grey horizontal plaster and the upper, lighter and more plain plaster, increasing towards the corner. The colour elements on the façades also contribute to its unusual character: the blue/cyan coloured penthouses and the striped parts of the bay window. Façades facing the yard as well as the penthouses and balconies have been given a distinct and powerful colouring which emphasises the joyful character of the building. The organisation of the dwellings responds to the building's L-shaped form, with the entrance from the street and the generous stairwell towards the yard. All flats are rather spacious and characterised by open areas connecting kitchen and living room, while passages along the façade lead to the bedrooms. They have large windows and glass doors towards south and east, where the balconies are located, in order to bring in as much light as possible. Large windows also to the north and west open up the view over the sea. Bay windows are situated in the extension of the living rooms to open views to the surroundings. The organic shaped store, laundry, etc make a smooth transition between the different parts of the flats. All flats have separate laundries as well as spacious bath rooms and saunas. Wood is used generously on floors while other surfaces have a light colour finish."
Ralph Erskine

## Karmebäck und Krüger

**Project** Terraced housing
**Architect** Karmebäck und Krüger, Berlin
**Structural engineer** Tyréns, Stockholm
**Landscape consultant** Stefan Wallmann
**Client** Packwerk
**Photography** © Leif Rosas, redstar, Helsinki

Six varying terraced houses form a very special atmosphere of sea and the waterside life in the inner part of the City of Tomorrow. The architects have drawn their inspiration from the old warehouse buildings that line the quaysides of so many European ports, but there is also a resemblance to the boathouses of a Bohuslän fishing village. The terrace is situated in the western part of the area, sheltered by the higher buildings that surround it. Contact with the water is maintained by the line of sight from the alleyways, and from the upper windows there is a view clear out over Öresund. The building takes the form of a solid stone house with individual colours in the façade. The robust character is repeated in the interiors with an open and flexible floorplan in three well-lit storeys. Five of the six houses are divided centrally by a light and communications shaft, where light enters via rooflights. High, narrow gable windows also contribute to the flow of natural light that reaches well into the interior. Movement between the two halves of the house is via wooden bridges around the light and communications shaft. Kitchens and living rooms in a unit are on the entry floor, with the kitchen facing the alley and the living room facing the little terrace garden. The more private rooms are on the second and third floors, with the bathroom on the second. The design features raw, steel-polished concrete floors, thinly-plastered walls that show the gaps between the chalky sandstone building blocks, and clinker flooring in the entrance hall and wet rooms. The plastered façades are formed individually in combination with colours on the windows and outer doors.

# NYRÉNS

**Project** Flats
**Architect** NYRÉNS Arkitektkontor ab, Stockholm
**Creative team** Chief architect: Johan Nyrén; Project architect: Marika Axén; Participating architect: Tomas Lewan, Natalie Stratakis; (Interior design) Chief architect: Karin Nyrén; Participating architect: Karin Broms, Kristina Jonasson, Maria Karatsaidou, Matti Klenell, Lars Pettersson
**Structural engineer** J&W Byggprojektering
**Main contractor** NCC ab
**Project management** Jacobsson & Widmark Projektstyrning
**Electrical engineering** J&W Sjölanders
**Landscape consultant** Bengt Isling, Jacob Almberg, Ingela Martinsson, NYRÉNS
**Client** Wihlborgs Fastigheter ab
**Photography** Åke E:son Lindman AB; Staffenbilder

The basis of the project's formation is the site and the location towards the wharf and the sea, a house that acknowledges the view and the daylight and protects the sunny yard. Towards the inner alley the yard is clearly defined by a long building. The façades are made of brick in order to cope with the exposed position, light yellow bricks towards the wharf and richly red towards the yard. The window sections are made of oak and the roofs are green – sedum covered. The sedum makes the roofs cool in the summertime. The wharf house is built around a light stairwell with a view over the channel. The interior of the flats is all natural material, in order to achieve beauty and durability. All apartments have exits to a balcony or terrace. Non-existent structural walls within the flats create possibilities for different types of planning. The flats on the first floor can be connected to the premises on the entrance floor, which creates maisonettes and makes it possible to combine work and living. On the top floor in the wharf house there are two large maisonettes with several balconies and roof terraces. A third type of flat is designed in the back-yard house, which is built like a terrace house with three small ground-floor flats. The back-yard house can also be used as a studio or workroom. The courtyard is the common oasis of the flats, screened off from the neighbouring houses with brick walls. It is built around a lower levelled lawn, surrounded by a large pergola with rich vegetation and narrow channels with running water. Car parking is located under the wharf house and is reached through the stairway of the house and the elevator.

## Mario Campi

**Project** The Entrance House
**Architect** Mario Campi, Lugano and Zurich
**Associate architect** Arne Jönsson, Architektlaget, Helsingborg
**Main contractor** Skanska Bostäder
**Landscape consultant** Karin Möllfors
**Photography** Basil Büby

A plain, taut building with projecting roof-edge, which will replicate the hard line of the horizon, forms the entry to the City of Tomorrow. The asymmetrical windows give life to the clean, white façades. A house built out over the street in the form of a gate gives an easy, floating impression. One T-shaped and one U-shaped four-storey building are enclosed, together with a lower garden lying along the terrace. The apartments are characterised by wide variation. There are no load-bearing walls, which makes for a flexible dwelling and allows for individual room placings. There is a range from two to six rooms to choose from. The terraced section in two storeys contains four dwellings of around 130 m² plus a cellar flat. All apartments have winter garden rooms which convert to wind-protected balconies in the summer. The large windows admit light well into the interior of the apartment. The building is constructed with load-bearing steel pillars, prefabricated concrete walls, and wooden infill walls in plastered façades. Windows, doors, railings, and roof soffits are in natural aluminium. On the terrace roof, sedum grows; other roofs are felted. The architects emphasise the significance of communication with the public rooms in many ways. The entry to the building is turned outwards in order to enrich the street life. From the streets and alleys, one can look into the garden through the glass doors of the stairwell. The alley between the houses also gives views and contact between inhabitants and visitors.

## West 8: Sund Garden

**Project** Sund Garden
**Architect** West 8, Rotterdam
**Creative team** Adriaan Geuze, Sabine Müller, Rudolph Eilander
**Completion** 2001
**Client** Bo01 City of Tomorrow, Malmö

The knowledge that the contemporary landscape is for the most part artificial and made up of different components, both designed and undesigned, allows West 8 the freedom to respond by positing its own narrative spaces. The basic ingredients are ecology, infrastructure, weather conditions, building programmes and people. The aim is to incorporate the awareness of these various aspects in a playful optimistic manner that stimulates the desire to conquer and take possession of space. Gardens form the only exception. The organised world of commerce, functionality and efficiency finds its necessary counterpart in specific spaces that appeal to uncertainty, mortality, desire and perversity. Gardens are enclosed and withdrawn from the world. It is here that the human dwellers can literally retreat into themselves. Situated on a landfill area, the secret garden dreams of the sea. It consists of an enclosed dark forest cut into the shape of a 12-metre cube. It is a mysterious garden to find your way through and move in. Walking in the garden you find a big shell. If you look up you see the sky through three holes cut into a thick layer of seashells. Parts of huge rocks lying on the surface are visible. It is possible to climb up through the garden to this level using ladders. Up here the atmosphere is different. The floor is covered with shells and several smooth rocks stick up to sit down on and relax. Two big shells lie on the surface and collect water. The garden enables an imaginary relationship between the ocean and the Swedish forest.

## sandellsandberg: Orangery

**Project** Malmö Bo01 exhibition; Orangery Pavilion
**Architect** sandellsandberg, Stockholm
**Creative team** Thomas Sandell, Boel Hellman, Gabriella Gustavsson
**Photography** © Åke E:son Lindmann AB, Stockholm

This pavilion is a temporary shelter for weather and wind, an exhibition café in a future Orangery environment. The whole complex is like an island imbedded in a Salix wood. The ground is covered by white marble gravel. On the gravel, outside, stand different rows of exotic fruit trees and inside are kiwis hanging from the pillars to give space underneath for seating guests. The whole shelter construction is demountable. The façade consists of eight metre-high plexi-glass sheets in aluminium frames. Every third glass pane is divided in half so that the lower part is able to slide upwards to function as entrances to the building. Due to restrictions in economy along the building process the upper floor of the pavilion is missing in this version, but could be added in the future, when the building is used as a part of a school canteen. This light blended environment frames the crisp green exotic garden surrounded by blue Swedish summer sky.

*Wiese (Meadow) IVa*
2001
Duratrans in light box
Part of a Triptych,
145 x 218 cm each

## Stefan Altenburger

**Date of birth** 1968
**Place of birth** Zurich
**Place of residence** Zurich
**Representation** Galerie Peter
Kilchmann, Zurich
**Courtesy** Galerie Peter Kilchmann

**Recent exhibitions**
**Solo** *(landschaft)*, Galerie Peter Kilchmann,
Zurich (2000) > *I Don't Remember Anything*,
Huis a/d Werf Beeldende Kunst, Utrecht,
Netherlands (1999) > *Move*, Container,
Amriswil, Switzerland (1999) > *March 99,
Mars 99, März 99*, L'Espace d'Art
Contemporain, Demingy, France (1999) >
*Happy, Happy, Joy, Joy*, Galerie Peter
Kilchmann, Zurich (1998) > **Group** *Music
and Art; Rock, Pop and Techno*, Museum
of Contemporary Art, Sydney (2001) > *Big
Nothing*, Staatliche Kunsthalle, Baden-
Baden, Germany (2001) > *Missing*,
Kunstraum Walcheturm, Zurich (2000) >

*Art Unlimited,* Art Basel, Switzerland (2000)
> *Internationales Videoprogramm,* Galerie
Barbara Thumm, Berlin, travelled to
Badischer Kunstverein, Karlsruhe,
Germany; House of Contemporary Arts,
Trafó, Budapest; Gallery for Contemporary
Art Bunkier Sztuki, Krakow; Lux Centre,
London (2000)

**Description of work** "My main interest is
the perception of reality through a medium.
More precisely I focus on the transformation
in meaning and sense of information
represented in different media. This
includes video, photography, sound and
digital information. I try to construct or find
situations where the information becomes
entropic, where the subject of observation
is disappearing or dissolving."

**Creative inspiration** "A lot of artists, some
with single works, some with their whole
biography. But I'm mostly inspired by
everyday observations in my surroundings,
including movies, TV, music culture, science
and mass culture." Stefan Altenburger

**01**
*Up In Smoke (White) VI*
C-Print on aluminium
120 x 169 cm

**02**
Stills of the video *Low Gravity*
2001
DVD, 5 mins
Edition of 10

**03**
Still of *Promenade*
2001
Cibachrome on plexi-glas
30 x 42 cm
Edition of 10

**01 - 04**
*Parallel*
2001

**05**
*Prop*
2001
Neon
19 x 57 x 15.24 cm

**06**
*Room Service*
2001
Two videos and photographic set
Dimensions variable

**07, 08**
*Director's Cut (Fool for Love)*
2001
Multimedia projection
17 mins, 2 secs

# Runa Islam

**Date of birth** 1970
**Place of birth** Dhaka, Bangladesh
**Place of residence** London
**Representation** Jay Jopling/
White Cube, London
**Courtesy** Jay Jopling/White Cube

**Recent exhibitions**
**Solo** Director's Cut (Fool for Love), White
Cube, London (2001) > Screen
Test/Unscript, fig-1, London (2001) >
**Group** Squatters, Museu de Serralves,
Oporto and Witte de With, Rotterdam (2001)
> Gymnasium, Kunstverein, Bregenz, Austria
(2001) > Idea Festival. Video in the City,
Centrum Hedendaagse Kunst Maastrict
(2001) > Please Disturb Me, Great Eastern
Hotel, London (2001) > Whitechapel
Centenary 1901-2001, Whitechapel Art
Gallery, London (2001) > In/SITE/out.
Inquiries into Social Space, Apex Art, New
York (2001) > Century City, Tate Modern,
London (2001) > Video, Barbara Gloss
Galerie, Munich (2001)

"Directors Cut (Fool for Love) was inspired
by an experience working for a very difficult
auteur theatre director last year. I found
myself more interested in watching him as
the subject than the play he was formulat-
ing. I made the work as a way of continuing
my interest in looking beyond the obvious
subject matter. Beyond the frame. The piece
was filmed in January in the Royal Court
Theatre, London, which was the only place
that responded to my request. I made the
work on one day with one rehearsal the day
before. I think this spontaneity is what keeps
the piece very alive. The film is installed
as a two-projection work, focusing always
on two points moving between diachrony
and synchrony.

"Prop was a piece made for the set
which acts as a signifier to give the relatively empty stage a sense of place. A neon
sign visualising a motel sign in perspective.
The set was very skeletal, resonating the
unformed quality of the play, which was
used in disjunctive parts. The actors were
all untrained, people I met or asked several
weeks preceding the filming.

"The theatrical is for me the starting
point of acting in film. Prior to making the
work, I researched works like Opening Night
by Cassavetes, Intervista by Fellini, and
Otto e Mezzo by Fellini, which all look at
the director as a dominant versus
vulnerable creator.

"Room Service was made a few weeks
after as a response to a request to make a
work after a stay in the Great Eastern Hotel,
Liverpool Street, London. I made a work
again in a manner to expose the workings of
a system. As in Director's Cut, we see the
way the piece is a film/art work and a play –
we are witness to the lights, the clapper-
board, the understudies. A behind-the-
scenes viewpoint, in Room Service we experience a morning in a hotel suite through
the indulgence of two chambermaids. The
girls use their time wisely to luxuriate in the
room as an illicit act. The video was made in
the room in which it was represented, and to
watch it the audience could also languish
on the bed or the chaise lounge.

"Parallel is being exhibited in both Porto
and Rotterdam and was filmed on sites in
these cities. The idea was to shoot the
same script in two different countries with
different native speaking casts." Runa Islam

*Five Angels for the Millennium
(Ascending Angel)*
2001
Video and sound installation
Dimensions variable

## Bill Viola

**Date of birth** 1951
**Place of birth** New York
**Representation** Anthony d'Offay
Gallery, London
**Courtesy** Anthony d'Offay Gallery

**Recent exhibitions**
**Solo** *Five Angels for the Millennium
and Other New Works,* Anthony d'Offay
Gallery, London (2001) > *Bill Viola, A*

*Retrospective,* Los Angeles County Museum
of Art (1998) > *The Messenger,* South
London Gallery (1997) > *Bill Viola: Buried
Secrets,* Venice Biennale (1995) > **Group**
*Spectacular Bodies,* Hayward Gallery,
London (2000) > *Encounters: New Art from
Old,* National Gallery, London (2000) >
*Between Cinema and a Hard Place,* Tate
Modern, London (2000) > *Modern Starts:
People, Places and Things,* MoMA, New York
(1999) > *The American Century,* Whitney
Museum of American Art, New York (1999) >
Lyon Biennale, France (1995)

Bill Viola's *Five Angels for the Millennium*
was inspired by a childhood accident in
which he nearly drowned: "I had no fear –
I was witnessing this extraordinarily
beautiful world with light filtering down,
green plants waving in the current, fish
swimming. For a moment there it was
like paradise – absolute bliss. I didn't even
know I was drowning until my uncle pulled
me out and I began spluttering and crying."

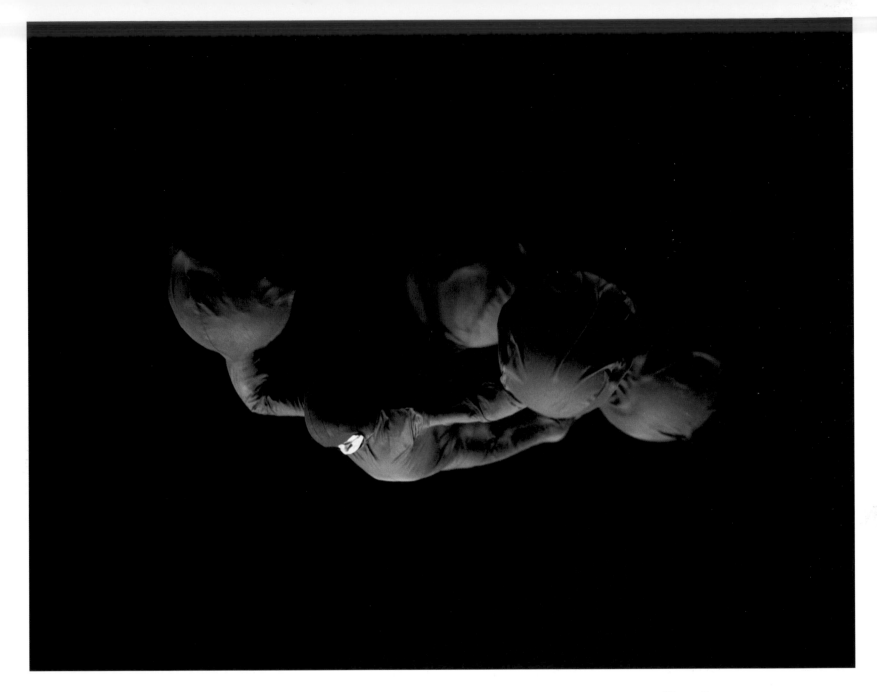

*Man on Air*
2001
Production still
From the series
*Man with Balls on Hands and Feet*
(1998-2001)

## Lars Siltberg

**Date of birth** 1968
**Place of birth** Stockholm
**Place of residence** Gothenburg,
Sweden
**Representation** Zinc Gallery,
Stockholm
**Courtesy** Lars Siltberg;
Zinc Gallery

**Recent exhibitions** *Le Printemps de*
*Septembre*, Toulouse, France (2001) >
Venice Biennale (2001) > *Way Out,*
Charlottenborg Museum, Copenhagen
(2001) > Mori Art Centre, Japan (2001) >
*Some Parts of this World*, Galleri Bakkeliti
Bambi, Helsinki (2000) > *Man with Balls on*
*Hands and Feet*, Zinc Gallery, Stockholm
(2000) > Rauma Biennale Balticum, Rauman
Taidemuseo, Finland (2000) > Hasselblad
Center, Gothenburg, Sweden (1999)

*Man with Balls on Hands and Feet* consists
of three films where a man dressed in an
awkward-looking futuristic jump suit with
large balls moulded onto his hands and feet
tries to defy the forces of gravity while
holding himself upright, first on ice, then in
a pool of water, and finally in a forceful fan-
generated vertical wind stream. There is of
course a slapstick quality in this piece that
immediately strikes the viewer, but on closer
scrutiny other aspects reveal themselves –
such as the relation between gravity, human
will power and the three 'phases' of matter
(solid, fluid, vapour). Just as in his other
works there is a translation between
incommensurable entities such as
psychology and natural forces, mediated

through different formal elements that
characterise the three pieces. In *Man on Ice*
(1998), Siltberg uses a fixed camera, and
presents the whole process in one take.
This technique produces a theatrical effect
(further enhanced by the lighting of the
scene) that corresponds to the solidity of
the ice. In *Man on Water* (1999) and *Man*
*on Air* (2001), Siltberg loosens the formal
austerity by using several angles and cuts,
thereby reproducing the more malleable
qualities of air and water. (Erik Van
Der Heeg)

*Capital*
2000
Stills from 16 mm/DVD
18 mins, 18 secs

## Sarah Morris

**Place of birth** UK
**Place of residence** London and
New York
**Representation** Jay Jopling/
White Cube, London
**Courtesy** Jay Jopling/White Cube

**Recent exhibitions**
**Solo** *Correspondence*, Nationalgalerie im
Hamburger Bahnhof, travelled to Museum
für Gegenwart, Berlin; Friedrich Petzel
Gallery, New York (2001) > *AM/PM*, Zurich
Kosmos Building, Vienna (2000) >
*Rumjungle*, White Cube², London (2000) >
Kunsthalle, Zurich (2000) > *Midtown* and

*AM/PM*, Philadelphia Museum of Art (2000)
> **Group** *Beautiful Productions. Art to Play,
Art to Wear, Art to Own*, Whitechapel,
London (2001) > Site Santa Fé (2001) >
*Playing Amongst the Ruins*, Royal College of
Art Galleries, London (2001) > *Hybrids*, Tate
Liverpool, UK (2001) > *Comfort: Reclaiming
a Place in a Virtual World*, Cleveland Center
for Contemporary Art, OH, USA (2001)

"I think my work reflects the desire for
power – its image and transparency – and
functions as its own ideology. The development of my work is probably a resonation
of all the environments I find myself in,
whether real or imaginary. The *Capital*
series developed as I became aware not
only that America was at the end of a
political era with the end of the Clinton

administration but an awareness that it
would be interesting to capture a sense of
Federalism and the matrix of bureaucracy
that Washington engenders.

"I use surfaces that are already loaded:
painting and gloss, film, and colour. I never
went to art school so I never had any hang-
ups about the attempt to paint. My work and
my art captures a naivety that anything is
possible. If I want to film the President in the
Cabinet Room this is in the realm of
possibilities. Power is accessible and
attainable. Maybe this is an American point
of view, but I have never viewed art as a
marginal activity.

"Inspirations range from Jackie O to
Thomas Pynchon. I have always viewed
my life as a narrative to be played out."
Sarah Morris

*Above The Grid*
2000
Video stills

*Interregna*
1999-2000
Video stills

*A la Claire Fontaine*
2001
Video stills

# John Pilson

**Place of residence** New York
**Representation** Nicole Klagsbrun
Gallery, New York
**Courtesy** Nicole Klagsbrun Gallery

**Recent exhibitions** *The Americans*, Barbican
Centre, London (2001) > Nicole Klagsbrun
Gallery, New York (2001) > *Video Jam*, Palm
Beach Institute of Contemporary Art, Lake
Worth, FL, USA (2001) > Raucci/Santamaria
Gallery, Naples (2001) > Venice Biennale
(2001) > *World Without Ground*,
Chase/Freedman Gallery, West Hartford, CT,
USA (2001) > *Ghosty*, 1000eventi Gallery,
Milan (2001) > *Some New Minds*, P.S.1
Contemporary Art Center, New York (2000)
> *MoMA 2000: Open Ends*, MoMA, New York
(2000) > *Above the Grid*, P.S.1
Contemporary Art Center, New York (2000)

"Much of my recent work has been set in
various corporate offices around New York
City. My attitudes about corporate culture
and corporate space were formed early.
As a child obsessed with science fiction, the
general idea was that you wanted a
button to push and somewhere to go.
We used to have to paste bottle caps on
the inside of the closet for the control
panels. Dad's office was where you found
the real buttons, the real, big, computers.
The office was outer space, outside the
home, above the street, daddyspace.
The office held mysteries.

"After graduate school, I found work in
a large investment bank on Wall Street. My
hours were late nights and weekends. I was
often alone in the powered-down dead zone
of empty corridors, enormous bathrooms
and silent waiting rooms punctuated by the
moans of displaced air from the elevator
bays. During these periods the space
became abstracted and easily adapted to
various imagined scenarios involving power,

submission, transcendence, isolation, and
ecstasy. The Utopia in the sky and its dark
secrets... always a favourite. It was toward
these ends that I began to take photographs
and make videos at work and in the work
spaces of others. Hitchcock often said that
many of his most sadistic dramas were
set in the home because that is where
"things happen". *Psycho* and *Marnie*
involve transgressions in the work place
and the spectres of imminent punishment.
My favourite chapter in the corporate hand-
book is the one on 'Unsolicited Backrubs'.
Work is where things don't or at least
shouldn't happen.

"In thinking about video, I am interested
in the artlessness of early art videos by
people like Vito Acconci and Bruce Nauman.
The static camera, the direct presentation
of a monologue or action. The point of view
represented by the camera was cool and
dispassionate... like a surveillance camera
or H.A.L. the computer. There is something
about the grim observance of silly behaviour

to which video seems naturally suited. My
reaction to the surveillance camera in the
corridor is always: 'Showtime!!' In the
elevator I like to invent behaviour that might
arouse curiosity but not necessarily alarm
from the security guard/viewer. Ritualistic
gestures at the patterns on the carpet... that
sort of thing.

"The people who appear in my work
are at work. They are seen within the
circumstances of their marketable skills.
As with every employee, there is always
more: more talent, more abilities, more to
capitalise upon. In one way or another these
individuals rub up against the cool world of
chrome, formica and glass that has been
designed for them. Sometimes there is
conflict and at other times... something like
grace. Lawyers sing, temps brawl and an
anonymous suit savours his anonymity in
a stall by wrapping his entire arm in toilet
paper. Although loosely scripted, I like to
think of my videos as field recordings."
John Pilson

*The Extension of Nothing, Removing the Floor in Pieces (2)*
2000
C-print
101.6 x 152.4 cm
Photograph: David Kelley

*The Extension of Nothing, Removing the Floor in Pieces (1)*
2000
C-print
152.4 x 101.6 cm
Photograph: David Kelley

*Falling at 1120 Ft above Sea Level*
2000
C-print
20.3 x 25.4 cm

## Patty Chang

**Date of birth** 1972
**Place of birth** San Francisco
**Representation** Jack Tilton/Anna Kustera Gallery, New York
**Courtesy** Jack Tilton/ Anna Kustera Gallery

**Recent exhibitions**
**Solo** Jack Tilton/Anna Kustera Gallery, New York (2001) > Entwistle Gallery, London (2001) > Fri-Art Centre d'Art Contemporain Kunsthalle, Fribourg, Switzerland (2001) > Baltic Art Center, Visby, Sweden (2001) > *Ven conmigo, nada contigo. Fuente. Melones. Afeitada*, Museo Nacional Centro de Arte Reina Sofia, Madrid (2000) >
**Group** *Video Jam*, Palm Beach Institute of Contemporary Art, FL, USA (2001) > *Casino 2001*, 1st Quadrennial of Contemporary Art, Stedelijk Museum Voor Actuele Kunst and the Bijloke Museum, Gent, Belgium (2001) > *Panic*, Julie Saul Gallery, New York (2001) > *WET*, Luise Ross Gallery, New York (2001) > *Transsexual Express Barcelona*, Centre d'Art Santa Monica, Barcelona (2001)

**Description of work** "I was interested in the ground falling out from under you and how walking on water bypassed this hazard."

**Materials used** "In this series I use a mirror, because everybody's got one."

**Creative inspiration** "When I was 12 my cousin sent me a book of Egon Schiele's nude drawings, and at the time I was also very into David Copperfield, the magician." Patty Chang

*The Bunny Lake Collection*
2001
Photographic sequences

## Georgina Starr

**Date of birth** 1968
**Place of birth** Leeds, UK
**Place of residence** London
**Representation** Emily Tsingou
Gallery, London
**Courtesy** Emily Tsingou Gallery

### Recent exhibitions

**Solo** The Bunny Lakes, Städtische
Ausstellunghalle am Hawerkamp, Munster,
Germany (2001) > The Bunny Lake
Collection, Pinksummer, Genova, Italy (2000)
> *The Bunny Lakes are Coming*, Anthony
Reynolds Gallery, London (2000) > Popping
up in Oostellingwerf, Friesland, Germany
(1999) > Tuberama, Ikon Gallery,
Birmingham, UK (1998) > **Group** *Il dono*,

*offerta ospitalita insidia*, Palazzo delle
Papesse, Centro Arte Contemporanea, Siena
(2001) > Venice Biennale (2001) > *Angst*,
Kunstwurk, Leewarden, Netherlands (2001)
> *Song Poems*, Cohan Leslie and Browne,
New York (2001) > *Music and Art; Rock, Pop
and Techno*, Museum of Contemporary Art,
Sydney (2001)

"My new work (*The Bunny Lake* series) is
partly inspired by two movies: *Targets* by
Peter Bogdanovich and *Bunny Lake is
Missing* by Otto Preminger. Both these films
have themes that are rather dark and
violent, and both are partly set in domestic
environments which seem staged or theatrical. In the films, and also in my own work,
there are various crossovers. All involve
young psychologically disturbed individuals,
white open-top cars, drive-in movie theatres,
children, murder, and suicide.

"[The series developed] from a
combination of the half-remembered films,
conversations and incidents involving my
younger sister. I wanted to develop the idea
of the Bunny Lake character becoming
plural, i.e The Bunny Lakes. After auditioning
lots of children, I then went on to record
some songs (a version of *Misty Roses* by
Tim Hardin) with one of them, which then
led to a new video work. From this I
developed a series of photo works and
ideas for a performance. I then began
designing a collection of dresses, and
made a catwalk show also involving more
children as The Bunny Lakes *(The Bunny
Lake Collection)*. At the moment I've just
finished customising a car, which I'm about
to start filming for a new work on 16 mm."
Georgina Starr

*Bantar Gebang*
2000
Location shot
35 mm colour film, sound
10 mins
Edition of 3

*Chun Tian*
1994
16 mm colour film, sound
3 mins
Installation: Casino Luxembourg (June 1998)
Edition of 3

*I'm Coming Home in Forty Days*
1997
16 mm colour film
15 mins
Edition of 3

*Of Three Men*
1998
Location shot
35 mm colour film, sound
10 mins
Edition of 3

## Jeroen de Rijke/Willem de Rooij

**Date of birth** 1970; 1969
**Place of residence** Amsterdam
**Representation** Galerie Daniel Buchholz, Cologne
**Courtesy** Galerie Daniel Buchholz

**Recent exhibitions**
**Solo** Kunsthalle, Hamburg (2001) >

The National Museum of Contemporary Art, Oslo (2001) > Galerie Rüdiger Schöttle, Munich (2000) > *Bantar Gebang*, Bureau Amsterdam, Stedelijk Museum, Amsterdam (2000) > Galerie Daniel Buchholz, Cologne (1999) > **Group** Yokohama Trienale, Japan (2001) > *Squatters*, MuseuSerralves, Portugal (2001) > *Casino 2001*, SMAK, Gent, Belgium (2001) > *Deliberate Living*, Greene Naftali Gallery, New York (2001) > *Anti-Memory*, Museum of Art Yokohama, Japan (2000)

*Untitled (Car)*
1998
Fibreglass, cellulose paint, car
headlights, transformer
approx. 460 x 205 x 140 cm

*Girl on a Rug*
2001
Jesmonite and enamel paint
Girl: 185 x 50 x 50 cm
Rug: 260 x 160 x 5 cm
Edition of 3

## Kerry Stewart

**Date of birth** 1965
**Place of residence** London
**Representation** Stephen Friedman
Gallery, London
**Courtesy** Stephen Friedman Gallery

**Recent exhibitions**
**Solo** Project Space, Tate Liverpool, UK
(2001) > Marianne Boesky Gallery, New
York (2001) > *The Window Box*, Milton
Keynes Gallery, UK (2000) > Royal Festival
Hall, London (1999) > Stephen Friedman
Gallery, London (1998-99) > **Group** *Girl*,
New Art Gallery, Walsall, UK (2000, touring)
> *Conversations*, Milton Keynes Gallery, UK
(2000) > *Corps Social*, Ecole Nationale
Supérieure des Beaux-Arts, Paris (1999) >
*this was now*, The Travelling Gallery,
Scotland (1999) > *Alice*, The Nunnery,
London (1998)

*They Went on Holiday to France*
2001
Jesmonite, enamel paint and
iron metal work
Person 1: 180 x 60 x 64 cm
Person 2: 177 x 35 x 58 cm
Metal grill: approx.
50 x 5 x 40 cm
Edition of 3

*Plantes Vertes*
1997
Mixed media
Dimensions variable
Exhibition: Contemporary Art
Center, Brétigny, France

## Michel Blazy

**Date of birth** 1966
**Place of birth** Monaco
**Place of residence** Paris
**Representation** Galerie Art:
Concept, Paris
**Courtesy** Galerie Art: Concept

### Recent exhibitions
**Solo** CCAC Institute, San Francisco (2001) >
Art Statements, Art Basel, Switzerland
(2001) > Collège Marcel Duchamp,
Chateauroux, France (2001) > *Les animaux
en voie de disparition,* Art: Concept, Paris
(2000) > *Univers en expansion: Le clos des
chutes: La chute des colonnes,* Museo de
las Artes, Guadalajara, Mexico (2000) >

**Group** + *vrai que nature,* CAPC Musée d'Art
Contemporain, Bordeaux (2001) > *La nature
n'existe pas,* Speelhoven, Baudouin
Oosterlynck, Aarschot, Belgium (2001) >
*Voyager à la verticale,* Maison de la Villette-
Parc de la Villette, Paris (2001) > *Sensitive,*
Printemps de Cahors, France (2000) > *The
Greenhouse Effect,* Serpentine Gallery,
London (2000)

"[My work is] about the observation of
things from everyday life. For example, one
day, my son forgot to put his yoghurt in the
fridge. The mould came and it was the
beginning of a new work called *la maison
de Mucor* which I am still developing.

"It's a bit weird, but my sculptures
develop by themselves. When I use food
in my installations, insects come, and I
discover this new form, and work with

insects. It's a kind of loop, the work
develops by itself and I try to follow this
development, the natural development
of my work.

"I use any kind of everyday materials.
I have had to experiment with those
materials to develop my work. I need to
use them for other purposes such as
cooking, or making bricolage... I try to
avoid barriers between life and the studio,
as this way I can de-condition the material.
An industrialised object comes alive in so
many different ways.

"My main influences are my father as a
gardener and my mother as a cook. The
gestures I use are simple and on the border-
line of the artistic thing. But if you want
some art references, my influences are very
large, from Wegman to Filiou, Christo or
Fischli & Weiss." Michel Blazy

*Spyrogires,* 2000
Hot glue, cotton, lentil seeds,
water, string
Dimensions variable
Exhibition: Serpentine Gallery,
London

*Mur de poils de carotte,* 2000
Carrot and potato purée
on the wall
Dimensions variable
Exhibition: CAPC, Bordeaux

*Le voyage des météorites*
1999-2000
Mixed media
Dimensions variable
Exhibition: Nagoya City Art Museum, Japan

Exhibition view: *Les animaux en voie
de disparition,* Collège Marcel
Duchamp, Chateauroux, France
2001
Mixed media
Dimensions variable

01

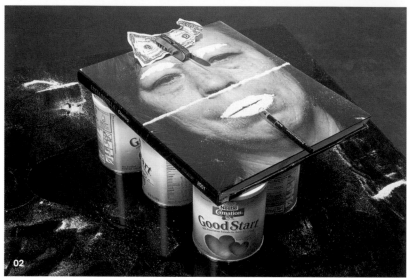

02

03

# Meyer Vaisman

**Date of birth**  1960
**Place of birth**  Caracas, Venezuela
**Place of residence**  Barcelona
and New York
**Representation**  Patrick Painter
Gallery, Santa Monica
**Courtesy**  Meyer Vaisman;
Patrick Painter Gallery

## Recent exhibitions
**Solo** *Surrogate Mothers*, Patrick Painter
Gallery, Santa Monica (2001) > Gavin
Brown's Enterprise, New York (2000) >
Patrick Painter Gallery, Santa Monica (1999)
> Galeria Camargo Vilaca, São Paolo
(1999) > Jablonka Gallery, Cologne (1999)
> **Group** *Almost Warm and Fuzzy: Childhood
and Contemporary Art*, P.S.1 Contemporary
Art Center, New York (2000) > *Insite 2000*,
San Diego and Tijuana, Mexico (2000) >
*Ultra Baroque*, San Diego Museum of
Contemporary Art, travelled to Modern
Museum of Fort Worth; Walker Art Center,
Minneapolis; SFMoMA, San Francisco (2000)
> Bienal de São Paulo (1998) > III Bienal
Barro de America, Museo Alejandro Otero,
Caracas, Venezuela (1998)

"Sometimes [my work] stems from a
thought, but sometimes it stems from a
feeling. In this case, I was feeling kind of
dead so I decided to portray myself that
way. It took me a while to decide to
proceed, given that I was profoundly
overcome by a severe case of the creeps.

"I've used pretty much everything: clay,
stuffed turkeys, plastics, eggs, wood, canvas,
stainless steel, polymers, underwear, my
parents' clothing, etc, etc. Since I let the
idea define the look and feel of the work,
I'm free to use whatever works best.

"Mixing and matching, I'd say my main
influences are the subjects of my most
recent works: Teresa Henriquez, Lucia
Bonilla and Barbara Fischer, my shrink.
There's also a nanny I had who lives in a
small town (in the Basque Country) whom
I'd like to contact. Artistically: Goya, Manet
and Robert Smithson come to mind. Lately,
however, I've been deeply touched by
Matthew Herbert (aka Dr. Rockit, aka Radio
Boy) as well as by Losoul and Isolee."
Meyer Vaisman

01
*Teresa Henriquez / Cooking & Cleaning
(After Mantegna)*
2001
Plexiglas, fabric, frames, and
laser sintering models
152.4 x 167.6 x 127 cm

02
*Lucia Bonilla / Cleaning
(After Helio Oiticica)*
2001
Plexiglas, baby formula, cans,
pocket knife, dollar bill and
handmade book
91.4 x 76.2 x 76.2 cm

03
*Barbara Fischer / Psychoanalysis &
Psychotherapy (After Michelangelo)*
2001
Fast cast, fibreglass, fabric,
leather, glass, and metal on
wood pedestal
213.4 x 111.8 x 108.6 cm

*AVL Table & Multi-Woman Bed*
2001
Installation view

*Darkroom*
2001
Installation: P.S.1 Contemporary Art Center, New York

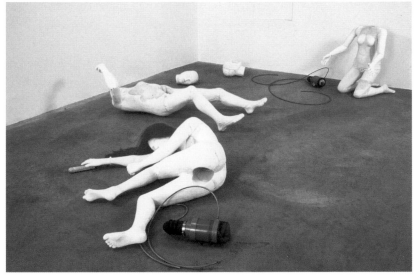

*Sex Machine*
2001
Foam dolls, latex, computer, metal
Installation view (detail)

## Joep van Lieshout/Atelier van Lieshout

**Date of birth** 1963
**Place of birth**
Ravenstein, Netherlands
**Place of residence** Rotterdam
**Representation** Jack Tilton/
Anna Kustera Gallery, New York
**Courtesy** Jack Tilton/
Anna Kustera Gallery

**Recent exhibitions**
**Solo** Gio Marconi, Milan (2001) > Jack
Tilton/Anna Kustera Gallery, New York
(2001) > *Darkroom*, P.S.1 Contemporary Art
Center, New York (2001) > Agency
Contemporary Art Ltd, London (2000) >
Stichting Grafisch Atelier Utrecht,
Netherlands (1999) > **Group** *Half-om-half:
Kunst vee geschiedenis*, Van Reekum
Museum en Historisch Museum Apeldoorn,
Netherlands (2001) > *Against Design, Works
that Blur the Boundaries of Art, Architecture
and Design*, Museum of Contemporary Art,
San Diego (2001) > *Just What is it That
Makes Trailer Homes So Different, So
Appealing?*, Center for Curatorial Studies,
Bard College, Annandale-on-Hudson, New
York (2001) > *An Ideal Home*, Victoria &
Albert Museum, London (2000) > *More
Works about Buildings and Food*, Fundicao
de Oeiras Hanger K7, Portugal (2000)

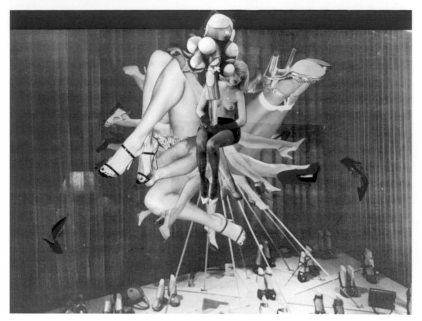

*Exciting Directions*
2001
Collage
37 x 47 cm
Collection: Boijmans Van
Beuningen Museum, Rotterdam

*Italy '89*
2001
Mixed media
34 x 32 x 42 cm

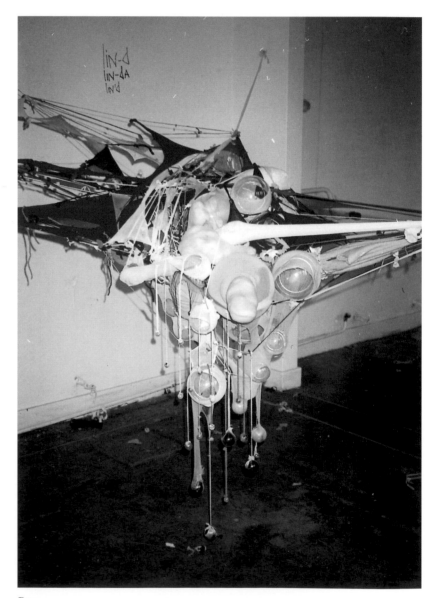

*Roy*
2000
Mixed media
1.6 x 10 x 4.5 m
Collection: Valerie Shields,
London

## Madeleine Berkhemer

**Date of birth** 1973
**Place of birth** Bergen op Zoom,
Netherlands
**Place of residence** Rotterdam
**Representation** Cokkie Snoei
Gallery, Rotterdam; Zinc
Gallery, Stockholm
**Courtesy** Zinc Gallery

### Recent exhibitions
**Solo** Zinc Gallery, Stockholm (2001) > *The Village of Milly-Molly-Mandy*, Cokkie Snoei Gallery, Rotterdam (2000) > *City Projects*, Torch Gallery, Amsterdam (2000) > *Sexxx*, Pracownia, Warsaw (2000) > *Respire –*

*HOTEL NEW YORK*, P.S.1 Contemporary Art Center, New York (1999) > The Modern Institute, Glasgow (1999) > *I Spy*, Witte de With, Rotterdam (1998)

Madeleine Berkhemer explores the body in every way possible and imaginable. She invites her viewers to look beyond the exterior. This, however, demands complete surrender of her viewers. He (or she) is required to passively watch Berkehemer almost ruthlessly change 'the body' into a battlefield. Whoever shies away from this, can no longer participate. This is unfortunate (for those involved), but so be it. Those, on the other hand, who dare to go with the flow will – after having been turned inside out – feel reborn!

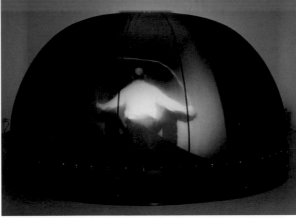

01

01
*On Hold*
2001
7 mins video loop
Inflated back-projection pvc,
rotating LCD-projector,
DVD-projector, steel base
2 x 4 m

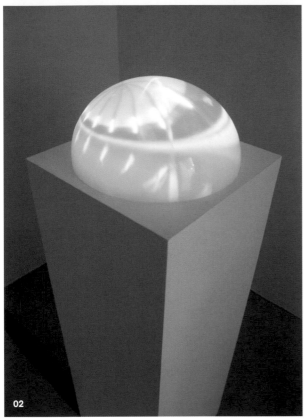

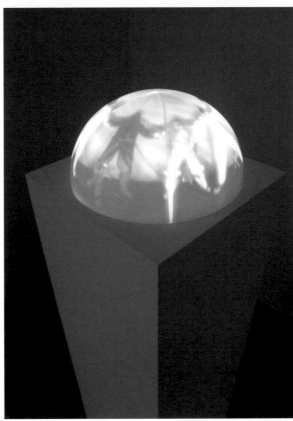

02

02
*Peptalk*
1999
Installation view
3.5 mins video loop
LCD-projectors, DVD players,
wood, plexiglas
45 x 155 x 155 cm

# Bigert & Bergström

**Date of birth** Collaboration
since 1986
**Place of birth** Stockholm
**Place of residence** Stockholm
**Representation** Zinc Gallery,
Stockholm; Galerie Barbara
Thumm, Berlin
**Courtesy** Zinc Gallery, Stockholm

**Recent exhibitions**
**Solo** Zinc Gallery, Stockholm (2002) >
Galerie Barbara Thumm, Berlin (2000) >
*Climate Chambers II*, Swedish Pavilion,
EXPO 98, Lisbon (1998) > *Love is in the Air,*
Galerie Barbara Thumm, Berlin (1997-98) >
**Group** *The Future Is Now!*, Louisiana
Museum for Modern Art, Humlebæk,
Denmark (2001) > Yokohama Triennale,
Japan (2001) > Kwangju Biennial, Korea
(2000) > Venice Biennale (1993) > EXPO 92,
Tequila Flashlightbar III, Swedish Pavilion,
Seville, Spain (1992)

Bigert & Bergström's closest kin are 18th-
century naturalists whose world was half-
wondrous and half-rational; the world of
colour theory and spatial conundrums, of
mapping cognition and drawing the effects
of the sun on the retina after closing your
eyes. It's almost strange that Bigert &

Bergström's inside-out video domes were
not invented in the 18th century. The domes'
inverted spatiality seems perfect for an age
obsessed with the relationship between perspective, spatiality, and subjectivity.

Unlike the countless artists who are
today seduced by the cutting edge of technology, Bigert & Bergström love the dull
edge of the knife because you can fit more
life on that edge. They implicitly know that
the essence of technology is a relationship
toward the world and toward other human
beings. In that sense, Bigert & Bergström
address the essence of technology in a way
that is impossible for all the shiny new
digital artists of today. (Sina Najafi)

01

02

## Ricky Swallow

**Date of birth** 1974
**Place of birth** San Remo, Australia
**Place of residence** Melbourne
**Representation** Karyn Lovegrove
Gallery, Los Angeles
**Courtesy** Karyn Lovegrove Gallery

**Recent exhibitions**
**Solo** *Matrix 191 For those who came in late*,
University of California, Berkeley Art
Museum (2001) > *Plastruct*, Karyn
Lovegrove Gallery, Los Angeles (2000) >
*Unplugged*, Darren Knight Gallery, Sydney
(2000) > Dunedin Public Art Gallery, New
Zealand (2000) > *Individual Ape*, Hot Rod
Tearoom, Oslo (2000) > **Group** Andrea
Rosen Gallery, New York (2000) > *Drawn
from Life*, Marianne Boesky Gallery, New
York (2000) > *Terra Mirabilis/Wonderful
Land*, Centre for Visual Arts, Cardiff (2000) >
*Brand New Master Copy*, UKS Galleri, Oslo
(2000) > *Rent*, Overgaden Gallery,
Copenhagen (2000)

"These works came out of fooling around
with casting techniques after working a lot
with more hand-constructed or model forms.
It was at a stage where I wanted to address
colour or the lack thereof, after looking at
my work in reproduction...

"I came across the Apple computer logo
and realised how dated it had become, in
favour of the white one. In a funny way it
seemed to mirror the way that I'd worked
previously by re-rendering coloured objects
through monochrome model replicas, somehow silencing them. I acquired the perfect
apple, took the bite and cast it in the
colours of its former face. It became like a
geological process, building these coloured
layers up in the mould, towards a perfect
form. It felt like a new form at the same time
as one that may have decorated company
offices a decade ago, a scrambled history. I
also wanted to make something that was
literally the visual record of its making, after
working on models where all the work is
rendered invisible in the final stages.
"The black-and-white version works both as
a reproduction of an earlier artwork by the
artist, as well as a more uninitiated form. It's
the version you'd see on the screen in a
black-and-white computer manual – it also
extends the nature of reproduction in my
work, a technological extinction; the grey
one is I guess a fossilised version of the
coloured one.
"The skull keyrings followed the apples
and continue this idea of a stratified form, a
commemorative model, in this case of homo
sapiens in the light of disappearance. Like
the Apple logo I like how the skull as an
image is so familiar it disappears and
becomes what you make it." Ricky Swallow

**01**
*Apple 2000*
2000
Pigmented resin

**02**
*Apple 2001*
2001
Black-and-white pigmented resin
9 x 7 cm

**03**
*The First One Now*
2000
Pigmented resin, wire

**04**
*We Are the Sedimentary Ones/Use Your
Illusions Vol. 1-60* (detail)
2000
Pigmented resin, keyrings

03

04

*12 Renumerated Workers* (Detail)
2000
Cardboard, wood, second-hand chairs
12 boxes, each 137.2 x 88.9 x 58.4 cm
12 chairs, dimensions variable

## Santiago Sierra

**Date of birth** 1966
**Place of birth** Madrid
**Place of residence** Mexico City
**Representation** Ace Gallery, New York
**Courtesy** Ace Gallery

**Recent exhibitions**
**Solo** *Visitors Transported Between Two Points of Guatemala City*, Belia de Vico Arte Contemporaneo, Guatemala City (2000) > *12 Remunerated Workers*, Ace Gallery, New York (2000) > *Documents*, Ace Gallery, Los Angeles (2000) > *Eight Ft Line Tattooed Over Six Paid Persons*, Espacio Aglutinador, Havana (1999) > *24 Concrete Blocks Moved Continuously During One Working Period by*

*10 Remunerated Workers*, Ace Contemporary Exhibitions, Los Angeles (1999) > **Group** Venice Biennale (2001) > *Concentration of Illegal Workers*, BF 15 Gallery, FIAC, Paris (1999) > *Representar/Intervenir*, Ex Teresa Arte Actual, Mexico City (1999) > *Frequent Stops*, Museo Carrillo Gil, Mexico City (1999) > *Made in Mexico, Made in Venezuela*, Art Metropol Gallery, Toronto (1998)

**Description of work** "Being a very 'synthetic' person, I work with two subjects which are very interconnected and between which it is hard to distinguish: with relationships between people in their hatred and their lives, and in the sale of their lives on the labour market. Some of the works reproduce the aesthetic of the clash between the social classes, with the overturning of cars, picket lines and other

aggressive acts against public or private elements. On the other hand, I have sought extreme working situations where the worker sells their body in a public context, defining themselves as object and unadorned merchandise."

**Materials used** "I look for things that are the most easily recognised, the most abundant, common and freely available. Very often it's the body of the worker."

**Creative inspiration** "Definitely the violence generated by the Mexican systems of exploitation, which recently I have discovered in more places, and having not-so-evident methods. They have been [central to my influences] because of their [obscene] cruelty and [society's] happy acceptance of them." Santiago Sierra

*Untitled (Upstairs)*
2000-01
Plaster, wood, steel

*Monument*
2001
Resin and granite
9 x 5.1 x 2.4 m
Photograph: Gautier Deblonde

## Rachel Whiteread

**Date of birth** 1963
**Place of birth** London
**Place of residence** London
**Representation**
Anthony d'Offay Gallery, London
**Courtesy** Anthony d'Offay Gallery

### Recent exhibitions
**Solo** Guggenheim Museum, Berlin, travelling to Solomon R. Guggenheim Museum, New York (2001) > Scottish National Gallery of Modern Art, Edinburgh (2001) > Serpentine Gallery, London (2001) >
*Fourth Plinth Project,* Trafalgar Square, London (2001) > Holocaust Memorial, Judenplatz, Vienna (2000) > **Group** *Public*

*Offerings,* Los Angeles Museum of Contemporary Art (2001) > *The Language of Things,* Kettles Yard, Cambridge, UK (2001) > *Shadow of Reason,* Galleria d'Arte Moderna Bologna, Italy (2000) > *Le temps vite,* Centre Georges Pompidou, Paris (2000) > *Wounds,* Moderna Museet, Stockholm (1998)

*Monument* is a replica of the stone plinth, cast in water-clear resin and inverted on top of the original. The mould was not made directly from the plinth, as it is a listed monument and therefore it is not possible to take a cast of it. The mould was constructed to the same dimensions. It is cast in two hollow sections which sit on top of the other and approximately 11 tons of material were used to make it.

# ÅBÄKE

Åbäke is a collective of four graphic designers, established in July 2000. We are Swedish, French, British, and French. We have been trained at Högskolan för Design och Konsthantverk (Gothenberg, Sweden), École Nationale Supérieure des Arts Décoratifs (Paris), Central Saint Martin's (London), Royal College of Art (London), Brighton University (UK), School of Visual Arts (New York) and Taike (Helsinki). Our commissioners are Swedish, Japanese, Algerian, Belgian, Danish, Italian, American, French, British and ourselves. They are singers, painters, photographers, architects, bands, record labels, furniture designers, curators, fashion designers, DJs, magazines, teachers, internet companies, and pen manufacturers.

## inga-lills bröd

6 st limpor eller många runda bullar

1 liter ljummet vatten
100 – 150 g jäst

4 dl brun farin
3 ägg
1 msk salt
3 1/2 (ca 1,9 kg) rågsikt
eller 2 liter rågsikt och 1,5 liter vetemjöl

– rör ut jästen i lite av vattnet. Tillsätt resten av vattnet
och de övriga ingredienserna.
– arbeta degen smidig och låt den jäsa ca 30 min.
– Knåda den sedan på bakbordet och arbeta in ytterligare
ca 3 dl rågsikt.
– dela degen i 6 lika stora bitar och forma till limpor.
– låt dem jäsa ca 1 tim.
– grädda dem i 225 graders ugnsvärme i 15 minuter.
– mums

## inga-lills bread

6 loaves or many small round ones

1 litre of luke warm water
100 – 150 grams yeast

4 cups of brown sugar
3 eggs
1 Tbsp salt
3 1/2 litres (approx 1,9 kilo) wholemealflour
or 2 litres wholemealflour and 1,5 litre flour

– put yeast in some of the water and make it even.
– add the rest of the water and the rest of the ingredients.
– work the dough even and nice, then let it rise for about
30 minutes.
– work with the dough on the table, add another 3 cups
of flour.
– divide the dough into 6 same size bits and make them into
shapes of loaves.
– let them rise for 1 hour.
– 225° in the oven for 15 minutes
– yummy

*Martin Gamper/alias_gampermartino*

**Page 160-161**
**Title** Village fête
**Date** July 2000
"Second-hand big letters (one week after they where used in the Feet First dance festival, see top images, page 161) for sale at the Village Fête summer 2000, Victoria & Albert Museum, London."

**Page 161 (top)**
**Title** Feet First
**Date** July 2000
"Signage, maps and decoration for the Finsbury Park one-day dance festival. Big letters following an A4 grid were created using scrap paper as templates."

**Page 162**
**Title** Air – Mini Rich
**Date** Spring 2001 onwards
"It appears that designing graphics for T-shirts is a common graphic design job. Our friends Rei and Alex are the parents

of little Mini Rich (six weeks old as we type this information).

"We want to customise T-shirts for Mini according to her growth. In a few years, customisation won't be necessary when she will be able to wear a 'normal' size shirt.

"The item shown is the first of the series and features our design for the French band Air."

**Page 163**
**Title** Mamma Inga-Lills bread recipe
**Date** Spring 2001
"Bread made after Mamma Inga-Lills recipe and font made for French band Daft Punk (based on existing logotype originally designed by Guy-Manuel de Homem Christo)."

**Page 164**
**Title** Martino Gamper
**Date** Spring 2001 onwards

"Swapping project: we make graphics for furniture designer Martino Gamper. He does furniture for our studio."

**Page 165**
**Title** Peter Jensen
**Date** Spring 2001 onwards
"Swapping project: we make graphics for fashion designer Peter Jensen. He makes garments for us."

**Page 166**
**Title** Sexymachinery
**Date** Summer 2000 (issue 1)
"A magazine in collaboration with co-editors from the Architectural Association. It is based on contributions from photographers, artists, designers, writers… In order to respond to the variety of the submissions, six different formats of paper – including a cover in real wallpaper and different papers – were chosen (from postcard to poster)."

**Page 167**
**Title** Simap
**Date** Spring 2001
"Packaging and catalogue for Simap, an Algerian pencil company."

**Page 168-169**
**Title** Source
**Date** Winter 2000 onwards
"Philippe Ascolli is the head of the Source UK record label. Philippe is French. At the first meeting we attended, he typically complained about British weather, food, traffic, etc… We wanted him to become more British than a Brit and therefore based his 'visual communication' on the very English crest. We consequently designed ads, sampler CDs, greeting cards, flyers, concert backdrops, slide projections, T-shirts, and posters looking more or less 'royal'. The size of the print decided on the number of elements we used."

Peter jensen

studio 1C / 2
Shacklewell studios
18 - 24 shacklewell lane
E8 2EZ
t: 07930 232 935

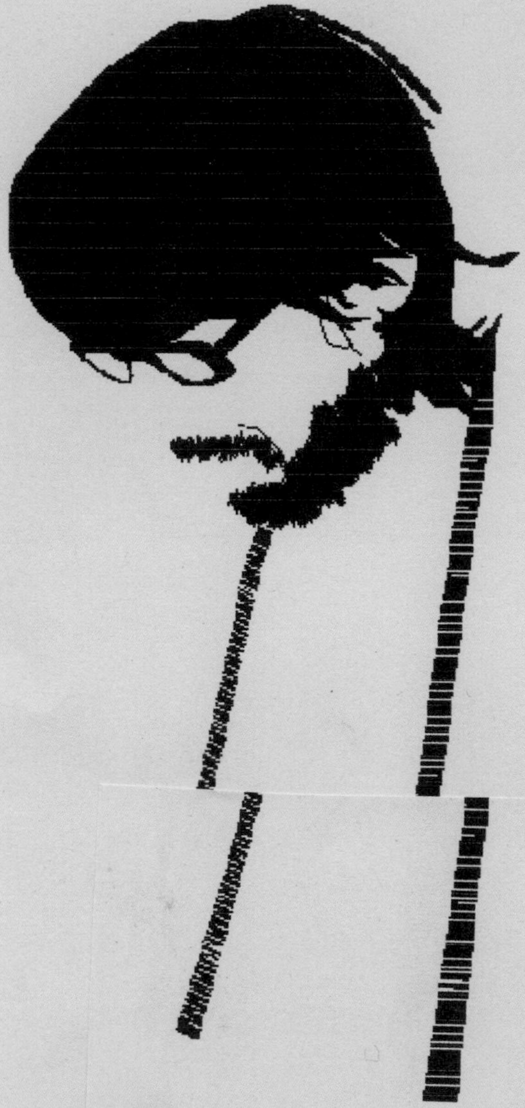

L London

I had this dream
once that I went
to heaven Just for
a Second. The first
person I met was Andy warhol
and I said
"Andy, Can I have a Cookie
from your minne mouse cookie
Jur"? and he said YES.

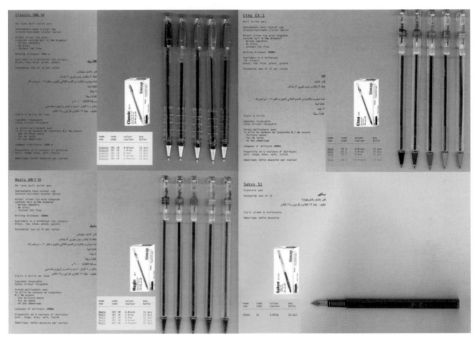

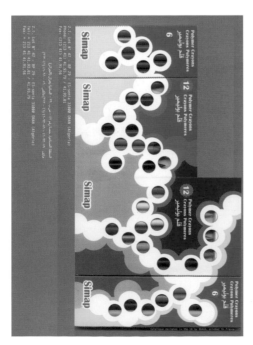

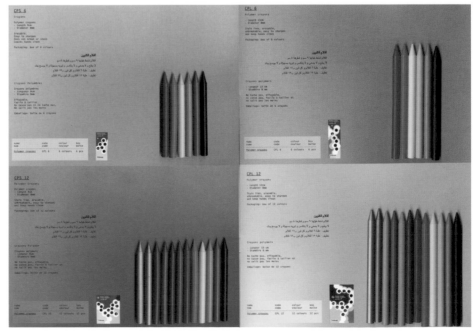

Saatchi & Saatchi: Sony *Brick Wall; New York; Jumper*

**Agency** Saatchi & Saatchi, London
**Creative director** Dave Droga
**Art director** Andrew Clarke
**Copywriter** Ross Ludwig
**Account director** David Sharrod
**Photography** Gina Garan,
First Base

**Client** Sony
**Product** Walkman
**Medium** Press, poster
**Exposure** UK
**Date** June 2001

Introduced but quickly discontinued almost 30 years ago, the Blythe doll has made something of a comeback recently. Firstly as the subject of photographer Gina Garan's book, *This is Blythe,* and now as the spokesmodel for the next generation of Sony Walkman.

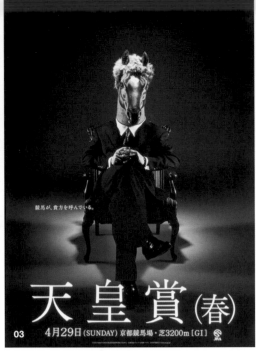

Dentsu: JRA *Takamatsunomiya Kinen; Oka Sho; Tenno Sho;*
*Fukushima Keiba; February Stakes*

**Agency** Dentsu Inc., Tokyo
**Project** Grade 1 Races
(images 01-03)
**Creative director** Kiyoshi Shimada
**Production** Taki Corporation,
Tokyo
**Art director** Shigenobu Kozuka
**Copywriters** Toshiyuki Okano,
Minoru Kato
**Creative producer** Reiko Kanda
**Photography** NAKA
**Design** Akira Okada,
Takuy Shimizu

**Project** Grade 1 Race and other
(images 04-05)
**Creative director** Kiyoshi Shimada
**Production** Taki Corporation,
Tokyo; Dentsu TEC Inc.
**Art directors** Shigenobu Kozuka,
Shunichi Sato
**Copywriters** Toshiyuki Okano,
Minoru Kato
**Creative producer** Reiko Kanda
**Photography** Yoshito Imaizumi
**Illustration** Eric White
**Design** Akira Okada,
Takuya Shimizu
**Client** Japan Racing Association

**Exposure** Japan
**Medium** Press, poster
**Date** January-April 2001

Visitors to the racetrack have been
declining steadily over the last few years
owing to the sluggish economy in Japan
and this has prompted the targeting of
a younger audience who have yet to make
their first trip. The horse-faced characters
were used to make young people feel more
disposed towards horse racing and to
stress that it is not just an old folks' form
of entertainment.

Mad Dogs & Englishmen: Haribo *Earring; Necklace*

**Agency** Mad Dogs & Englishmen, New York
**Creative directors** Dave Cook, Guy Seese
**Art director** Dan Lucey
**Copywriter** Mike Ludwig
**Account director** Janique Helson

**Photography** Fritz Kok; Unit C.M.N.A., Inc.
**Client** Haribo
**Product** Gummi Bears
**Medium** Press
**Exposure** USA
**Date** April 2001

Taxi: Flow 93.5 *Afro; Equalizer*

**Agency** Taxi, Toronto
**Creative directors** Zak Mroueh,
Paul Lavoie
**Art directors** Christina Yu,
Lance Martin
**Copywriter** Christina Yu
**Account director** Gary McGuire

**Illustration** Christina Yu,
Christian Borstlap
**Client** Flow 93.5
**Product** Radio station
**Medium** Poster
**Exposure** Canada
**Date** February 2001

Internet radio programmed by Volkswagen.
© 2001 Volkswagen, 1-800 DRIVE VW or VW.COM

radiovw.com | Drivers wanted.

Arnold Worldwide: VW *Flying Monkeys;*
*Orange Sounds; Space Robot*

**Agency** Arnold Worldwide, Boston
**Chief creative officer** Ron Lawner
**Creative director** Alan Pafenbach
**Art director** Chris Bradley
**Copywriter** Carl Loeb
**Account director** Collen McGee
**Illustration** Jago (*Space Robot*);

Fred Deacin (*Orange Sounds*);
Kid Acne (*Flying Monkeys*)
**Client** Volkswagen of America
**Product** Radio VW Internet Radio
**Medium** Press, poster
**Exposure** USA
**Date** June/July 2001

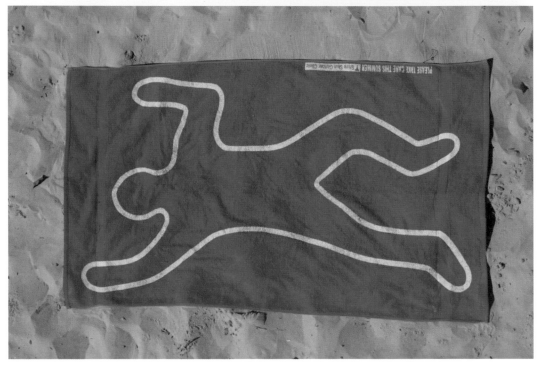

## Colenso BBDO: Shire Skin Cancer *Bernadette; Towel*

**Agency** Colenso BBDO, Auckland
**Creative director** Mike O'Sullivan
**Art directors** Leo Premutico,
Guy Rooke
**Copywriters** Leo Premutico,
Guy Rooke
**Illustration** Guy Hastings,
Antonella Napoli
**Client** Shire Skin Cancer Clinic
**Product** Skin Cancer Awareness
**Medium** Outdoor
**Exposure** Australia
**Date** Summer 2001

The aim of this campaign is to convince people to take care of themselves in the sun but instead of telling them, it shows what will happen if they do not.

Murals of people sunbathing were painted on walls and exposed to the sun. The skin was painted in acrylic paint on an enamel surface, and the sun did the rest. Within weeks the skin had cracked and peeled, much like the effects that the sun has on real skin overexposed to the elements.

The contrast between the beautiful original images and the degradation of the paint also helped to make the message more powerful. The towels simply act as a timely reminder about the dangers of long-term exposure to the sun.

WAR VICTIMS IN EUROPE NEED YOUR HELP + Australian Red Cross

J Walter Thompson: Australian Red Cross *Camouflage*

**Agency** J Walter Thompson, Melbourne
**Creative directors** Simon Greed, John Mescall
**Art director** Simon Greed
**Copywriter** John Mescall
**Account director** Susan Foley

**Photography** Steve Diffey
**Typography** Glenn Birznieks
**Client** Australian Red Cross
**Product** Australian Red Cross
**Medium** Press, poster
**Exposure** Australia
**Date** June 2001

Saatchi & Saatchi: monster.com *Do Something About It*

**Agency** Saatchi & Saatchi, London
**Creative director** Dave Droga
**Copywriter** Justin Barnes
**Account directors** Ben Callis, Justin Barnes
**Photography** Patrice Hanicot
**Typography** Scott Silvey

**Art director** Ben Callis
**Client** monster.com
**Product** Recruitment website
**Medium** Poster
**Exposure** UK
**Date** May 2001

Forsman & Bodenfors: Volvo *Freezer*

**Agency** Forsman & Bodenfors,
Gothenburg, Sweden
**Art directors** Anders Eklind, Mikko
Timonen, Andreas Malm
**Copywriters** Johan Olivero,
Filip Nilsson
**Account directors** Olle Victorin,
Eva Carlheim-Müller

**Photography** Henrik Bonevir
**Client** Volvo Cars Sweden
**Product** Volvo Cross Country
**Medium** Print
**Exposure** Sweden
**Date** March 2001

You will be more demanding after the Ford**focus**.

J Walter Thompson: Ford *More Demanding*

**Agency** J Walter Thompson, Brazil
**Creative director** Pedro Feyer
**Art director** Marcelo Prista
**Copywriter** Cassio Faraco
**Account director** André Gustavo
**Photography** Claudio Elizabetsky,
Fernando Zuffo

**Client** Ford Motor Company
**Product** Ford Focus
**Medium** Poster
**Exposure** Brazil
**Date** March 2001

# Foster and Partners: Chesa Futura

**Project** Chesa Futura,
St Moritz, Switzerland
**Architect** Foster and
Partners, London

The Chesa Futura apartment building in the Engadin Valley fuses state-of-the-art computer design tools and traditional, indigenous building techniques to create an environmentally sensitive building.

Although its form is novel, it utilises timber construction – one of the oldest, most environmentally benign and sustainable forms of building.

In Switzerland, building in timber makes environmental sense for a number of reasons. It is culturally sympathetic, reflecting local architectural traditions, and it contributes to the established ecology of felling older trees to facilitate forest regeneration. Furthermore, wood is an entirely renewable resource; it absorbs carbon dioxide during its growth cycle; and if indigenous timber is used, little or no energy is expended in its transportation. The larch shingles that make up the

building's skin will respond to weather, change colour over time, and appear as an organic part of the landscape.

The building consists of three storeys of apartments and two underground levels for car parking. Its bubble-like form is a response to the site and local weather conditions. The site has a very limited ground footprint and is spectacularly located on the edge of a slope, looking down over the village towards a lake. The curved form allows windows to wrap around the façade, providing panoramic views of the lake and surrounding mountains. The building has balconies to the south, which

benefit from sunlight, and it is closed at the back where it faces the mountains and the coldest weather, providing insulation through its thermal mass.

In order to maximise views, the building has been lifted above the ground on eight piloti. Raised buildings have a long architectural tradition in Switzerland, where snow lies on the ground for many months of the year. The fact of touching the ground lightly is expressed in the concept for the landscaping beneath the building, which will reinstate the rocky texture and scale of the mountain landscape.

## Shigeru Ban: Day-care Centre

**Project** Day-care Centre,
Odate, Akita, Japan
**Architect** Shigeru Ban Architects,
Tokyo
**Creative team** Shigeru Ban,
Nobutaka Hiraga, Soichiro
Hiyoshi, Keita Sugai
**Structural engineer** Norihide
Imagawa, Koh Sakata; TIS
& Partners
**Main contractor** Shelter
**Completion** May 2001
**Key dimensions** 131.2 m$^2$
**Client** Imai Hospital
**Photography** © Hirai Hiroyuki

"After the Japan Pavilion, EXPO 2000 Hannover, the Unochiyo Memorial Museum in Iwakuni-City was the second collaboration with Prof. Frei Otto. The site for this project was a scenic zone, and the client requirement was to design a Japanese-styled building with tile roofing.

"One of the main ideas during the design process was to have a rational structural solution for parabola-style roofing rather than applying a form decoratively. The structural solution was to use 'Ajiro' (wicker-work) with thin LVL (Laminated Veneer Lumber) and suspend it. As a result of the structural system, the roof naturally formed a curve suspended from its two ends, much

like traditional Japanese architecture.

"On the other hand, for this day-care centre, the main structural idea was to make a long arch that extends to form a tunnel with developed compressive stresses on the LVL Ajiro structure. From the structural idea, daylight enters the interior space from between the vertical and horizontal LVL members. Difficulties involved in resolving the issue of structure included the material's tendency to thicken under compression. 'Magewappa', the special product of Odate, proved to be a more feasible alternative.

"Odate has heavy snowfall, and building roofs are required to be able to bear a load of 450kg/m$^2$ of snow. In order to avoid the weight of the snow, a pitched roof was built over the LVL arches at an angle of 45 degrees. The LVL's rigidity was increased by using space-framing with a lattice member between the circular LVL and the square pitched roof.

"For the roof structure, a layer of FRP and corrugated steel folded plates was used over the LVL members to allow light through.

"The gaps between LVL members were covered with glass, and the space between the roof and LVL forms a double skin to maintain the interior environment.

"Similar to the paper structure, I found that thin LVL can also form the structure for a big span, and use significantly less wood compared to the usual arch of glue-laminated wood." Shigeru Ban

## Softroom: Designworks

**Project** Designworks, London
**Architect** Softroom, London
**Creative team** Dan Evans,
Oliver Salway
**Completion** late Summer 2001

Situated in Broadwick Street, in the heart of London's 'medialand', and due to open late Summer 2001, the new flagship store for menswear label Designworks is set to make a bold impression. An unusual, stage-like window-display, incorporating an accessories vitrine and discreet metal signage, recalls the traditional shopfronts of Bond Street and Savile Row, yet presents the merchandise in a totally contemporary setting. Colour plays a leading role in the interior, with contrasting blocks underlining the message that Designworks' clothing covers both casual and contemporary formal wear.

## sauerbruch hutton architects: TV World

**Project** TV World, Hamburg
**Architect** sauerbruch hutton
architects, Berlin/London

On an area in south-eastern Hamburg which was formerly used as an army barracks, an 'edutainment' park is planned in conjunction with premises already in use by Studio Hamburg, a TV production company. This

park will allow the visitor to see behind the scenes of the world of television. A further part of the site is dedicated to Studio Hamburg's own expansion, and other areas will accommodate a Congress Hotel, and future 'Ice' and 'Water' worlds. The scheme regards the whole site as a large park in which the various parts are scattered as 'islands' around a central space. In the southern zone of the site there is a public park forming a buffer to the neighbouring residential area. New north-south and east-west connections form pedestrian and

cyclist routes across the site.

The actual TV World theme park can literally be understood as a 'world' in which the various islands are distributed as individual 'countries'. Each island is seen as a set which contains its own attraction – for example, a museum, a stunt hall, TV show hall, water and fun ride – which are either housed in the open air or in covered halls. The boundaries of these sets are conceived as 10-12-metre high 'green façades' – mesh fencing with planting, poplar trees, etc. Between the sets there

is a continuous, flowing garden space – whilst within each set an individual atmosphere is created by means of its internal backdrop and its particular activity. This spatial situation allows the visitor to spring from one set the next, rather as one might 'zap' between television channels. The garden space between the sets is of a tactile, restful, park-like character, which offers a welcome contrast to the visual density of the conglomerate sets.

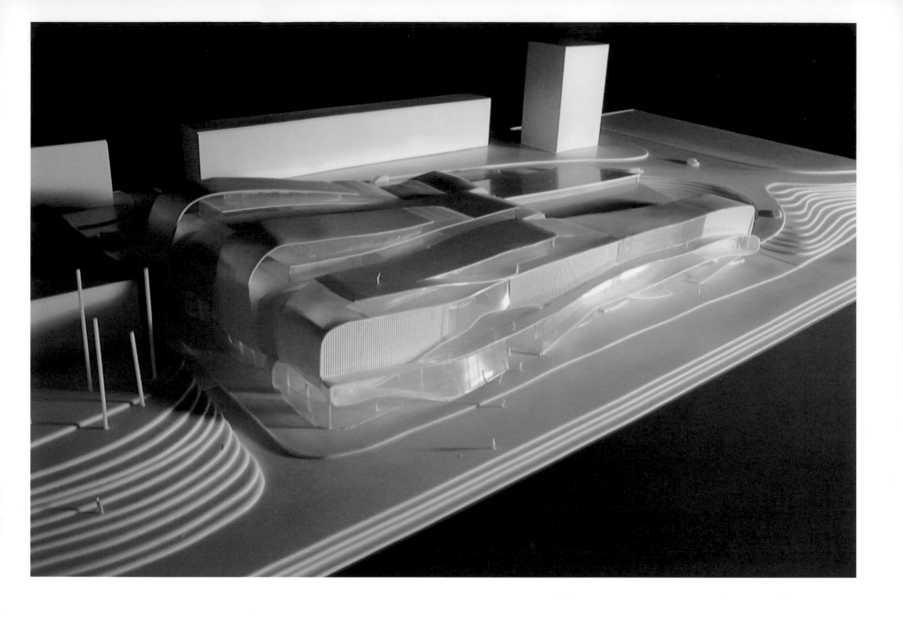

## Oman & Videcnik-OFIS architects: 'Cinema Paradiso'

**Project** Cinemaplex,
Maribor, Slovenia
**Architect** Oman & Videcnik-OFIS
architects, Ljubljana
**Creative team** Rok Oman, Spela
Videcnik with Josip
Konstantinovic, Tinka Prekovic,
Ivana Sehic, Blaz Razpotnik
**Structural engineer** Elea, Ljubljana
**Invited competition** June 2001
**Budget** £10 million
**Key dimensions** 17,000 m²
**Client** Kinematografi Maribor,
Slovenia

The Cineplex is located in the city centre
of Maribor, Slovenia. It is an urban hybrid
of cinemas, restaurants, bars, retail

provision, and underground parking. The site
is unique: the river bank is an extension of
the city public promenade. Therefore the
urban approach is a very sensitive response
– with a fragmented structure that rises
from the river landscape.

The cinema halls are separated and
the surfaces containing public program
are wrapped around them. The wrapping
surfaces roll around the halls in a similar
way to a film strip rolling through a
projector. And the performance on this
public filmstrip is provided by the visitors.

The strong appearance of the building
is exaggerated also by using multimedia,
projected onto the main elevation at night.
Film extracts and commercials mix with
the moving images performed by the
visitors inside the palace and attract the
people outside.

The roof is visible from almost all river
bridges that represent the main car and

pedestrian entrances to the city centre.
Therefore it is treated in a special way as
the fifth façade of the building. Similarly,
the roof is defined by fragmented strips
that form terraces, gardens and an open
cinema auditorium. The interior is formed
as sequences of programmatic paths and
entrances into diverse interior programs.
It is extremely perforated and forms
galleries, voids and opened plates. The
commercial programs are therefore
exposed into various directions and attract
for example restaurant guests into the
cinema lobby or cinema visitors into media
shops. Detailed studies of acoustics,
projection corners and visibility were made
as part of the approach to the formal
design. The cinema hall forms, the wave-
like public surfaces and wrapped acoustic
walls are results of those studies and
contribute to maximum functionality
and efficiency.

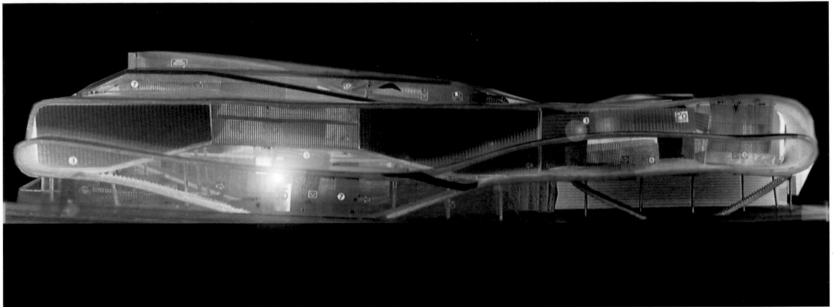

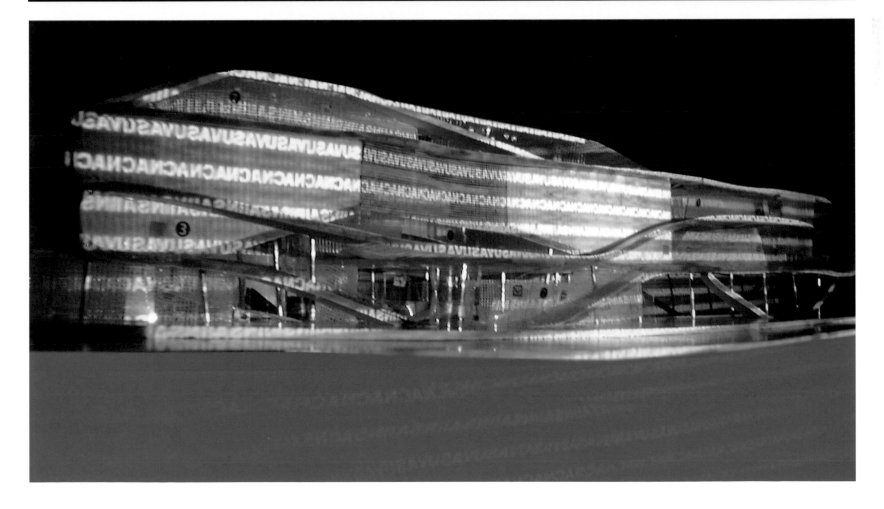

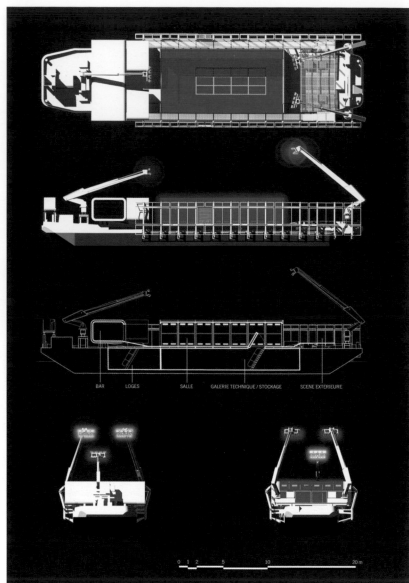

BAR    LOGES    SALLE    GALERIE TECHNIQUE / STOCKAGE    SCENE EXTERIEURE

0  1  2    5      10                    20 m

## Didier Fiuza Faustino: Floating Theatre

**Project** AMJ, 'Arteplage
Mobile du Jura': Temporary
Floating Theatre, Three Lakes
region, Switzerland
**Architecture creative team** Didier
Fiuza Faustino, Pascal Mazoyer
**Competition** February 2001
**Completion** March 2002
**Client** EXPO 02, national
Swiss exhibition

"The intervention is not limited to the
container's outlines, it soaks altogether in

the arteplages, leads the visitor out of his
intentions, houses itself in Expo 02's logic."
(excerpt from the competition programme)

"The project, an original medium rich in
diversity, soft and light, is a tool favourable
to any form of experimentation. It is being
materialised in three spaces, the trace,
the cage and the attractor, which are
complementary and indivisible. All
movements of the Arteplage Mobile du
Jura are conditioned to the situation of
the public within the project. The Arteplage
Mobile du Jura is a spatial and temporal
device. Three following sequences distil
desire and doubt, blurring usual landmarks
of the body, preparing minds to have access
to a renewed critical vision of reality, of

Expo 02, of Switzerland, and to action and
reaction. The Arteplage Mobile du Jura is an
almost innocuous device where all of whom
would get lost in it, and say: 'To feel it so
close to me, so brotherly at last, I have felt
that I had been happy, and still was.'
(Albert Camus)

The Arteplage Mobile du Jura is not a
cynical device serving subversion. Its
assumed stake is that each individual who
has chosen to go on board is able, in this
very place, and in Jean Genet's words, to
'deny our universe and its values, in order to
act on it with a supreme freedom'."
Didier Fiuza Faustino

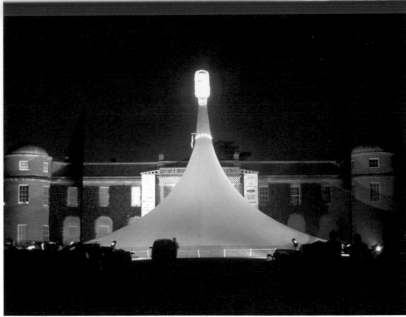
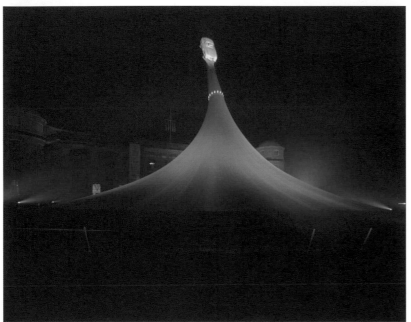

## Judah Ltd: Mercedes-Benz

**Project** Mercedes-Benz
Central Display, Goodwood
Festival of Speed,
West Sussex, UK
**Architect** Judah Ltd, London
**Completion** July 2001
**Budget** £125,000
**Photography** Rob Brown

Following his annual excursion into designing and producing the dazzling central displays for various marques such as Ferrari, Porsche, Audi and Jaguar for the Goodwood Festival of Speed, this year designer Gerry Judah took the 40 x 30 metre elliptical lawn in front of Goodwood House, Chichester, West Sussex and with the use of tensile fabric, stretched it 25 metres up into the air to balance a polished silver Mercedes-Benz 300 SL Gullwing. The sculpture contained, internally and externally, banks of pre-programmed lights, which from sunset produced a rippling effect, making the entire form appear to hover. To celebrate the 100th anniversary of Mercedes-Benz, this display, including an internal steel structure by Edwin Shirley Staging, silver tensile membrane by Architen Landrell, and lighting by Patrick Woodroofe, was erected for the duration of the festival, 6-8 July – becoming the most spectacular installation in the automobile calendar.

## Sheppard Robson: Toyota Headquarters

**Project** Toyota Headquarters,
Epsom, UK
**Architect** Sheppard Robson, London
**Creative team** Partner: Tim Evans;
Project architect: Philip Doyle;
Rodi MacArthur, Ed Jackson,
Rupert Evers, Michael Chadwick,
Frank Peacock, Fred Renton,
Tom Alexander, Barry Kendell;
Interiors team: Glenn Vaus,
Mark Thompson, Lara Ford,
Hannah Foden
**Structural engineer** Whitby Bird
& Partners
**Building services** ARUP
**Quantity surveyor** Davis Langdon
& Everest
**Project manager**
Insignia Richard Ellis
**Landscape consultant**
Derek Lovejoy Partnership

**Main contractor** Takenaka (UK) Ltd
**Budget** £25 million
**Key dimensions** 14,000 m²
**Client** Toyota (GB) Ltd
**Photography** Morley von Sternberg

The architectural concept developed by
Sheppard Robson was generated by two
primary objectives – to create a building
that would sit well within the landscape and
appear to extend into its parkland setting;
and secondly, to develop a flexible and
dynamic workplace for Toyota staff with a
variety of different work environments that
would improve interaction and motivation
whilst supporting both traditional and evolv-
ing workstyles. The building takes the form
of four two-storey office wings radiating out
into the landscape from an 80-metre long

glazed 'street', which houses all circulation,
informal meeting spaces and support
services. The street links the offices and
connects to a three-storey entrance rotunda
containing a staff restaurant, conference
facilities, computer suite and fitness centre.
Acting as a showcase for the company as
well as a meeting and greeting area for
staff and public, the street provides space
for the dramatic display of Toyota cars
both at floor level and suspended from
the 14 metre-high ceiling.

Central to the success of the design is
the fact that it has been designed as one
large single compartment on two levels
with an area in excess of 10,000 m². This
has resulted in a vast physically open
environment, which mirrors Toyota's
aspiration for an open work culture – an
environment without barriers. The principal
of work freedom led to the creation of
work places throughout the site – in the
café, restaurant, street, external courtyards,

and even by the lake.

The building structure comprises
exposed pre-cast and hidden in-situ
reinforced concrete elements to create a
unique hybrid solution, which is clad
predominantly in a glazed and aluminium
curtain walling system. The process of
on-site assembly and prefabrication relates
the building's construction and detail design
to Toyota's motor manufacturing processes
and engineering vocabulary.

The exposed concrete structure, by
providing a cool ambience, also promotes
the building's adoption of a low-energy
environmental strategy. This includes a low
level ventilation system, natural ventilation
and passive solar shading. The office floor
plate has been restricted to 15 metres to
enable offices to be naturally ventilated
during the mid-seasons via openable
windows within the glazing panels of
the façades.

## Geoffrey Reid Associates: Farnborough Airport

**Project** Farnborough Airport, UK
**Architect** Geoffrey Reid
Associates, UK
**Creative team** Bob Daziel, Colin
Calderhead, Matthew Bedward,
Luke Zuber, Anne Kelly, Eric
Guibert, Rudy Darmawan, Karen de
Waal, Paul Green, Stuart Barlow
**Structural and services engineers**
Buro Happold
**Infrastructure** Gibb
**Construction manager**
Bovis Lend Lease
**Landscape consultant**
Derek Lovejoy Partnership
**Budget** £50 million
**Key dimensions** 4,000 m²: terminal
**Client** TAG Aviation

The core of the proposals is to integrate
three functionally diverse buildings of vastly
different scales, engineered with a coherent
family of details and materials, so as to
avoid the piecemeal appearance so often

associated with airport development. The
sculptural form of the tower reflects the
client's desire to create a landmark focus
for the airport. The integration of the tower
and support building has been resolved by
using a seamless brushed aluminium skin –
inspired by aircraft and boat-building
technology – as a cloak which is extruded
up the stem of the tower before flaring
outwards to support the visual control room.
An illuminated lift rises behind the glazed
section of the tower elevation facing the
terminal. The largest of the buildings is
the 300 x 45-metre hangar. It is located
adjacent to the terminal building at the
northern perimeter of the site. Their
relationship is necessitated from a desire
to have a close interaction between the
active hangar, terminal building and waiting
aircraft. This context is significant in creating
a sense of arrival at Farnborough's airport.
The architectural aspiration for the hangar
was the creation of an effective structural
solution, the form of which captured the
undulations of the surrounding hills. It is
constructed in three 93-metre wide bays,
each of which is spanned by an optimised
arched structure supporting a 'floating'

natural aluminium roof skin.

The terminal building is the operational
and administrative centre of the airport and
also provides conference facilities for the
executive travellers. Most passengers never
enter the terminal and instead of checking
in are escorted in their own cars directly to
the waiting aircraft.

Geoffrey Reid Associates has created a
'theatre of aviation', a grandstand with views
of the dynamic activities of the airport, yet
maintaining a functionality and scale
appropriate for the privacy often demanded
by the client's customers. Conceived as a
single entity, the terminal building is a
powerful form that will evoke a sense of
flight and contribute to the overall
experience. The building comprises three
levels with varying sized floor plates
constructed in concrete to contribute to
the thermal mass, with an air displacement
system for ventilation. An uninterrupted,
lightweight metal skin envelops the spaces
within, with windows simply inserted to
relate to the spatial planning of each of
the floor plates.

## Peter Ebner + Franziska Ullmann: Stairway to Heaven

**Project** Stairway to Heaven, Vienna
**Architect** Peter Ebner + Franziska Ullmann, Vienna
**Creative team** Peter Ebner, Franziska Ullmann, Klaus Bollinger; Bollinger & Grohmann
**Budget** $150,000
**Size** 25 x 45 metres
**Client** MUQA: Museumsquartier
**Renderings** Michels

Visitors climb up between tall, just four-centimetre wide, iron plates made out of 'corten-steel', to reach a view at the top, uncertain of what it will be. The experience of having only the individual steps in front of you, with no view of the surroundings, but still having a hint of what is beneath, by climbing up semi-transparent steps, sharpens each visitor's concentration. The closer the ascending visitors come to the top, the further they 'rise' above the steel plates on the side. And slowly they start to experience the vista: a view that is supposed to show the travellers the glory of past epochs in conjunction with its current architectural inserts.

Once at the top, visitors can relax on the seats at the side of the platform. From there they can enjoy not only the view across the new museum quarter all the way to the 'Hofburg', but they are also right in the middle of the new museum quarter. Elevated from the ground one can enjoy the new construction in direct reference to the historic districts of Vienna.

On the way back down visitors are able to enjoy a vista of Vienna which is unknown to most travellers. They can see the backyard of the museum quarters with a great insight into the 7th District. This is the place where pomp and everyday life meet each other.

The Stairway to Heaven is supposed to be built as a temporary sculpture. The property this sculpture is on is, just like the steps of the stair, covered with steel gratings and epoxy-fillings. Owing to the translucent appearance of the epoxy, each visitor should be able to sense the originally rough character of the site.

It is the reduction to two materials – steel and epoxy – which creates a defined area of certainty within a heterogeneous surrounding.

## Llewelyn-Davies: Chongqing Airport

**Project** Chongqing Jiangbei
International Airport, China
**Architect** Llewelyn-Davies, London
**Structural, M & E engineers** ARUP
**Airport consultants** Speedwing
**Animation** Melon Studio, London

Chongqing Jiangbei International Airport is
located 21 kilometres from Chongqing and
is about to be developed into a modern
21st-century international airport to cater
for the expected eight million passengers
per annum in 2010 and a potential 15
million passengers later. The scheme design
solution proposes a first phase of around

65,000 m² with the flexibility for future
expansion. It will incorporate the best
modern standards of safety, functional
performance and quality and provide
flexibility for future use. The roof form
of the first phase terminal development
symbolises the surrounding hills of
Chongqing and will provide a new focal
point for Chongqing Jiangbei Airport. With
its futuristic design the new terminal will
become a catalyst for trade and will set
the standard for the future development
of the area. The design of the new terminal
is fundamentally very simple and achieves
good airport design standards in being
logical, customer-orientated and elegant.
Its success depends foremost upon its
capacity to handle passenger flows in a
simple, efficient and unambiguous way.

## Lifschutz Davidson Ltd: Dome Legacy

**Project** Dome Legacy, London
**Architect** Lifschutz Davidson Ltd
**Structural engineer** ARUP, London
**Quantity surveyor** Davis Langdon
& Everest
**M&E engineer, fire, acoustic and
daylight consultant** ARUP, London
**Transport consultant** Oscar Faber
**Lighting design** Speirs and Major
Lighting Architects Group
**Client** Legacy Plc;
Treasury Holdings Ltd
**Image** © Hayes Davidson, London
**Animation** Melon Studio, London

Legacy's proposal is to transform the
Dome into a large cluster of knowledge-
based businesses. Conference space will
also be provided for use by the occupants
and the other third-party users for product
launches, showcases and exhibitions. The
new architecture within the Dome will
complement the image of the Dome itself.
The internal layout of space will promote

interaction between all of the occupiers.
The ancillary retail, leisure and restaurant
areas, including health and fitness centres
and an hotel, will provide the ideal scope for
the occupants to interact. The environment
of the interior will be humanised by the
widespread use of natural materials
including stone, gravel and timber in the
hard landscaping and extensive areas of
trees and shrubs linking the buildings
together at ground and terrace levels. In
initial phases, trees will be used not just to
create parks and to line boulevards but also
to fill empty space to provide containment
for the emerging community. In later phases
the number of trees may be reduced by
replanting elsewhere but the remainder
will remain as essential components of the
environment of the Dome – providing a
natural canopy to streets and courtyards
and helping to clean and filter the air.
Trees will be planted in containers
concealed in the raised floor and plugged
into an irrigation system. External alterations
include the cutting in of clear roof panels
to 10-20 per cent of the surface area.
Clear panels will be either ETFE foil 'pillows'
or glass, subject to detail design.

## OMA/Rem Koolhaas: CCC

**Project** Cordoba Congress
Centre, Spain
**Architect** OMA/Rem Koolhaas,
Rotterdam
**Creative team** Catarina Canas,
Fernando Donis, Thorsten Kiefer,
Rem Koolhaas, Roberto Otero,
Erik Schotte, Sibylle Waelty
**Completion** 2006
**Budget** 50 Million Euro
**Key dimensions** 35,500 m²
**Relevant awards** Winners,
invited competition

Taking full advantage of the potential site,
the project transforms the east-west strip
across the Miraflores peninsula into a linear
volume that acts as promenade, mall, and
mixing chamber – a take-off point for the
Cordoba Experience.

First, the site is thickened into a long
block that marks the threshold of the
Miraflores neighbourhood and defines a
southern edge for the planned fluvial park.
A horizontal slice through the slab allows
the necessary activities – congress centre,
auditorium, retail, hotel – to be contained
along a continuous trajectory running the
full length of the building. The transparency
of this middle zone establishes the building
as a linear viewing platform, looking out
over the park, the river and the historic
centre beyond.

Functioning as a programmatic
sandwich, the upper and lower layers fold or
converge to respond to different interior/
exterior pressures along its length:
separating to accommodate the conference
hall and auditorium; converging to define
the hotel lobby; lifting to allow Miraflores
Park and the street to continue through to
the specified site. To the south, the main
volumes of the conference centre and
auditorium project from the slab; a ramp

between the two marks the formal entrance
to the complex.

The 360-metre length of the building
is conceived as a promenade, a coherent
sequence of programs and views. Bridging
the east and west banks of the river along
its length, the project spans the new site
to become a route, the crucial link is the
trajectory that moves visitors in and out
of the historic centre. A series of ramps
channel the public seamlessly through
the building, absorbing all circulation
into a sequence of visitors' centre,
auditorium, conference hall, retail, and
hotel. A roof terrace accommodates
additional leisure activities: mini golf,
outdoor cinema, and lookout.

Taking its place within the urban
fabric of the city, the siting of the CCC
organises the now disparate elements of
Miraflores, river and historic centre into a
coherent urban grouping that extends the
benefits of Cordoba's tourist industry to
the rest of the city.

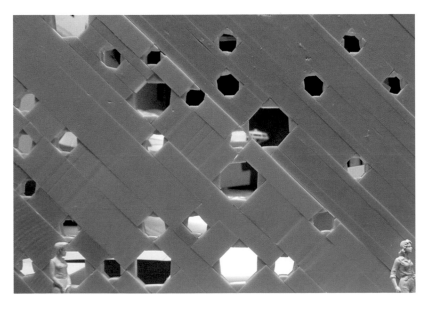

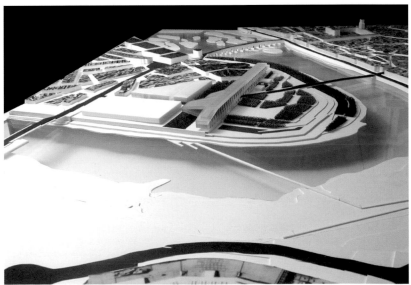

# Hamzah & Yeang: World Science and Trade Centre

**Project** World Science and Trade Centre, Beijing, Masterplan
**Architect** T.R. Hamzah & Yeang Sdn Bhd, Selangor, Malaysia
**Associate architect** North-Hamzah-Yeang Engineering Design Co Ltd, Beijing
**Creative team** Principal in charge: Dr Ken Yeang; Project architect: Andy Chong; Design architects: Ridzwa Fathan, Kenneth Cheong; Design team: Renee Lee, Shahrul Kamaruddin, Amy Chong, Antony Ridgers, Angie Foong, Beng Hin, Ng Chee Hui, Joris Tan, Lena Ng
**C&S and M&E engineers; landscape and environmental design consultant** Battle McCarthy Consulting Engineers and Landscape Architects, London
**Quantity surveyor** Davis Langdon & Seah; Kuala Lumpur, Hong Kong
**Feng-shui master** Master Jerry Too

**Commencement** February 2001 (design)
**Key dimensions** 690,798 m², built area; site area 9.21 Ha
**Client** Hong Kong International Development Co Ltd
**Model maker** Lim Swee Ming, Technibuilt Sdn Bhd
**Photography** K.L.Ng Photography

The proposed development has the following design features: a grand entrance from East Sanhuan North Road with the placement of two twin-tower office blocks on the eastern site boundary representing 'gateway towers', as the massing concept. The proposal has a central plaza as a focus for public cultural activities and functions, centrally located between the apartment blocks on the west and commercial buildings on the east. The all-year round weather-protected public cultural plaza has an operable roof that provides natural ventilation when external conditions are favourable. An internal rapid transit system is proposed for express movement of users from one part of the development to another in weather-protected conditions bypassing street activities below. The proposal adopts the strategy of separating pedestrians from vehicular traffic.

The buildings are serviced by a perimeter ring road on Basement 1 level, freeing the ground level of the development to be used as pedestrianised areas. The traditional Chinese art of Feng Shui is considered and taken into account in the planning and orientation of buildings. The apartments are located in three tower blocks of varying heights. Apartments are served by an internal rapid transit system line located on Level 2. The offices are configured as twin towers with bridge connections at selected floor intervals. The hotel and serviced apartments are located in the same building block. They share common facilities – the health club, restaurants, and business centre. The Convention Centre is predominantly below street level and faces the cultural plaza to its north. On the topmost floor is an Expo pavilion.

The development has a linear 'green belt' park that connects to all parts of the development via landscaped ramps and bridges, providing pedestrians with a safe vehicle-free environment for movement between buildings within a park environment. Each apartment has a garden terrace with adjustable glass shutters that encloses the space in winter, becoming greenhouses. In summer they open up to encourage natural cooling and ventilation of the internal spaces, while in mid-seasons they can be adjusted to suit external conditions. The apartment towers have landscaped sky terraces and common facilities at selected floor intervals of the tower which serve as communal spaces for its occupants. The bridge-over levels in the office towers are treated as 'parks in the sky' with lush planting and extra high ceiling height. These serve as recreational and relaxation spaces which contain cafés and shops. Large moveable vertical screens between the towers modify the internal environment by deflecting or scooping wind into the atrium space.

## Terry Farrell & Partners: Lots Road Power Station

**Project** Lots Road Power Station
Development, London
**Architect** Terry Farrell &
Partners, London
**Creative team** Design director:
Aidan Potter; Project director:
Dennis Dornan; Design team:
Andrea Armellini, Nigel Bidwell,
Jeremy Boole, Bobby Desai, Chris
Dyson, David Holt, John
Letherland, Jan Loecke, Steve
Middleton, James Patterson,
Michaela Ruffatti, Roger
Simmons, Mike Stowell
**Structural engineer** Waterman Group
**Environmental engineer** Waterman
Environmental
**Cost consultant** ECHarris
**Services engineers** Hoare Lea

**Transport consultants** Symonds
**Planning consultants** Montagu Evans
**Developer and project manager**
Circadian (Joint Venture Taylor
Woodrow Capital Developments &
Hutchison Whampoa)
**Landscape consultant**
Randle Siddeley
**Completion** 2008
**Budget** £350 million
**Key dimensions** 140,000 m²; 700
residential units

Situated on a wide concave bend of the
Thames, the Lots Road Power Station
occupies a highly visible location which,
after a century of industrial use, has
remained largely undeveloped. Together
with Battersea and Bankside, the majestic

building is one of three great power stations
on the Thames. At its completion in 1904,
Lots Road was the biggest generating
station in the world. Around 135 metres
long, 54 metres wide and 42 metres tall at
the roof's apex, the building is colossal, and
its four chimneys were, at 83 metres, the
highest in Europe.

Terry Farrell & Partners' proposals focus
on the retention and conversion of the
historic power station building, which will
be decommissioned, decontaminated and
cleared of internal plant. The shell will then
be transformed into a unique mixed-use
development comprising community uses,
a doctor's surgery and dental practice,
local shops, loft offices, an internal street
reminiscent of the Galleria in Milan, live-
work units and private apartments. The
ground level will be opened up to create
permeability across the site from Lots Road
to the river and creek, while the tops of the
two remaining chimneys will be converted to

house public viewing galleries offering
spectacular views of the Thames and
across London.

Two new residential towers located
on either side of the creek entrance form
a powerful visual grouping with the power
station. Residential buildings, arranged in
sequential blocks to continue the
permeability from Lots Road, follow the
creek's curve, creating a broad public
frontage to the new water garden. Social
housing is principally arranged in a new
low-rise building adjacent to the power
station, carefully designed to mitigate the
scale of the existing building, act as a
counterpoint to the northern tower, and
create a courtyard at the eastern end of
the power station. This building also
contains a crèche and a local museum.

The riverside scheme will create an
expanded village centre to a true mixed-use
urban quarter within walking distance of
local transport, rail network and bus routes.

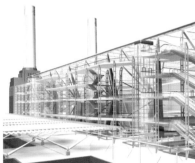

## Nicholas Grimshaw & Partners: Battersea Power Station

**Project** Battersea Power Station and Jetty, London
**Architect** Nicholas Grimshaw & Partners, London
**Creative team** Director: Chris Nash; Design team: Simon Beames, Annelie Kvick, Theo Lorenz, Tim Shennan
**Structural engineer** Buro Happold with Atelier One
**Quantity surveyor** Gardiner & Theobald
**Services engineer** Roger Preston & Partners
**Fire safety** Fire Check Consultants
**Acoustic consultant** Fleming & Baron
**Acccess** Selwyn Goldsmith
**Landscape consultant** Charles Funke
**Budget** £150 million (approx.)
**Key dimensions** 120,000 m²
**Client** Parkview International London plc

Nicholas Grimshaw & Partners intends to highlight the architectural virtuosity of the landmark building while providing inspiring and viable proposals for its reuse, to include a mix of entertainment and retail facilities, with a theatre as the principal attraction. To the east and west, public atria link the power station to hotels, providing routes to the riverside and also access for arrivals from the new station to the west. Visitors arriving by car and coach will enter the building from a new square to the south. The interconnection of the access points from each approach is achieved through a universal floor surface. This accommodates disparate levels to allow free-flowing circulation and forms the base of a huge public space termed the 'Agora'. Cuts into the floor plane give views down to the lower levels of the 'Underworld', housing a multiplex cinema suite. The Agora acts as a gathering point for an auditorium and children's theatre. Two new floors make up the 'Roofworld' above the east and west wings, with views down into the public space and out across the city. A multimedia

façade replaces the dilapidated existing brickwork of the west wall of the Boilerhouse, bringing daylight into the building. A further three floors, dubbed the 'Upperworld', sit above the Agora to complete the scheme. The development will be supported by a major new transport infrastructure that integrates road, river, rail and pedestrian access to the site. This will include a new railway station for a dedicated shuttle service from Victoria station, and a riverside jetty, also designed by NGP, providing Riverbus services to key points in Central London and the city. The jetty will comprise two levels above the existing deck. River boats will be accessible via a series of glazed pods arranged in pairs on a central pivot in a see-saw configuration. When one pod is at its highest point the other will be at river boat level. This will effectively empty and fill the boat with one pivotal movement.

The scheme was awarded detailed planning consent in May 2001.

## Camenzind Gräfensteiner: Tyre-Fitting Shop/Art Exchange

**Project** Tyre-Fitting Shop/Art
Exchange, Zurich
**Architect** Camenzind
Gräfensteiner, Zurich
**Creative team** Stefan Camenzind,
Michael Gräfensteiner,
Susanne Zenker
**Art installation** Martina Issler
**Budget** 0.9 Million Swiss Francs
**Client** IWAG Distribution
**Photography** Peter Würmli,
Martina Issler

The new Tyre-Fitting Shop/Art Exchange is
situated on a brownfield site adjacent to the

lake of Zurich, between the railway station
of Zurich-Wollishofen, a bus-stop and the
main access road into the centre of Zurich.
The client was looking for a highly efficient
tyre-fitting workshop with a strong visual
identity. The location of the site and its use
as a tyre-fitting workshop is typical of many
cities that are encircled by a semi-industrial
periphery serving the workforce commuting
between their urban place of work and the
surrounding suburban residential green belt.
The semi-industrial fringe acts as a filter
between an increasingly disassociated world
of work and leisure that has developed into
a finely tuned mirror of today's socio-
economic changes. In this stark environment
we find petrol stations, 24-hour shops,
night-clubs, factory outlets and start-up
companies of every kind which are served

by a never-ending stream of people.
Movement is the key which drives this
environment. We therefore conceived the
entire façade of the first floor of this tyre-
fitting building as a four-sided, 200 square-
metre interactive communication surface.
Sponsored by tyre manufacturers, young
artists are given the opportunity to
challenge the borders of art by taking their
work out of the gallery and placing it into a
commercial, fast-moving environment.

Challenging the conventional frontiers
of art and commerce, the building becomes
a marker of the cultural identity of today.
The building acts as a drive-by gallery for
passing vehicles and trains and engages
even more powerfully with pedestrians
waiting for buses or trains. This is the first
building of a series of cultural markers we

intend to place around Zurich, acting as
the new cultural gateway to the city. The
building is split into two levels, with the
workshop on the ground floor and tyre
storage on the first floor. Here, metal panels
were set back from the glass façade to
create a 50-centimetre wide access space,
in which to install artwork.

The architects were also responsible
for the quantity surveying, as well as site
management. This guaranteed a highly
successful and fast transition from the first
concept to the final construction in just
five months.

# MARTINA
# HOOGLAND IVANOW

Martina Hoogland Ivanow was born in Stockholm in 1973, and now lives and works between London, New York and Stockholm.

The work on the following pages was produced for *Colors* magazine, for an issue on old people's communities: "This series is from the Stage, an old people's home in St. Petersburg, a retirement home for old actors. It was for me a celebration of the old with their stories and life experience, easily forgotten in our society. These people have in some cases experienced the First and Second World Wars, the fall of Communism, near-death experiences and in many cases survived their own children and are still optimistic about life. The building and its people had an amazing atmosphere, a sense of loss of time and the beauty of living in your memories from the past."

Martina's work has been shown in exhibitions worldwide, including the recent *Jam – London/Tokyo* exhibition at the Barbican in London. She has been published in numerous magazines including *The Face, Arena Hommes Plus, Dazed & Confused, Visionaire, Self Service* and *Big.* In 2000, she also completed two pop promos for Queen Adreena. She has chosen to work with a camera because "it can document and pay attention to the magic in reality. I am mainly inspired by 'real' subject matter, subjects that are timeless and will always be important to us."

Martina Hoogland Ivanow is represented by Z Photographic in London and New York.

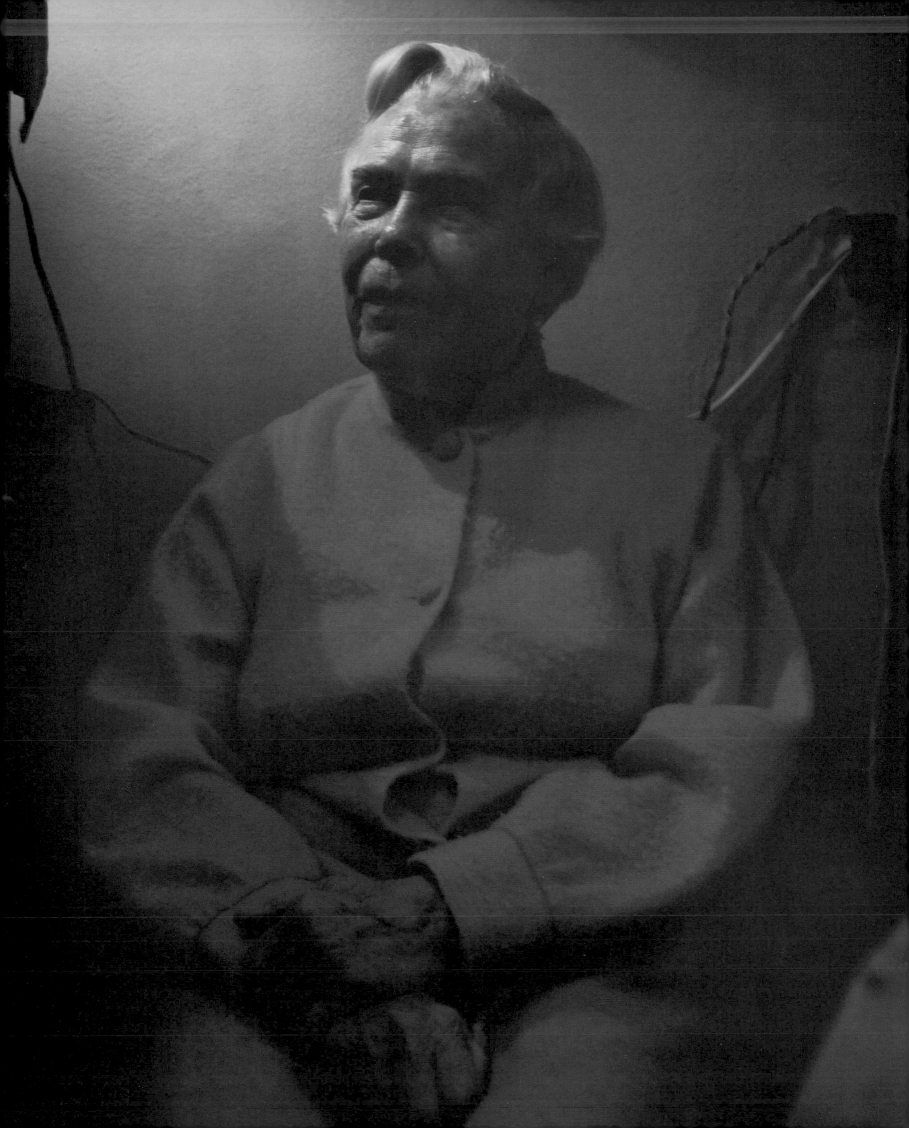

## Wieden + Kennedy: Nike *Freestyle*

**Agency** Wieden + Kennedy, Portland, OR, USA
**Creative directors** Hal Curtis, Jim Riswold
**Art director** Hal Curtis
**Copywriter** Jimmy Smith
**Account director** Rebecca Van Dyck
**Agency producer** Vic Palumbo
**Production** HSI, Los Angeles
**Director** Paul Hunter
**Director of photography** Max Malkin
**Producer** Nina Huang

**Editor** Adam Pertotsky; Rock Paper Scissors, Los Angeles
**Music composers** Afrika Bambaataa, Planet Rock Music; Jeff Elmassian, Endless Noise; Steven 'Boogie' Brown, Breakthru Productions
**Client** Nike
**Product** Nike Basketball
**Medium** TV
**Exposure** USA
**Date** February 2001

A combination of the unmistakeable sounds of Afrika Bambaataa and the skills of several NBA players and street dancers have created this choreographed classic for Nike.

The dribbling, shuffling and shooting sounds of the players are all integrated into this commercial, which at times feels more like a pop promo. Accompanied by the visuals from the rhythmic moves of the dancers and players alike this ad seems to be a homage to the street culture that surrounds basketball.

Hollywood all day , every day

## Dentsu: Star Channel *Rocky; Titanic*

**Agency** Denstu Inc, Tokyo
**Creative agency** Tugboat, Tokyo
**Creative directors** Takuji Nakamura
(Dentsu), Yasumichi Oka
(Tugboat)
**Production** Tohokushinsya Film
Corporation, Tokyo
**Director** Shinya Nakajima
**Client** Star Channel Inc.
**Product** Star Channel
**Medium** TV
**Exposure** Japan

'The magic of Hollywood, all day every day' is certainly apparent in the lives of two extraordinary Japanese office workers. Their daily lives are injected with excitement as scenes from classic movies infiltrate their normal routines. In one spot the first man is seen working at his desk, the office is swelteringly hot and a fly buzzes annoyingly around his head. He becomes more and more irritated as the sweat drips from his forehead and the fly divebombs his desk.

His patience finally breaks and he goes for the fly. He snaps his fist at it, and niftily catches it in his palm. The insect is finally defeated. From the other side of the office, a timid co-worker sees this triumph. Then, as we cut back to the first worker, the music from *Rocky* begins to play. He stands, holds his fist aloft and cheers. He looks across the office, where his co-worker is making his way towards him through the crowds. His face seems to have become bruised, and he begins to cry uncontrollably. Finally his colleague flings himself into his arms and they celebrate together.

In the second spot *Titanic* gets the same hilarious treatment.

## Mother: Organics *I'm so Fab*

**Agency** Mother, London
**Creative team** Mother
**Production** Hungry Man, London
**Director** John O'Hagan
**Director of photography**
Simon Archer
**Producer** Jeremy Bannister
**Post production** MPC, London

**Editor** Scott Crane;
The Quarry, London
**Audio post production** Jungle
Studios, London
**Client** Lever Fabergé
**Product** Organics shampoo
**Medium** TV
**Exposure** UK
**Date** June 2001

A young girl's obsessive hair admiration is the focus of this shampoo campaign that sees a welcome departure from the clichéd ads of the past. The young woman feels that her hair is so gorgeous she must indulge every hair-flicking opportunity. Any reflective surface becomes a mirror in which she can admire her beautiful locks, toss her hair and flounce ridiculously. In the final scene she shakes her head vigorously in front of a large window, behind which a national TV chatshow is being filmed. Her actions are witnessed by the millions of viewers.

## Lowe Lintas: EOC *Time of the Month*

**Agency** Lowe Lintas, London
**Creative team** Jeff Curtis,
Wayne Hanson
**Account director** Helen Rae
**Agency producers** Anthony Falco,
James Stoker
**Production** Itinerant
Films, London
**Director** Chris Beckles
**Director of photography** Angus Hudson

**Producer** Fiona Campbell
**Post production** The Mill, London
**Editor** Bill Smedley
**Client** Equal Opportunities
Commission
**Product** EOC
**Medium** Cinema
**Exposure** UK
**Date** April 2001

This cinema ad was created from a press brief originally to highlight the pay gap between men and women. It ran in April as a national campaign shown during films such as *Bridget Jones's Diary*. The ad shows a woman in an office environment showing all the symptoms of PMS – she throws things around her desk, bangs items down and looks thoroughly miserable. A male colleague makes a joke about how it must be her 'time of the month'. However it is revealed that the reason for her distress is far from biological, it's the fact that her monthly pay is 18 per cent lower than her male counterparts.

## EURO RSCG WORKS: Citroën *Black Smoke*

**Agency** EURO RSCG WORKS, Paris
**Creative directors** Frédéric Temin, Guillaume de la Croix
**Art director** Fabrice Delacourt
**Copywriter** Olivier Desmettre
**Account directors** Patrick Benveniste, Patrick Chambeau
**Agency producer** Pascale Petit
**Production** 1/33 Productions, Paris
**Director** Kinka Usher
**Producer** Sophie Jacobs

**Client** Citroën
**Product** C5 2.2 Hdi 136 Hp (Particulate Filter)
**Medium** TV
**Exposure** France
**Date** May 2001

The inspiration behind this striking 30-second commercial for the launch of the Citroën C5 is the fact that Citroën's unique Particulate Filter removes diesel particles so that your lungs no longer have to.

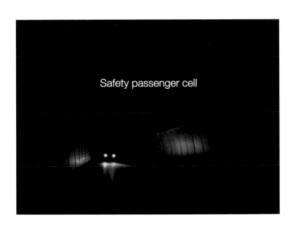  

## Jung von Matt an der Isar: BMW *Magic Car*

**Agency** Jung von Matt an der Isar, Munich
**Creative directors** Bernhard Lukas, Till Hohmann
**Art director** Gudrun Muschalla
**Copywriters** Till Hohmann, Bernhard Lukas
**Agency producer** Moritz Merkel
**Production** Arden Sutherland-Dodd, London
**Director** Paul Arden
**Director of photography** Nic Knowland

**Producer** Nick Sutherland-Dodd
**Post production** Moving Picture Company, London
**Editor** Bryan Dyke
**Music** Karl Jenkins Music, London
**Composer** Karl William Pamp Jenkins
**Client** BMW
**Product** C1
**Medium** TV
**Exposure** Pan-European
**Date** April-June 2001

In keeping with the genre of car advertising, we see the as-yet-unidentified car driving through the night. As it makes its way through the darkness the shots of the car are accompanied by copy lines describing the cars advantageous features, such as ABS and seatbelts. These however don't sound too fantastic until the main headlights of the 'car' move off in opposite directions, to reveal the BMW C1 motorbike, and the fact that what used to be available only in cars is also now available on two wheels.

## Abbott Mead Vickers·BBDO: Guinness *Dream Club*  ↘ ●

**Agency** Abbott Mead Vickers·
BBDO, London
**Creative director** Peter Souter
**Art director** Walter Campbell
**Copywriter** Walter Campbell
**Account director** Casper Thykier
**Agency producer** Yvonne Chalkley
**Production** Academy, London
**Director** Jonathan Glazer
**Director of photography** Dan Landin
**Producer** Nick Morris
**Post production** Computer Film
Company, London
**Editor** Sam Sneade
**Audio post production** Sound Tree
Music & Wave, London
**Client** Guinness
**Product** Guinness
**Medium** TV
**Exposure** UK
**Date** May 2001

This is the fourth execution in the award-winning 'Good Things Come To Those Who Wait' campaign. *Dream Club* features an extraordinary dream quest to illustrate Guinness's message that the ultimate experiences are always worth waiting for. The ad focuses on The Dream Club, a group of champion dreamers who have dreams beyond imagination. Fuelled by Guinness, the club's champion sets out to experience the ultimate dream, the one that will reveal the true meaning of life. The ad tells the story of his dream quest, from the moment he nods off, to the final revelation. In his search, our hero's dream world and reality combine around the pint of Guinness he orders.

Like the previous films in the campaign, *Dream Club* was written by AMV's award-winning creative Walter Campbell. The 60-second ad was directed by Jonathan Glazer, who previously directed *Swimmer* and *Surfer* through Academy.

## Bartle Bogle Hegarty: One 2 One *Life is...*  ↘ ●

**Agency** Bartle Bogle Hegarty,
London
**Creative directors** John Hegarty,
John O'Keefe
**Art director** Alex Grieve
**Copywriter** Adrian Rossi
**Account director** Paul Bradbury
**Agency producer** Tania McKenzie
**Production** Another Film
Company, London
**Director** Steve Reeves

**Director of photography** Andrzej
Sekula
**Producer** Tim Marshall
**Post production** The Mill, London
**Editor** Paul Watts;
The Quarry, London
**Client** One 2 One
**Product** One 2 One
**Medium** TV
**Exposure** UK
**Date** May 2001

This new campaign stars the British actor and director Gary Oldman. The multi-layered commercial is an ensemble where several characters act out an interwoven narrative. The spot was directed by Steve Reeves and shot by *Pulp Fiction*'s director of photography Andrzej Sekula, filming took place over five days in and around Los Angeles to achieve a feature-film quality and a unique sense of scale. The commercial centres on the fact that 'Life is made of One 2 Ones', which is the company's new strapline.

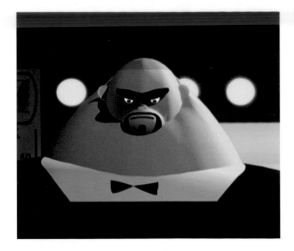

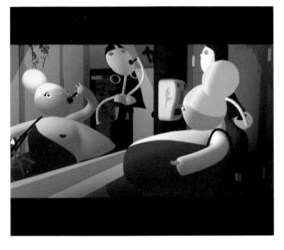

## BMP DDB: Vodafone *Night out*

**Agency** BMP DDB, London
**Creative team** Dan Hubert,
Amber Casey
**Agency producer** Lucy Westmore
**Production** Studio AKA, London
**Director** Mic Graves
**Producer** Angela Cocker
**Post production** FrameStore, London
**Editor** Murray Butler
**3D animation** Dominic Griffiths,
Boris Kossmehl
**3D model building** Andy Stavely,
James Gaillard
**Client** Vodafone
**Product** Vodafone Youth

**Medium** Cinema
**Exposure** UK
**Date** July 2001

To advertise downloadable ring tones, this
humorous 60-second film depicts party
girls Mandy and Stacey on a night out
clubbing. After prowling the nightclub and
eyeing up several of the available men
they spot the man of their dreams.
However they soon discover that this
animated love god is definitely not on the
market thanks to the personalised ring on
his mobile – the gay anthem *YMCA*, by the
Village People.

## Deutsch: Elements *Woodland Creatures*

**Agency** Deutsch Inc., New York
**Creative director** Cheryl Van Ooyen
**Art director** Tuesday Poliak
**Copywriter** Mark Koelfgen
**Agency producer** Nicole Lundy
**Production** Passion Pictures,
London
**Director** Russell Brooke
**Producer** Hugo Sands
**Post production** Soho 601, London
**Editor** Judd Parson; Tape House
Editorial, New York

**Audio post production** Howard
Schwartz Recording, New York
**Music** Raymond Loewy, New York
**Animation** John Robertson,
Tim Sanpher
**Client** Snapple Beverage group
**Product** Elements
**Medium** TV
**Exposure** USA
**Date** June 2001

This new campaign for the launch of
Elements energy drink centres on four
woodland creatures. Each has their own
particular personality – ranging from the
socially-conscious Happy Squirrel to the
self-centered Sinister Rabbit. Grumpy
Gopher, leads the life of an old man and Mr.
Weasel is true to his name. Elements is the
catalyst that keeps them going on the
bizarre, everyday adventures that only these
animated creatures could have.

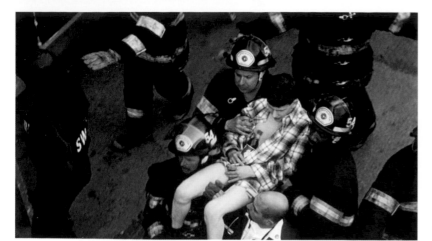

## Mother: Dr Pepper *Emergency*

**Agency** Mother, London
**Creative team** Mother
**Production** Hungry Man, London
**Director** Brian Buckley
**Product** Dr Pepper
**Medium** TV
**Exposure** UK
**Date** April 2001

'What's the worst that can happen?' is the new strapline for Dr Pepper soft drink. This campaign, shot in the style of a teen 'coming-of-age' movie plays on the potential humiliations that lie in wait at this tender and impressionable age. A teenage boy goes up to a refridgerator rammed full of bottles of Dr Pepper – he reaches for one as he thinks to himself 'What's the worst that can happen?'. He pulls the bottle from the shelf and is instantly buried under a

mound of groceries as they fall from the surrounding shelves. Before he can pull himself free of the rubble the cashier has called 911. The emergency services arrive and, much to the boy's horror and embarrassment, decide that the only way to save him is to cut him out of his trousers and underwear. The boy cringes in disbelief as he sits naked from the waist down, only to have his nightmare compounded by the news reporters and TV crews who have gathered outside to get the latest on this drama, which in this short space of time has become a national story. As he leaves the supermarket on a stretcher, one reporter calls out to his camera "Here is butt-naked boy!" Before long the streets are lined with banners and streamers wishing the 'butt-naked boy' well, and he is recognised on the television by several of his high school peers. In the end it all becomes too much for the teenage misfit – he jumps from the stretcher and runs off with only his bottle of Dr Pepper to protect his modesty.

## Saatchi & Saatchi: Telecom New Zealand *Flat Out*

**Agency** Saatchi & Saatchi New Zealand, Wellington
**Creative** Gavin Bradley
**Account directors** Ian Christie, Andrea Hammond
**Agency producer** Olivia Woodroffe
**Production** Flying Fish NZ
**Director** Gregor Nicholas
**Director of photography** John Toon
**Producer** Elly Toft, Mark Matthews
**Post production** Digital Post, Auckland
**Editor** David Coulson
**Animation** Jason Bowden
**Client** Telecom New Zealand
**Product** Brand image
**Medium** TV
**Exposure** New Zealand
**Date** April 2001

This ad aims to show the benefits of global communication through Telecom New Zealand. A young girl looks out from her dark, dreary basement flat at an equally depressing London street, obviously homesick for warm New Zealand days. She sighs as her computer pings to let her know she has email. She rushes over to the computer and smiles when she sees it's from her mum. She smiles even more as she starts to look at the attachments and prints them out one by one. She lays them all on the floor, labels them and then begins to stick them on the wall. Before long she has finished her task, and she steps back to reveal a huge picture of her parents' garden, with the glowing sunset and beach now brightening her room.

## TBWA: Levi's *Belly Button*

**Agency** TBWA Chiat/Day, San Francisco
**Creative director** Chuck McBride
**Associate creative director** Jon Soto
**Art director** Jeff Labbe
**Copywriter** Susan Treacy
**Account director** Peter Randeria
**Agency producer** Betsy Beale
**Production** Partizan, Los Angeles
**Director** Michel Gondry
**Effects** Olivier Gondry; Twisted Laboratories, Los Angeles

This new ad for Levi's 'Make Them Your Own' advertising theme features singing belly buttons peeking out of the low-slung, hip-hugging Superlow jeans, singing a version of the Diana Ross hit *I'm Coming Out*.

The 30-second commercial, which features a variety of young female bodies dressed in Levi's Superlow jeans with exposed mid-drifts and singing belly buttons, was directed by Michel Gondry and produced by Partizan. Special effects from Olivier Gondry helped create realistic singing belly buttons using a unique computer program specifically designed to achieve this.

## Verba DDB: Audi *Hair*

**Agency** Verba DDB, Milan
**Creative director** Stefano Longoni,
Enrico Bonomini
**Art director** Andrea Maggioni
**Copywriter** Luca Gelmuzzi
**Account director** Germano Zung
**Agency producer**
Guiseppe Brandolini
**Production** BRW & Partners, Milan
**Director** Federico Brugia
**Director of photography**
Alessandro Bolzoni
**Producer** Stefano Quaglia
**Post production** Anteprima
Video, Milan
**Editor** Fabrizio Rossetti
**Audio post production** Ariete
Edizioni Musicali, Milan

**Client** Audi
**Product** Audi A2
**Medium** TV
**Exposure** International
**Date** April 2001

A women leaves the hairdressers. She
looks stunning, due mostly to the fact that
she is wearing a very striking asymmetric
fringe. Inside the salon several other women
seem to be sporting a similarly strange hair-
cut. Is this the latest scary fashion trend?
We then see a woman sitting at the chair.
The hairdresser goes to trim her a very
straight fringe, but just as the scissors cut
through her hair she abruptly turns her head
to the side – her attention drawn to the
beautiful Audi A2 that is parked outside.

## Cliff Freeman & Partners: Finishline *Don't Walk*

**Agency** Cliff Freeman & Partners
**Creative director** Eric Silver
**Art director** Guy Shelmerdine
**Copywriter** Grant Holland
**Account director** Livia Tuzzo
**Agency producer** Ed Zazzera
**Production** Partizan, Los Angeles
**Director** Traktor
**Editor** Dick Gordon;
Mad River Post, New York
**Client** Finishline
**Product** Trainers
**Medium** TV

**Exposure** USA
**Date** March 2001

Continuing the theme of previous ads, this
new commercial shows again the dedication
of Finishline employees to ensure that you
get the best possible run out of your training
shoes. *Don't Walk* sees a young employee
stopping on-coming traffic, so that his customer can continue her run uninterrupted,
by throwing himself in front of the next
car to come along.

## Forsman & Bodenfors: Mer *Birth*

**Agency** Forsman & Bodenfors,
Gothenburg, Sweden
**Art director** Andreas Malm
**Copywriters** Jans Enhage,
Oscar Asketof
**Account director** Anders Härneman
**Production** Gorgeous, London
**Director** Frank Budgen
**Producer** Simon Copper
**Client** Mer
**Product** Pear juice
**Medium** TV
**Exposure** Sweden
**Date** April 2001

A young couple look forward to the birth of
their first child, however there seems to be
an unhappy edge to the expectant mother's
demeanour. Her thoughts seem to be
elsewhere – perhaps with another lover. On
the day she goes into labour, they rush to
the hospital in eager anticipation of the
happy event. Finally the child is handed to
the new mother, who cradles it contentedly
in her arms, devotion, love and happiness
finally shining in her eyes. As the father pulls
back the blanket to reveal his firstborn his
shock becomes apparent – his beloved wife
has given birth to an infant pear. The ad
then cuts back to the local pool maintenance guy, a strapping human-sized pear.

 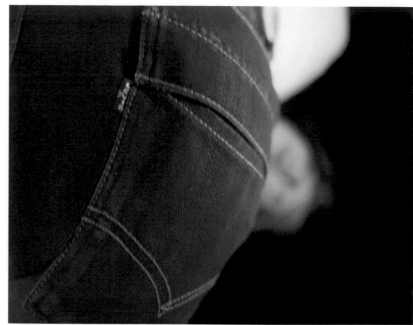

## BBH Asia Pacific: Levi's *Photocopier*

**Agency** BBH Asia Pacific, Singapore
**Creative team** Steve Elrick, Scott McClelland, Lisa Glasgow
**Account directors** Richard Thompson, Chikako Nishiwaki
**Agency producer** Rebecca So
**Production** San of Nexus Films
**Director** Jake Night
**Director of photography** Richard Stuart
**Producer** San Takashima
**Music** Plump DJ
**Client** Levi Strauss Asia Pacific
**Product** Levi's

**Medium** TV, cinema
**Exposure** Japan, Asia
**Date** March 2001

A young guy dances in front of a black background. He pushes his body against the clear surface below him, twisting and turning against the glass. We then cut to a shot of the man from above, and realise that he is lying on top of a giant photocopier, making sure that he has a copy of his Levi's Originals.

## BBDO Chicago: Wrigley's *Whatever Comes Out... It's Cool*

**Agency** BBDO Chicago
**Group creative directors** Jim Hyman, Gail Pollack
**Creative directors** Elaine Perri, Gwen Dawkins
**Art director** Elaine Perri
**Copywriter** Gwen Dawkins
**Account director** Andrea Templeton
**Agency producer** Charles Sheldon
**Production** Wild Brain, San Francisco
**Directors** John Hays, Marcos Sorensen (*Beat Box*); Mike Smith (*Joke*);

Gordon Clark (*Mirror*); Ed Bell (*Urban Hip Hopper*)
**Producer** Bill Weir
**Assistant producer** Kristian Barowsky
**Client** Wm. Wrigley Jr. Company
**Product** Winterfresh chewing gum
**Medium** TV
**Exposure** USA
**Date** June 2001

'Wrigley encouraged each of our directors to pitch design and technique ideas that appealed to them on a personal aesthetic

level. They were inspired to pursue challenging, experimental looks." Bill Weir, Wild Brain

Each of the six 30-second spots in this diverse campaign is an artistically-driven piece of experimental animation with a unique style, design, animation technique and execution. They provide the audience with a viewing experience that is like a short film or art piece. The campaign shows teens involved in a number of everyday activities in which they express themselves creatively or personally, to us and their peers, in a confident, fun and natural way. All the spots feature the Winterfresh tagline 'Whatever Comes Out... It's Cool.'

**Agency** Fallon, New York
**Creative directors** James Barrett, Kevin Roddy
**Art director** Chris Brignola
**Copywriter** Matt Vescovo
**Account director** Victor Kimble
**Agency producer** Nancy Gentry
**Production** Harry Nash, London
**Director** Fredrik Bond
**Director of photography** Adam Kimmel
**Producer** Helen Williams
**Post production** Quiet Man, New York
**Editors** Gavin Cutler; McKenzie Cutler, New York
**Client** Conseco
**Product** Financial services
**Medium** TV

**Exposure** US
**Date** April 2001

Continuing in the vein of past Conseco commercials, these new spots go to even lower depths to show how pensioners are having to save money due to their lack of savings. In one spot a family waits at a luggage carousel for their suitcases. They seem a little more concerned than the other passengers and soon begin to ask, "Have you seen Grandma?". You presume that Grandma is lost in the airport, but all of a sudden they spot her. They grab a piece of luggage and open it up. Inside, Grandma is neatly curled up. She unfolds herself and smiles at her grandchildren. Of course, the next task is to find Grandpa...

St Luke's: Clarkes *Berdoing*

**Agency** St Luke's, London
**Creative director** Kate Stanners
**Art director** Nick Simons
**Copywriters** Ruth Jackson
**Account director** Dan O'Rourke
**Agency producer** Andy Palmer
**Production** Blink, London
**Director** Mark Denton
**Director of photography** Rob Hardy
**Producer** Jane Fitch
**Post production** Rushes, London
**Editor** Joel; Cut & Run, London
**Audio post production** Warren; Wave Music, London
**Client** Clarkes Shoes
**Product** Autumn Range

**Medium** TV
**Exposure** UK
**Date** April 2001

While dining in a restaurant a young woman looks down through the crystal-clear glass table top at her brand-new shoes. She looks at them with great admiration, but is disturbed to see that something has become stuck to the bottom of one. She reaches down quickly to remove the offending item – only to embarrassingly hit her head and face on the glass table top.

**Agency** Abbott Mead Vickers·
BBDO, London
**Creative director** Peter Souter
**Art director** Paul Brazier
**Copywriter** Nick Worthington
**Account director** Annie Gallimore
**Agency producer** Kate Taylor
**Production** Outsider, London
**Director** Paul Gay
**Director of photography** Paul Gay
**Producer** Jason Kemp
**Post production** MPC, London
**Editor** Alister Jordon OBE
**Audio post production**
750mph, London
**Client** Dulux

**Product** Paint
**Medium** TV, cinema
**Exposure** UK
**Date** May 2001

This commercial continues the award-winning 'You find the colour, we'll match it' campaign for Dulux Paints. The ads show women gaining inspiration for the perfect paint colour in unexpected places. In this execution a plasticine man, who is living a happy and fulfilled life in an art display in a school corridor, is beheaded by a primary school teacher as his horrified plasticine friends look on.

Arnold Worldwide: VW *Aqueduct*

**Agency** Arnold Worldwide, Boston
**Creative director** Alan Pafenbach
**Art director** Don Shelford
**Copywriter** Susan Ebling Corbo
**Agency producer** Paul Shannon
**Production** Bob Industries,
Venice, CA, USA
**Director** Dayton/Farris
**Director of photography**
Joaquin Baca-Asay

**Producer** Bart Lipton
**Post production** 525 Post,
Los Angeles
**Editor** John Hopp; Jigsaw,
Santa Monica
**Client** Volkswagen of America
**Product** Beetle
**Medium** TV
**Exposure** USA
**Date** April 2001

As the host of an educational show, a British narrator is pontificating on the amazing strength of the arches of the Roman Aqueducts. As he's rambling on about the virtues of arches, a new Beetle drives up in the background, perfectly mimicking the shape of the arch. A tourist pops out of the sunroof, snaps a picture, and drives off without the narrator ever knowing what has happened.

## Ogilvy & Mather: The Samaritans *Foot and Mouth*

**Agency** Ogilvy & Mather, London
**Creative director** Steve Dunn
**Art director** Mat Doman
**Copywriter** Ian Heartfield
**Account directors** Craig Burleigh,
Henry Debenham
**Agency producer** Sarah Roche
**Production** S.V.C, London

**Directors** Mat Doman, Ian
Heartfield, Steve Dunn
**Editors** Nick McChearty,
Nick Robson
**Product** The Samaritans
**Medium** TV
**Exposure** UK
**Date** May 2001

This moving commercial shows the appalling emotional strain that British farmers have been under during the foot and mouth crisis that has gripped the British countryside. The ad aims to raise awareness, and underline that their plight has not gone unnoticed and that there is someone out there to help them.

## Abbott Mead Vickers·BBDO: *The Economist Freedom of Knowledge*

**Agency** Abbott Mead Vickers·
BBDO, London
**Creative director** Peter Souter
**Art director/copywriter** Tom Carty
**Account director**
Victoria Zimmerman
**Agency producer** Yvonne Chalkley
**Production** Gorgeous, London
**Director** Tom Carty
**Director of photography**
Alex Barber

**Producer** Siska Faulkner
**Post production** The Mill, London
**Editor** Paul Watts;
The Quarry, London
**Audio post production** Sound Tree,
London; The Tape Gallery, London
**Client** The Economist
**Product** Magazine
**Medium** TV
**Exposure** UK
**Date** May 2001

A new commercial for *The Economist* tells the moving and incredible story of how Nelson Mandela and his fellow inmates tricked the authorities into supplying *The Economist* while they were in prison on Robben Island. In Mandela's book *Long Walk to Freedom* he explains that they were kept in a timeless state and deprived of all news of the outside world. The only books they were allowed were those relevant to a field of study. So, when one inmate, Mac Maharaj, asked for *The Economist* because he was studying economics, amazingly the authorities complied and Mandela and his friends were able to read the news they

hungered for. This was short-lived however, as the authorities soon realised their mistake and it was withdrawn.

The ad juxtaposes the simple and poignant narrative account from Mandela's book with arresting and surreal images. The authenticity of the story is enhanced because it is narrated by Mac Maharaj. He spent 12 years in prison with Nelson Mandela, and most of his life in the struggle for democracy in South Africa.

## Mother: Pimms *Happy Together*

**Agency** Mother, London
**Creative team** Mother
**Production** Harry Nash, London
**Director** Ringan Ledwidge
**Product** Pimms
**Medium** TV
**Exposure** UK

A group of friends demonstrate that Pimms is the drink that brings people together, in these simple but sweet commercials. In fact they are all so happy together that they remain stuck to one another wherever they go, much to the amusement and bemusement of the people around them.

## Cliff Freeman & Partners: Mike's Hard Lemonade *Lumberjack*

**Agency** Cliff Freeman & Partners,
New York
**Creative director** Eric Silver
**Art directors** Guy Shelmerdine,
Scott Vitrone
**Copywriters** William Gelner,
Ian Reichenthal
**Account director** Shana Brooks
**Agency producer** Ed Zazzera
**Production** Partizan, Los Angeles
**Director** Traktor

**Post production** Quiet Man,
New York
**Editor** MacKenzie Cutler, New York
**Product** Lemonade
**Medium** TV
**Exposure** USA
**Date** April 2001

Horrific power-tool and building-site accidents form the basis of this stomach churningly realistic series of ads for Mike's

Hard Lemonade directed by Traktor. In one spot, a lumberjack sets about a fallen tree with a large chainsaw. Suddenly he has mistakenly cuts off his own foot, which with the help of some amazing post production, looks uncannily real. He laughs as his colleagues gather around him, and complains that his wife has only just bought the boots he's wearing. They all then head off to enjoy an ice-cold bottle of Mike's Hard Lemonade. Other spots include impalings and Killer whale encounters.

## Leo Burnett: Heinz *Channel*

**Agency** Leo Burnett, London
**Creative directors** Nick Bell, Mark Tutssel
**Art director** Rob Nielson
**Copywriter** Jack Stephens
**Account director** Christian Dean
**Agency producer** Angela Zabala
**Production** Rogue Films, London
**Director** Johan Tappert
**Director of photography** Baz Irvine

**Producer** Charlie Crompton
**Post production** MPC, London
**Editor** Adam Jenkins; Final Cut, London
**Client** Heinz
**Product** Salad Cream
**Medium** TV
**Exposure** UK
**Date** June 2001

*Channel* plays on the 'Booze Cruise' journeys made by British people to buy quality wine from France in large quantities. Here the cultural roles are reversed. A Frenchman leaves his cottage to make an epic journey across the Channel to England. He explains that he makes the journey twice a year to buy a dozen cases to have with meals. In England he is seen pulling into a supermarket and then filling his van up with Heinz Salad Cream. The ad ends with the strapline 'Vintage 1914'

## Ogilvy & Mather: Imperial Margarine *Spud*

**Agency** Ogilvy & Mather, Toronto
**Creative directors** Janet Kestin, Nancy Vonk
**Art directors** Ian Letts, Chris Ward
**Copywriters** Michael Gelfand, David Ross
**Account director** Justin Stephenson
**Agency producer** Brenda Surminski
**Production** Industry Films, Toronto
**Director** Todd Lincoln

**Director of photography** Morgan Susser
**Producer** Trudy Turner
**Post production** School, Toronto
**Editor** David Hicks; School, Toronto
**Audio post production** Pirate Radio & TV, Toronto
**Client** Unilever Canada
**Product** Imperial Margarine
**Medium** TV
**Exposure** Canada
**Date** March 2001

A suicidal spud is the hero of the latest commercial for Imperial Margarine. The ballad *I'm All Out of Love* by Air Supply rings out as the baked potato sits atop the microwave. It wimpers gently as it gazes down at an empty tub of margarine. Distraught, the potato wriggles to the edge of the microwave before hurling itself onto a two-pronged fork, ending his margarineless misery. The strapline reads, 'Imperial Margarine. Food is nothing without it.'

## Malcolm Moore Deakin Blazye: MTV *Eggcentric*

**Agency** Malcolm Moore Deakin
Blazye, London
**Creative directors** Guy Moore,
Tony Malcolm
**Art director** Nick Williamson
**Copywriter** Gary Ruby
**Account director** Ed Chilcott
**Agency producer** Helen Routledge
**Production** Gorgeous, London
**Director** Tom Carty
**Director of photography**
Peter Thwaites
**Producer** Ciska Faulkner
**Post production** Final Cut, London
**Editor** Rick Russell
**Audio post production** Wave, London
**Client** MTV

**Product** MTV Hits
**Medium** TV
**Exposure** UK
**Date** June 2001

We follow several days in the life of a
strange young man and his passion for
eggs. He indulges in eggs for breakfast,
lunch, dinner, eggs for his dog, eggs for a
mobile, a cheese board – his life is nothing
but eggs. It is not until the very end of the
spot that the reason behind his excesses
are revealed. He needs the egg boxes to
sound-proof his sitting room so that he can
listen to MTV Hits as loud as he likes.

## Merkley Newman Harty: Mercedes *Modern Ark*

**Agency** Merkley Newman Harty,
New York
**Creative directors** Andy Hirsch,
Randy Saitta, Marty Orzio
**Art director** Sivan Ben-Horin
**Copywriter** Stephanie Crippen
**Account director** Alex Gellert
**Agency producer** Rachel Novak
**Production** HSI Productions,
New York; Gerard de Thame
Films, London
**Director** Gerard de Thame
**Director of photography** Mick
Coulter

**Producer** Fabyan Daw
**Post production** Smoke & Mirrors,
London
**Editor** Richard Learoyd;
Cut & Run, London
**Audio post production** Amber,
New York
**Client** Mercedes Benz USA
**Product** Mercedes Benz
**Exposure** USA
**Date** March 2001

A remake, on an equally grand and striking
scale, of the Bible story of Noah shows what
the modern-day equivalent of the essential
items to be taken onto the ark two-by-two
would be. The usual suspects of elephants,
giraffes and kangaroos are accompanied by
classical works of art, Apple Macs, a fridge
of Häagen-Dazs ice-cream and of course
the Mercedes – which enters last before the
rain begins to fall.

## FCB: Ripolin *Colour Therapy*

**Agency** FCB, Paris
**Art director** Carole Denis
**Copywriter** Bertrand Gruyer
**Account director**
Jean Claude Pierrat
**Agency producer** Sylvie Pierre
**Production** Wanda, Paris
**Director** Who?; Great Guns, London
**Director of photography**
Nic Knowland
**Producer** Christophe Bichot
**Post production** MPC, London
**Editor** John Smith;
White House, London
**Client** Ripolin

**Product** Paint
**Medium** TV
**Exposure** France
**Date** May 2001

We enter the room of a young man who is being threatened by a group of vicious looking gangsters. One holds a gun to his head, while another gives the order to fire. However the gun-toting criminal just can't seem to pull the trigger. He looks at his boss and shrugs his shoulders, his problem being that he finds the colour of the paint on the walls so lovely that he just can't get angry.

## John Doe: AT5 *Builders*

**Agency** John Doe, Amsterdam
**Creative team** John Doe
**Production** John Doe
**Directors** Benito Strangio,
Herman Poppelaars
**Director of photography** Benito
Strangio
**Post production** Martijn van
Waveren; Condor, Amsterdam
**Sound design** Geert van
Gaalen, Studio de Keuken,
Amsterdam; Kees Kroot,
Kroot Geluid, Amsterdam

**Client** AT5
**Product** TV station
**Medium** TV
**Exposure** Netherlands
**Date** May 2001

Dutch television station AT5 has been renovated. Not just its programming but its entire appearance too. To make the public aware of these changes, John Doe made 30 commercials that were broadcast in the two weeks prior to the launch.

The commercials revolved around the two builders who were responsible for the renovation work. All the effort and hard work, or perhaps their mishaps, flirtations and general incompetence, could be seen daily. The pair managed to set off several destructive events in true Laurel and Hardy style.

The commercials ended with the line: 'One moment please. See you on the 15th of May.'

## Modernista!: MTV *We're Watching*

**Agency** Modernista!, Boston
**Creative directors** Lance Jensen,
Gary Koepke
**Art director** Will Uronis
**Copywriter** Shane Hutton
**Account director** Mike Densmore
**Agency producer** Colleen Wellman
**Production** Satellite Films,
Los Angeles
**Director** Brian Beletic
**Director of photography**
Joaquin Baca-Asay
**Producers** Charles Wolford,
Phillip Dechmendy
**Post production**
Cosmo Street, Los Angeles
**Editor** Roeben Katz

**Music** Ben Mor; Master Grip,
Los Angeles
**Client** MTV, New York
**Product** MTV Brand
**Medium** TV
**Exposure** USA
**Date** March/April 2001

The highly contagious nature of MTV is
explored in this series of commercials from
Modernista!. In one spot a girl worries
continually as to whether she has caught
MTV, as apparently one-in-four people now
have it. In another, those with MTV are seen
to be leading normal lives despite having it.

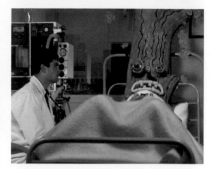

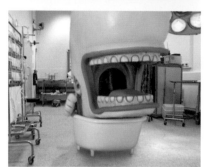

## Aardman: WWF *Biodiversity 911: Saving Life On Earth*

**Client** World Wildlife Fund
**Product** Charity
**Medium** Travelling Exhibition
**Exposure** USA
**Date** May 2001
**Agency** Aardman, Bristol, UK
**Production** Aardman
**Director** Luis Cook
**Director of photography** Sam James
**Producer** John Woolley
**Post production** Soho 601, London
**Audio post production** Wounded
Buffalo, Bristol, UK

The latest short film to come from Aardman
is a hospital drama with a difference. For
the last two years Aardman has been
working with the World Wildlife Fund USA
to make the film. The 12-minute production
was made in a real hospital whose patients
are not people but other living things,
ranging from poorly topsoil to injured
shrimp plasticine animated creatures
designed by the director Luis Cook.

From pollution to deforestation, from
climate change to wildlife trade, the patients
in the hospital have all suffered. In the
emergency ward the sick patients include
Babs Taylor, a Beluga whale infected by
toxic chemicals, and Sergeant Rock
Johnson, a rhino so scared of being hunted
for his horn that he now believes he is a
hippo and has ended up in the psychiatric
unit. The oldest patient is 265-year-old
Branche Du Bois, a Tulip poplar tree, who
has been cut down in her prime owing to
deforestation and sadly has little time left.

The film will form part of the WWF
exhibition due to travel around the USA
throughout the next three years.

Fallon: BMW of North America: *Chosen;*
*Follow; Ambush*

**Agency** Fallon Minneapolis
**Production** Anonymous Content
**Director** John Frankenheimer
(*Ambush*), Ang Lee (*Chosen*),
Wong Kar-Wai (*Follow*)
**Director of photography** Newton
Thomas Sigel (*Ambush*),
Frederick Elmes (*Chosen*),
Harry Savides (*Follow*)
**Producers** Aristides McGarry,
(*Ambush, Chosen, Follow*)
Robyn Boardman (*Ambush, Chosen*);
Jacky Pang Yee-wah,
Hong Kong Unit (*Follow*);
Robert van de Weteringe
Buys (*Follow*)

**Creative consultants** David Lubars,
David Carter, Joe Sweet, Bruce
Bildsten (*Fallon*);
**Writers** Andrew Kevin Walker
(*Ambush, Follow*);
David Carter (*Chosen*)
**Client** BMW
**Product** Cars
**Medium** Internet
**Exposure** International
**Date** May 2001

The latest effort for BMW is a star-studded
event made specifically to utilise the

growing internet market. *The Hire* project
consists of five short films by leading
Hollywood directors that were shown
exclusively on bmwfilms.com. Several outstanding directors joined up with Fallon
Minneapolis to create the films which were
written by Bruce Bildsten, David Carter and
Joe Sweet and several other scriptwriters.
The films were directed by John
Frankenheimer, Ang Lee, Wong Kar-Wai,
Guy Ritchie, and Alejandro Gonzáles
Iñárritu. Each film stars Clive Owen as a
hired driver who becomes embroiled in the
adventures of the passengers he carries, the
BMW he drives being as much a part of the
story as Owen himself. Some fantastic car
stunts and chases contribute to the overall
big-screen feel of these small-screen films.

# BLUE SOURCE

London-based creative communication agency Blue Source was set up in 1991 by Leigh Marling. "The business sort of came about as a result of the cultural explosion of acid house back in the late Eighties," recalls Leigh. "It may sound a bit cheesy and nostalgic, but there seemed to be so much creative energy everywhere at that time and like a lot of other people we thought 'why not.'" Marling was soon joined by his brother Seb and Alison, Seb's wife. The three were undaunted by their lack of formal training: "We didn't know anything about design or art direction, but we loved music and film. From there it was just a case of learning. Music has always been at the heart of Blue Source. Our personal inspiration became our business inspiration. We built a company around packaging and communicating music, and although we now work in many different fields, our work with music remains at the core of our identity and aesthetic."

In the last eighteen months this core value has been

strengthened by the company's highly successful expansion into music video production. But while most design-oriented companies have tentatively experimented in this field by animating graphics, all Blue Source's promos to date have been full-scale live-action projects. The quality of their video work has earned them recognition within the production industry as outstanding newcomers, with a flair for narrative and particularly strong casting and art direction. Rob Leggatt and Mark Tappin are the other key members of Blue Source's production team, yet when it comes directing individual projects, responsibilities are shared amongst the group. "Rob and I tend to work on stuff which is more narrative based," explains Leigh, "Rob and Mark on stuff which is more art direction driven. But really the whole Blue Source ethic is team-based and on our clip for Groove Armada the design studio helped out a lot on the animated sequences, so that one was a well-rounded collective effort."

Caterpillar Autumn/Winter 1999
Tokyo print advertising campaign
**Photographer** Stefan Ruiz

Far from limiting its scope, Blue Source's continuing commitment to music has won respect and kudos which attracts a diverse array of clients from adidas and Levi's to the Health Education Authority. So far the team has produced logos, graphic identities, music packaging, brand strategy, and consultancy, print advertising, TV and cinema commercials, publications, music videos, title sequences, and short films. It's a range of services and expertise that undoubtedly justifies Leigh's gung-ho optimism of ten years ago. "Every year since we started, we've learnt more and applied those lessons, and the work has got better," he confirms. "We aim to continue that trend. Also, Woody Allen's thing about 95 per cent of success being about turning up is true. We've worked our nuts off to get this far."

Shawn Lee *Monkey Boy* CD cover
**Illustrator** Kam Tang

**01**
**Title** *Out of Sight* promo
for Babybird
**Directors** Rob Leggatt,
Mark Tappin

**02**
**Title** *Sunset (Bird of Prey)* promo for
Fatboy Slim
**Directors** Rob Leggatt,
Leigh Marling

**03**
**Title** *Superstylin'* promo for
Groove Armada
**Directors** Rob Leggatt,
Leigh Marling

**04**
**Title** *The F-word* promo for Babybird
**Directors** Rob Leggatt,
Mark Tappin

...it's some kind of ritual.

She bought them...

So one day she left.

Now he dances to bring her back.

01

02

03

**01**
**Title** *Days Go By* promo
for Dirty Vegas
**Directors** Rob Leggatt, Leigh Marling

**02**
Backgrounds for TV show, *Banzai*

**03**
**Title** *Since I Left You* promo for The Avalanches
**Directors** Rob Leggatt, Leigh Marling

Teenage Fanclub
Start Again

01

Teenage Fanclub
Ain't That Enough

Teenage Fanclub
I Don't Want Control Of You

Teenage Fanclub
Start Again

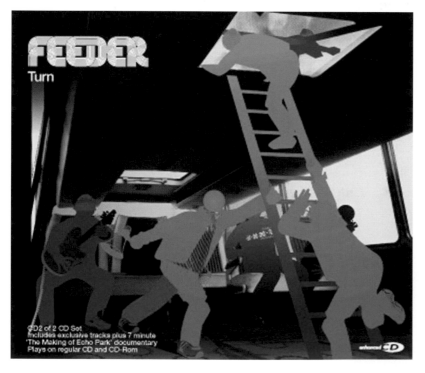

FEEDER
Buck Rogers

02

Teenage Fanclub
I Don't Want Control Of You

FEEDER
Turn

CD2 of 2 CD Set
Includes exclusive tracks plus 7 minute
'The Making of Echo Park' documentary
Plays on regular CD and CD-Rom

enhanced CD

GLOSS
NEW
YORK
BOY

03

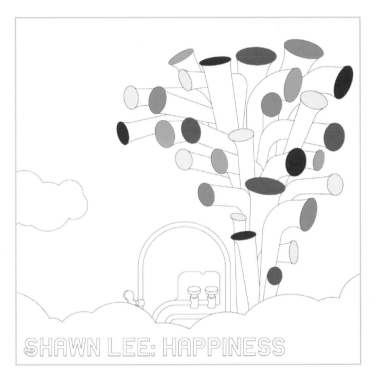

**01**
CD sleeve artwork for
Teenage Fanclub
**Photographer** Donald Milne

**02**
CD sleeve artwork for Feeder
**Illustrator** Roy Wilkinson

**03**
CD sleeve artwork for Gloss
**Illustrator** Julie Verhoeven

**04**
CD single artwork for
Shawn Lee *Happiness*
**Illustrator** Kam Tang

## RMX Extended Play

**Designers** Various
**Nationality** Australian, Swiss, German, Japanese, British, American
**Title** Rinzen presents RMX Extended Play
**Date** Remixing January to June 2001; book published September by Die-Gestalten Verlag, Berlin, 2001 (Europe), March 2001 (USA)

"RMX is a creative device paying homage to the concepts of manifold collaboration and spontaneous reinvention. Launching from a desire to produce exciting work in an unpredictable way, the project is a praxis for like-minded designers to create and re-create, generating outcomes that are as surprising to the creators as they are to the audience.

"In RMX, a series of six initial pieces are created by the six members of Rinzen, based on themes ranging from the relevant to the ridiculous. These are passed progressively to each player, being 'remixed' each step of the way – modified, added to, erased – with each participant not seeing the work before it's their turn to remix it. In this way, the stylistic and interpretive tendencies of the players are free to echo and clash in a series of Chinese-whispers-like translations – a self-perpetuating sequence full of collisions and surprises, conceits and transformations." Rilla Alexander, Rinzen

Each of the original pieces was remixed in 16 stages, and the book features 96 remixes. The players include: François Chalet, Deanne Cheuk, Designershock, eBoy, Extra Design, Filesharing, Ben Frost, Furi Furi Company, Futurefarmers, Hausgrafik, Evan Hecox, Mat Hinkley, IDN and Six Studio, Less Rain, Menu|Exit, Miamy of Sweden, Norm, North, Pony Loaf, Shynola, Standard Rad, Superfun, Sweden, Tomoko Takeue, The Designers Republic, The Office for Fun and Profit, Tycoon Graphics, Volumeone, and Wink.

**01**
*Maybe Later #3*
Remix: Rhys Lee (North) with
visible elements by
Steve Alexander (Rinzen),
François Chalet

**02**
*Happy Accident #6*
Remix: Steve Alexander (Rinzen)
with visible elements by
Designershock, eBoy, Ben Frost

**03**
*Magic Spray Potion #1*
Karl Maier (Rinzen)

**04**
*Magic Spray Potion #6*
Remix: Georgina Cullum (North)
with visible elements by The
Office for Fun and Profit,
Craig Redman (Rinzen)

**05**
*Magic Spray Potion #8*
Remix: Jason Groves (Shynola)
with visible elements by Sweden,
Georgina Cullum (North)

**06**
*Repeat Offender #14*
Remix: Adrian Clifford (Rinzen)
with visible elements by
Designershock, The Office for
Fun and Profit

**07**
*Repeat Offender #4*
Remix: Mat Hinkley with
visible elements by Norm,
Craig Redman (Rinzen)

**08**
*Magic Spray Potion #12*
Remix: Rilla Alexander (Rinzen)
with visible elements by Amy
Franceschini (Futurefarmers),
Mat Hinkley

Me Company:
*Kenzo: Mainline*
advertising campaign

**Art directors** Thomas Lenthal
(Kenzo); Paul White (Me Company)
**Title** *Kenzo: Mainline*
advertising campaign
**Date** August 2001
**Photography** Paul White
**3D models, rendering, compositing**
Jess Warren, Maarten Heinstra,
Garrett Honn (Me Company)
**Production** Kevin, CLM Ltd;
Alistair Beattie (Me Company)

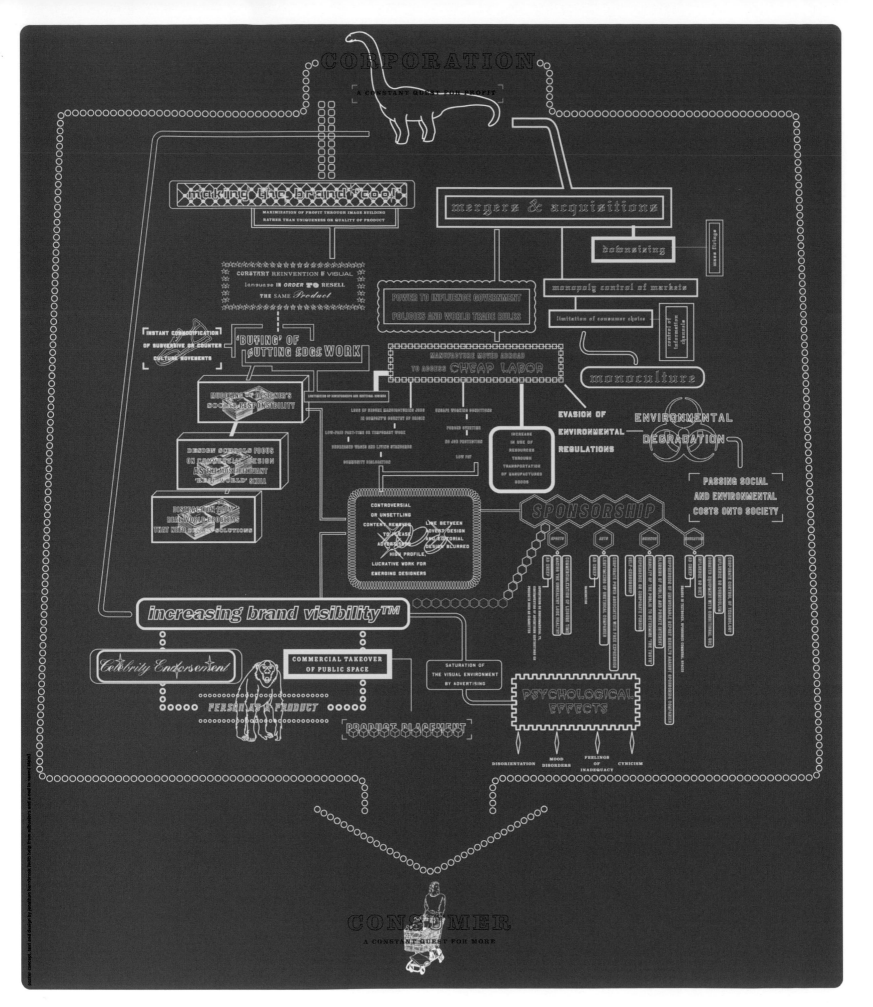

01

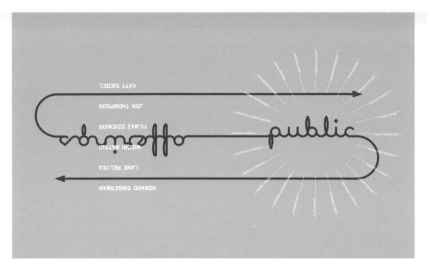

02

04

03

05

06

**Designer** Jonathan Barnbrook
**Nationality** British
**Country of residence** UK
**Title** *Adbusters* poster (01);
*Public Offerings* (02, 03, 05);
*Kohkoku* (04, 06)
**Date** 2001

"The *Adbusters* poster was created out of a desire to explain the method and the political implications of buying a manufactured object. The creation of the text for the poster was also part of the project.

"The *Public Offerings* project, for the Museum of Contemporary Art, Los Angeles, is an identity and catalogue of contemporary art from the 1990s. The catalogue has two front covers and was designed to be read equally easily from either direction:

images and artist biographies start from one end of the book, and essays begin at the other. All display fonts used were specially designed.

"*Kohkoku*, which means 'advertising' in Japanese, is a social issues magazine. The magazine, whose subtitle is 'future social design', changed to a square format from this issue to reflect the magazine's constructivist and communist ideals. A red square sits inside the Japanese character

for 'advertising' and a square font was designed for the project so that it could be used either across the page in English or down the page in Japanese. The artwork was created as ASCII art."
Jonathan Barnbrook

## Graphic Thought Facility: Habitat Autumn/Winter 2001 brochure

**Designer** Graphic Thought Facility
**Title** Habitat Autumn/Winter 2001
brochure: *BasicDeluxe*
**Date** May 2001
**Photography, digital retouching**
Huw Morgan
**Illustration** Alan Levet

"The brief was to reflect a new take on
luxury. Luxury through quantity. Basic
objects in luxury materials. Luxury items
mass-produced for everyday use. Luxury
through flexibility and added function.
Refined excess." Graphic Thought Facility
    The mirror box camera was designed
and made by Huw Morgan at Graphic
Thought Facility.

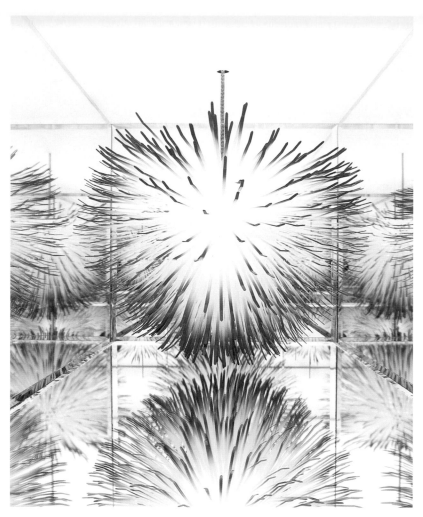

## BasicDeluxe

...is affordable designer classics.

Invest in the best for less. This season sees more must-have additions to the 20th Century Legends series, pieces from world-renowned designers exclusively re-issued, or newly commissioned by Habitat.

Must have 1... the ultimate clock (Mariner) from the 60s by Kenneth Grange, he who designed London's taxicabs.

Must-have 2... an ergonomically elegant plastic desk tidy (Otis) from the archives of Italian furniture producer Kartell.

Must-have 3... a black glass ashtray (Orb) by Marc Newson, the Australian designer responsible for some of London's most fashionable restaurants.

Must-have 4... a side cabinet (Forma) based on a 1948 design by Robin Day, Britain's Charles Eames, and his assistant Clive Latimer. It won first prize in a New York MoMA design competition but amazingly was never put into production. Until now!

"Robin Day is a classic BasicDeluxe designer. The consideration of comfort, ergonomics and function that goes into his work is amazing. It's what makes his furniture so beautiful."

Matthew Hilton, Head of Furniture Design

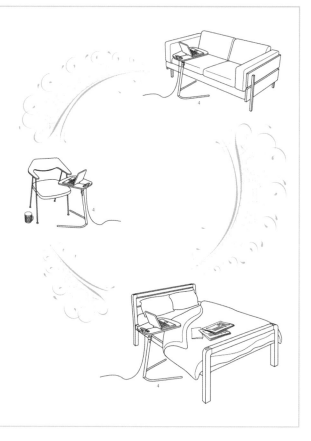

01

## Geoff Kaplan: AIACC poster; Free Time

**Designers** Geoff Kaplan at General Working Group, Gail Swanlund (AIACC conference poster), Pamela M. Lee at TimeSuck (Free Time)
**Nationality** American
**Country of residence** USA
**3D type** Paul Seymour (AIACC poster)

**Title** AIACC conference poster (04)
**Date** May 2001

"Who makes design current and valuable now? Permanent value seems significantly less important these days. Who assigns value to design? What determines its value? Not just what people will pay? Or is it? The new impresarios, entrepreneurs, and those designers viewed as cultural icons give their imprimatur, which creates value.

"Impresarios: Dakota Jackson (old), Philippe Starck, Marc Newson, Rem Koolhaas (the intellectual impresario, new). Entrepreneurs: Raymond Loewy, Charles and Ray Eames, Michael Graves (old), Karim Rashid (new). Cultural Icons: Morris Lapidus, Frank Gehry (on his way), Charles and Ray Eames, Rem Koolhaas (new).

"We want better – or at least, better looking, now! We are living in a time of tremendous prosperity, but we are anxious about its inevitable demise. Technology has been the vehicle for the boom in design currency and the currency of design; it has influenced the communication of design as repository of cultural values and image fascination/desire. It is the epitome of the idea of 'flow', dynamic change; it has changed our notion of temporality (24/7).

"The cult of celebrity/personality has raised designers' value – the more eccentric the better. Media-centric focus has been expedited by saturation through MTV, internet, 24/7 reporting, opinion-assessment, and talk show confessionals.

"Democratisation of design through market penetration of edgy design for the masses, media focus, internet marketing, graphic and video design, has set up a level of high expectation.

"Technology has also acted as a sys-temic model for producing design solutions, as well as a formal model (blobitecture has been made possible); the role of plastic has also increased (fondness for plasticity).

"Form has separated from function and image has become dominant. Interestingly, our consumer culture wants technology in digestible bites, and therefore we fetishise and reveal the complex through image, but want the function to be as easy as 1,2,3 (iMac with transparent monitor casing, but idiot-proof operation). Transparency is another by-product of the plastic, as well as the revealed object. The wrapper/skin is primary.

"With form and function disjuncture, the relationship between the human body and architecture, the designed object, etc, becomes significantly less anthropocentric. Or does it?" Geoff Kaplan

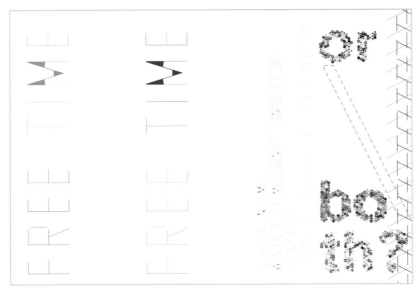

03

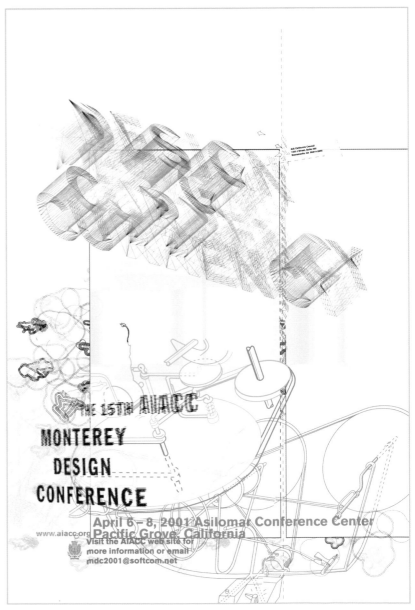

**Title** Freetime (01, 02, 03)
**Date** June 2001
"A break in time wrought by modernist sensibilities; or Leisure as enforced by its counterpart in Work? Or both? The temporal-industrial complex as now subjected to the so-called digital dialectic. The virtues of slowness in the age of mobility. Fight time with time." Geoff Kaplan

04

## DED Associates: *Do Not Inflate*; *Hybrids*

**Designers** Nik Daughtry,
Jon Daughtry
**Nationality** British
**Country of residence** UK
**Date of birth** 1970
**Title** Spreads from *Do Not Inflate [as this may impede your exit]* and *Hybrids – International Contemporary Painting*
**Date** September 2001, April 2001

*Hybrids*: "In March of this year the then newly appointed Director of Tate Liverpool, Christoph Grunenberg, announced that it was his intention to establish links with innovative design agencies in order to produce exhibition material. With his first project in mind and having seen [our book] *Travel Sickness* he approached DED for his first collaboration.

"DED set out to create a catalogue to accompany the exhibition that did not just merely present the artists' work, but also shared in the concern in extending the language of abstraction and figuration in unexpected and inventive ways."
Nik Daughtry
(Page size: 21.2 cm x 27 cm; 64 pp plus cover.)

*Do Not Inflate*: "Buckle up, check the view from the window and unwrap a boiled sweet. In this age of package holidays and international business, we're all seasoned travellers and we've seen the drill dozens of times. All we want to know is where the nearest door is.

"This book is the work of design deconstructivists and safety card fetishists DED and is a hymn to the on-board safety card. Extinguish all cigarettes, strap yourself in with a microwaveable dinner and do not inflate." Michael Evamy
(Page size: 21 cm x 21 cm; 64 pp plus cover.)

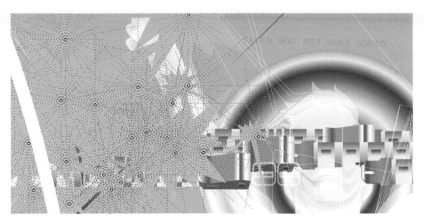
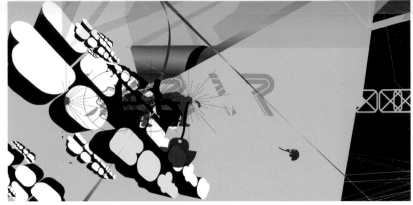
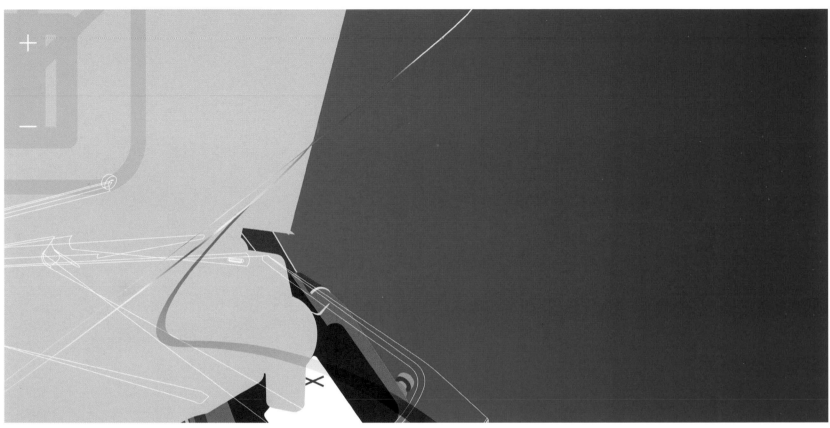
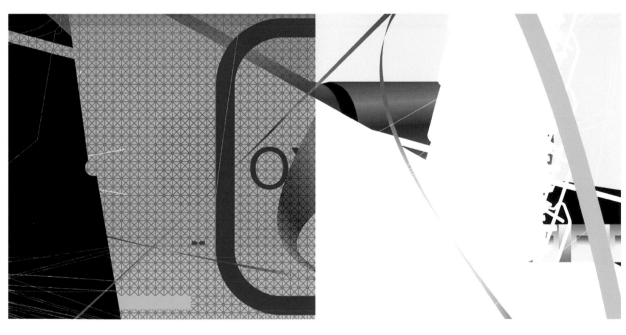

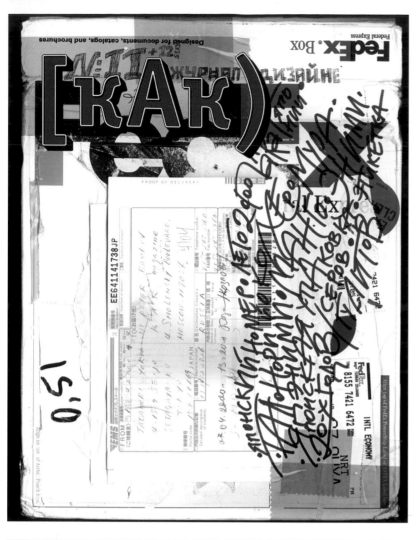

www.KAK.RU

## DesignDepot: [kAk) magazine

**Designers** Peter Bankov,
Katerina Kojoukhova
**Nationality** Russian
**Country of residence** Russia
**Date of birth** 1968, 1969
**Title** [kAk) magazine issues 11,
12, and 14
**Date** March and April 2001

[kAk) is a professional graphic
design magazine.

"For the cover of issue 11, we used a real envelope from Tadanori Yokoo, whose works we've published in this issue.

"Issue 12 is dedicated to Japanese design. As Japan is considered to be the country of the rising sun, we decided to draw this orange sun on the cover.

"Issue 14 is devoted to extreme design. The names of the designers featured – both from Russia and abroad – are in the shape of a flame. A match is a good symbol of everything extreme; the designers are presented in one issue, so they form one style, one flame." Peter Bankov

## Flong: Output of the Alphabet Synthesis Machine

**Designers** Golan Levin, Jonathan Feinberg, Cassidy Curtis at Flong Design Studio
**Nationality** American
**Country of residence** USA
**Date of birth** 1972, 1967, 1971
**Title** Output of the Alphabet Synthesis Machine
**Date** Expected launch date September 2001

"The Alphabet Synthesis Machine was commissioned by PBS, the American Public Broadcasting Corporation, as a featured online artwork for their Art21 site, http://www.pbs.org/art21/

"I very clearly remember the first time that I encountered an unfamiliar alphabet: it was an event that occurred in my family's synagogue when I was very small, perhaps four years old. I had just learned to read English, but it had not yet been explained to me that there could exist other writing systems apart from the one I knew. One evening during a ceremony, I asked my father what the funny black squiggles were in the prayer books we were holding. 'Sh!'; he said: 'That is how we talk to God'. Astonished, I became transfixed by the black squiggles, which no longer seemed quite so funny; but although I stared at them until I was dizzy, I could find no way to render them intelligible. Only later did I learn that these marks were Hebrew.

"Since that time, I have been pre-occupied by the possibility that abstract forms can connect us to a reality beyond language, and bridge the thin line between nonsense and the divine.

"Somewhere between the visual noise of television static, and the visual order of the text you are now reading, lies a fascinating realm of visual semi-sense. Precisely where do the borders of that realm lie? By studying that realm of semi-sense, I surmise that we may come to a deeper understanding of precisely how sense-making occurs at all. To do this, we have written software that attempts to generate artefacts that seem to make sense, but in fact, don't.

"The particular goal of this work is to bring about the specific feeling of semi-sense one experiences when one recognises – but cannot read – the unfamiliar writing of another culture. Our Alphabet Synthesis Machine is an interactive system in which a user guides an evolutionary genetic algorithm in order to create and explore coherent sets of abstract glyphs. Hopefully, these mark-like forms resemble the plausible alphabets of human civilisations with which we simply happen to be unacquainted.

"The Alphabet Synthesis Machine is a piece of interactive online software, written in Java and Perl. It allows users to create and breed their own synthetic alphabets, and produces TrueType fonts as output."
Golan Levin

## Arnaud Mercier: *Journey On*

**Designer** Arnaud Mercier at Elixirstudio/Blast Radius
**Nationality** French
**Country of residence** Canada
**Date of birth** 1972
**Title** *Journey On* for 'Mind the Banner' Project
**Date** Online April 2001
**Producer** NTT Data Corporation (www.nttdata.com)
**Soundtrack** Nordic Trax (www.nordictrax.com)

"This piece is an autobiographical journey. It could be anyone's journey. Take the time to look at what surrounds you, at simple things. Observe the fluidity: people are moving, things are moving, data is moving, and everything touches each other. This piece is a window on the world. Forget cultural and national boundaries. Disconnect. Turn off your computer. Go outside." Arnaud Mercier

The project is viewable as a Flash 5.0 movie, 320 x 320 pixels, 2.12 MB, duration approximately one minute. It was made using a Canon XL1 (video); the photographs were taken using a Lomo; design, editing and animation were completed on an Apple G4, with Adobe Illustrator, Adobe Photoshop, After Effects, and Flash 5.0.

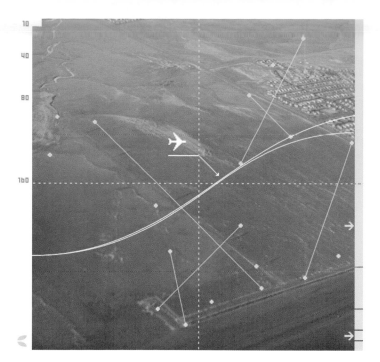

LOVE YOUR "?"

PHOTO / VIDEO AND DESIGN
ARNAUD MERCIER
ELIXIRSTUDIO.COM

1    2    REPLAY    CLOSE

AT
ELASTRADIUS
ELASTRADIUS.COM

SOUNDTRACK
EEN NEVILE, DESIGNER DRUGS
MORDICTRAX
MORDICTRAX.COM

THANKS TO
MIND THE BANNER PROJECT
ELASTRADIUS
ELASTRADIUS
LEE FELDMAN
LUKE MCKEEHAN
CELINE

JOURNEY ON
HIGH QUALITY VERSION
ELIXIRSTUDIO VANCOUVER, BRITISH COLUMBIA
MADE IN CANADA
MARCH 2001

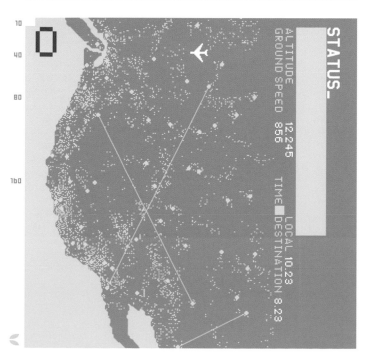

STATUS.
ALTITUDE      12.245
GROUND SPEED  856
                    LOCAL 10.23
TIME  DESTINATION 8.23

DEPRESSION PROCESS
ASPIRATION    AIRPLANE PORTANCE
DEVIATION
SURFACE

ENGINE RESPONSE

**Title** *Untitled:002-Infinity*
**Date** June 2001
**Country of residence** USA
**Executive producer** Steve Kazanjian
**Project producer** Eric Saks
**Project creative directors** Mike Goedecke, Eric Saks

"Belief started the *Untitled* series to encourage various creative people to collaborate on selected themes. Many design studios are working for clients and don't have anyone pushing them to create original artistic content just for themselves. The *Untitled* series breeds creative experimentation. Storytelling is also very important – storytelling that is visually designed. Sound is crucial, and the decision to include various sound studios was also key to the creative process. Some pieces begin with sound, others are created to the sound. The 28 pieces are authored to DVD for a random playing of interstital and programme material and will repeat with an infinite number of variations. *Untitled:002-Infinity* is the second in the ongoing series that was developed by Belief EXP, the experimental film division started by the artists at Belief. The final project is comprised of work by artists, film-makers, animators, typographers, and composers. Pieces are submitted as motion graphics, film, video, Flash, 3D animation, typographic treatments, photography, and composited still imagery. *Untitled:002-Infinity* premiered in Miami on 20 June at the Promax & BDA conference in an installation of live, mixed projections.

"*Untitled:002-Infinity* is dedicated to the memory of Claude Shannon, father of information theory and the digital age, 1916-2001." Mike Goedecke

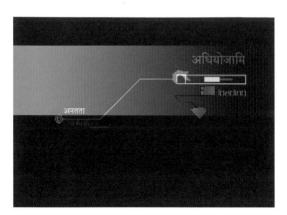  

## Belief: *Aparamitah*

**Creative director, designer, animator** Thomas Kurniady at Belief
**Nationality** Indonesian
**Country of residence** USA
**Date of birth** 1970
**Title** *Aparamitah*
**Date** First Shown: June 2001

**Producer** Eric Saks
**Photography** Eric Saks
**Sound design, music** Rob Cairns

"The piece is based on a modern art movement in conjunction with a traditional Balinese cultural movement, with reincarnation as a story base and segmentation of cremation, life, love, meditation, and the cycle of life. Other influences include flatness as a part of stage style – puppet/wayang symbolism merges with a global three-dimensional space for the visualisation of the complexities of life in digital techno culture. The elements of symbolism are: puppet/wayang as a symbol of humanity and a stage as a world that we live and explore; representation of cremation; and the symbol of the sword (Keris, a beautifully wrought sword imbued with spiritual power) from generation to generation." Thomas Kurniady

The project was created using Adobe Photoshop 6, Adobe Illustrator 9, After Effects 5 (for 2D-3D compositing), and 3D Studio Max (for 3D object and graphics elements).

 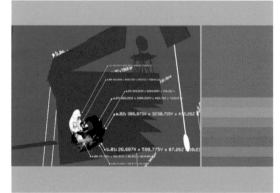 

## MK12 Studios: *MK12 Submission*

**Designers** Ben Radatz, Jed Carter, Shaun Hamontree, Tim Fisher, Matt Fraction at MK12 Studios
**Nationality** American
**Country of residence** USA
**Date of birth** 1968-75
**Title** *MK12 Submission*
**Date** April 2001
**Actors** John Dretzka, Dalton Carter

"According to quantum theory, reality can and does split itself into an infinite number of directions an infinite number of times per second. The path of one dimension as it advances through time may overlap that of another, weaving intricate meshes of half-realised worlds in which illogical combinations of objects and events become logically plausible. Our submission to *Untitled:002-Infinity* is a simulation of such a world, as seen from a god's eye point-of-view; an objective look at the third dimension from a higher plateau. Illustrated via shards of visual information spanning both Cartesian and relative timespace, scenarios unfold only under the most exact of circumstances. Apparent large-scale order forms and dissolves as the viewer's perspective shifts, creating a world that is entirely possible unto itself yet indistinguishable to an outside observer.

"In combining fragments from different locations both in time and space, environments are formed that lie somewhere between the past and the future, constantly shifting and never fully realised. It is only in these environments that linear time and solid matter are perceived, forming a paradox in which an infinite number of combinations emerge from a finite set of variables." MK12 Studios

Software used was MAYA 3.0, After Effects 4.0, Adobe Photoshop 6.0, and Adobe Illustrator 8.0 on Mac G3, Compaq and Aptiva workstations. The original format was 35 mm still photography.

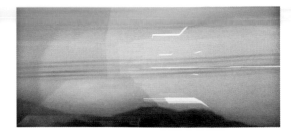

## Delapse: *From A-Z and back again*

**Designers** Johan van Wyk, Hilton Tennant, Garth van Heerden, Olivier Schildt, Michael van Straaten, Adrian Garces
**Nationality** South African
**Country of residence** South Africa

**Title** *From A-Z and back again*
**Date** June 2001
**Composer, sound designer** Kendall Reid, Michael van Straaten
**Sound engineer** Craig Dodds
**Producer** Aletta Alberts

**Production manager** Erna de Villiers
**Researcher, writer** Gerhard Greyvensteyn
**Technical director** Gustav Praekelt

"Our project focuses on the relation between order and disorder, which is interpreted as a process without beginning or end. Complex patterns – fractals – are self-similar and infinite; dissipative structure is a new complex structure; and only qualitative description becomes possible. The presence of multiple factors characteristic to the world of order-disorder is grounded in entropy, increasing disorder." Delapse

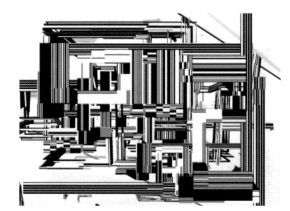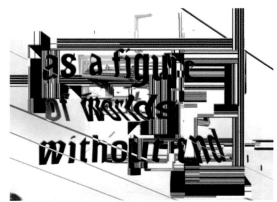

## General Working Group: *Paradox of the Infinite*

**Designers** Geoff Kaplan, R. Paul Seymour, Pamela M. Lee at General Working Group/Time Suck

**Title** *Paradox of the Infinite: the collapsing of space as a figure of worlds without end* for *Untitled:002-Infinity*

**Date** June 2001
**Music** Jon Huck

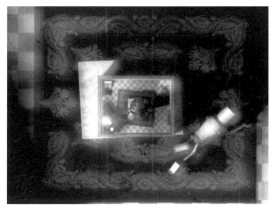

## Beezlebug Bit: *Welcome to the Universe*

**Designer** Lee Lanier at Beezlebug Bit
**Nationality** American
**Country of residence** USA

**Date of birth** 1966
**Title** *Welcome to the Universe* for *Untitled:002-Infinity*
**Date** March 2001

"The concept of 'infinity' brought to mind the endless cycle of birth, life and death. I thought it would be interesting to represent this with an 'endless zoom', where a camera flies through a universe within a universe within a universe that represents the various stages of a person's life.

"*Welcome to the Universe* is a one-minute computer animation created with Alias|Wavefront Maya, Adobe Photoshop, Adobe After Effects, and various pieces of music composition shareware running on a trio of custom-built PCs. It was literally a one-man job and took up my spare time over three weeks." Lee Lanier

## Mid-Tokyo Maps

**Creative directors** Hisayoshi Tohsaki (IMG SRC), Yoshiaki Nishimura (Living World), Naoki Sato (ASYL design)
**Design and development** IMG SRC (Jun Kuriyama, Momoko Takaoka, Yusuke Shibata, Rio Hashimoto, Jun Awano), ASYL design (Taku Enjohji, Yoko Washimine), Transform (Sayaka Umezawa, R. Tyler Shaw, Yoshiko Kanai)
**Country of residence** Japan

**Title** Mid-Tokyo Maps
**Date** Project due to be completed February 2002
**Producer** Hiroko Sakomura (Transform Corporation)
**Production** Transform Corporation, IMG SRC, ASYL design
**Client** Mori Building Co, Ltd
**Executive producer** Masahiro Watahiki (Mori Building Co, Ltd)
**Executive planner** Hitomi Namba (Mori Building Co, Ltd)

**Director** Hiroo Mori (Executive Director, Mori Building Co, Ltd)
**Publisher** Minoru Mori (President, Mori Building Co, Ltd)

Mori Building produces this website as part of its internet-based public relations activities. Mori Building Co, Ltd, an urban development company that got its start building and renting properties in Tokyo, is currently realising a massive 11-hectare redevelopment project in the Roppongi area. Mori Building firmly believes that Tokyo cannot simply maintain the status quo if it is to retain its world-class competitiveness. Mid-Tokyo Maps uses maps as an easily accessible way to explore Tokyo in its existing form — looking at, for instance, the easily forgotten land beneath Tokyo's asphalt; the size of Tokyo as a city; the use of vertical space; or the area and siting of open space (parks, plazas, and streets) — and inspires viewers to rethink their desires for future urban development.

## Slowmotion: *Robbery* titles sequence

**Designers** Jeff Miller
at Slowmotion
**Nationality** American
**Country of residence** America
**Date of birth** 1972
**Title** *Robbery* titles sequence
**Date** May 2001

"*Robbery* is a film about a well-known and highly skilled safe cracker in the present-day underground world of professional thieves. The criminal is called on by the American government to help execute a robbery against itself, in order to adjust the economy by displacing large amounts of cash distributed by the federal reserves.

"The sequence begins as the camera moves through an extreme close-up of a fingerprint. Numerals roll onto the screen in the same mechanical motion as the tumbler on a lock. The typography was derived from the ornaments and monetary classicism of American paper currency. As the camera moves through the lines of fingerprints, the letters turn into the titles of the film. The titles continue to change from numbers to letters until each is completely readable. After the title is seen, fingerprints are rubbed back over the words, similar to the way in which a police officer would roll a suspect's inky fingers onto paper. As the fingerprints are pressed into the letters, the title and letters seem to rub off, suggesting that whoever is at work here is carefully and systematically covering his tracks.

"A flatbed scanner was the most used piece of hardware, with software to scan in fingerprints and reproductions of paper currency.

"The type was set in Adobe Illustrator and animated using After Effects."
Jeff Miller

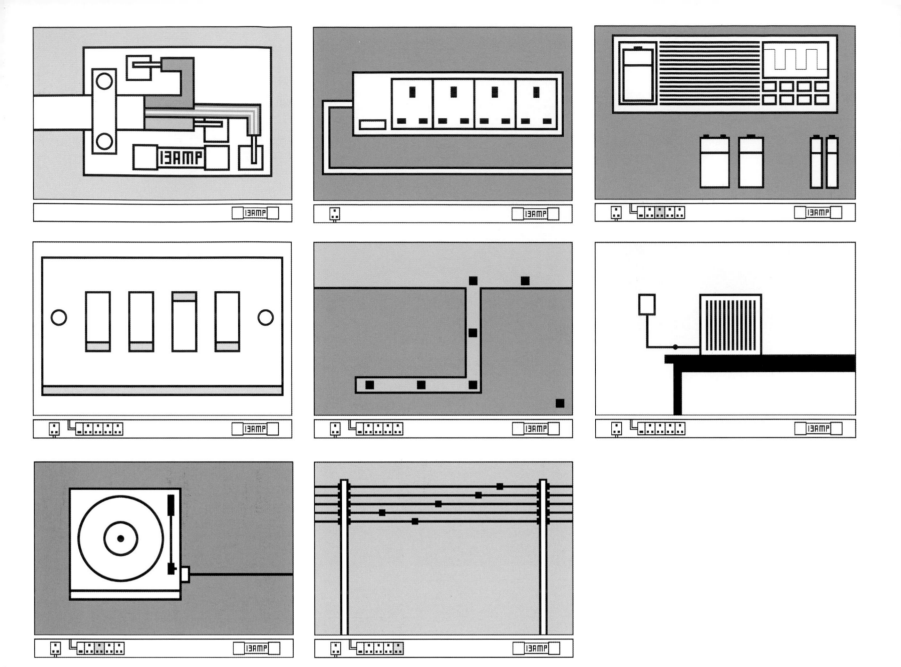

Friendchip: www.13amp.tv

**Designers** Anthony Burrill, Kip
Parker at Friendchip
**Nationality** British
**Country of residence** UK
**Date of birth** 1966, 1973
**Title** www.13amp.tv
**Date** June 2001

"13amp is a new record label, and this is the
website we designed for them. The first
release by the label isn't until the end of
the year, but to build interest in 13amp we
planned a website that evolved over the
summer. The first stage, shown here,
contains no text. It is a series of interactive
'sound toys', all based on the theme of
electricity. The second stage, launched in
July, has more interactive elements, plus a
message board. There is still no reference
made to the nature of 13amp, however.
Only when the label's first release is made
will the site contain any 'facts' about
musicians signed to the label."
Anthony Burrill

## Ippei Gyoubu: *Planet of the Fusion*

**Designer** Ippei Gyoubu
**Nationality** Japanese
**Country of residence** Japan
**Date of birth** 1974
**Title** *Planet of the Fusion*
**Date** Magazine on sale
1 July 2001

"*Planet of the Fusion* is serialised quarterly in a magazine published by Bijyutu Syuppansya in Japan. The action is set on Earth in the near future. Pollution has increased as a result of an increase in temperature: arctic ice has melted causing flooding. Moreover, destruction of the ozone layer continues and an artificial orange ozone layer is created.

"Humans cannot survive without a protection suit, and have made the most of gene technology, and 'fusion' man is the result of mixing human genetics with those of other living things. A new type of human is born. Through genetic engineering, humans succeeded in manipulating the genetic structures of other living things and have become able to survive on this unclean planet. However, some people refuse to undergo this operation on the grounds of religion or ethics. These 'originals' are the target of discrimination and violence.

"The hero of the story is called Yuuzow. He is a professional killer for a certain organisation. He is just the trigger man and knows nothing of his boss's identity. The purpose of the organisation is to erase 'originals'; Yuuzow, however, is only in it for the money. One day, he falls in love with an 'original' girl – someone he is supposed to kill. But seeing for the first time a human being without a protection suit, he experiences the shock of beauty. He promises to give up his profession and save the girl, but another hit-man gets to her first. Yuuzow vows revenge and a price is put on his head. But he learns that if someone in his position kills ten other wanted men, his criminal history will be erased. In addition, there are material benefits if he succeeds. Yuuzow decides to take up the challenge – but his purpose is to acquire information. What is the true purpose of the organisation? What is the secret of his boss's past? And what is the unexpected relationship between Yuuzow and his boss?

"The images are created by first drawing a picture with a pencil; then I scan it, and import it into Adobe Photoshop and Adobe Illustrator." Ippei Gyoubu

## Mysterious Al

**Date of birth** 1979
**Place of birth** London
**Place of residence** London
**Courtesy** Mysterious Al

**Description of work** "Everything I do is based 100 per cent on personal experience. Recently, my work has revolved around this group of monsters I met in a club in East Twickenham. They were really weird characters, and most of them were really difficult to get along with. I became friends with Salboas, though. He's sort of their unofficial leader. I helped him out with some posters for his election campaign (East Twickenham Mafia, 2000). Through hanging out with the monsters I gradually got introduced to the ROODS, the Low-wage Crew. They all suck at graffiti. I don't really know the ROODS, but they helped me out while I was being dumped by my girlfriend. And for that I thank them. The SMS guys, well they're my more recent stuff. Portraits. They carry text-messages from cell-phone to cell-phone. It's a whack job, but for 10p a shot it pays the bills. They move at sub-sonic speed, so I can only see them with stills from my digital camera.

"When I was a kid I used to write graffiti. I'm retired now, but graffiti concepts still interest me. The putting up of colours, the interruption, the coverage. I was never big into the elaborate paintings and wild-style. I liked the fast, messy stuff. Big three-letter dubs in red and white. I still use graffiti methods in paintings but my main influences are not artists or writers. They are the things I love. Mild summer nights. Walking to parties while it's still light outside, the rattle of the 6 am train, car batteries by the roadside, sliding into the slipstream of speeding police cars. Noises, dogs barking, sirens, the N9 night bus home, the District Line, the sound she makes as she sleeps, Kitchner fried chicken, Minidisc players, and dripping-wet paint-markers. These are the reasons that I write pages. They are the backbone of my paintings. I'm not so much celebrating any of these things, merely acknowledging them."

**Materials used** "In no particular order, paint-markers, oilsticks, emulsion, gloss paint, plaster, spraycans, varnish, vinyl, egg-whites, and a G4 super-Mac. Why? Well because they're the best materials for the job. I also use found objects as platforms for my paintings. I find good stuff while sifting the streets with a bottle of rum." Mysterious Al

*The Lorraine Motel*

*Cafeteria*

*Elian*

*Quang Duc*

*Wang Weilin*

*Meredes – Pl. de l'Alma*

*The Condo on Bundy*

*the Humiliation of Mr Banks*

*R. King*

*Screenshots Series*
Chromogenic prints from digital
files created in Photoshop
2000
All images: 57.2 x 76.2 cm

## Jon Haddock

**Date of birth** 1960
**Place of residence** Tempe, AZ, USA
**Representation** Howard House,
Seattle
**Courtesy** John Haddock,
Howard House

**Recent exhibitions**

**Solo** *Screenshots*, Howard House, Seattle (2001) > *No Absolutes*, Arizona State University Art Museum Experimental Gallery at Matthews Center, Tempe, AZ, USA (2000) > *Modifications*, Roberts & Tilton Gallery, Los Angeles (2000) > *Homemade*, Howard House, Seattle (1999) > **Group** *Cyborg Manifesto, or the Joy of Artifice*, Laguna Art Museum, Laguna Beach, CA, USA (2001) > *BitStreams*, Whitney Museum of American Art, New York (2001) > *Air Hockey*, Howard House, Seattle (1999) > *Not There*, Rena Bransten Gallery, San Francisco (1999) > *Too Small (To Stand on Their Own)*, Lead Gallery Annex, Seattle (1997)

"The *Screenshots*, *Modifications*, and *Resin* series all deal with the same interrelated themes. They are a reaction to the violence in our culture, as well as a claim of ownership. I'm not happy about having been subjected to gratuitous portrayals of violence as a child, but I acknowledge that those portrayals have shaped my world view, making me who I am. As a viewer, and as an artist, I expect to have the right to free use of material that is so integral to my person.

"I often modify existing photographs using Adobe Photoshop. When making prints I like the Cymbolic Sciences Lightjet 5000, which exposes photo paper directly from a digital file. Once I have thought of something I want to say, I try to package it in a clear and concise form. I lay out a plan for making the work, then execute it. In many instances the actual making of the work is fairly mindless and repetitive.

"My most direct influence has been the KLF. Without the *Manual* (http://www.hairybob.org/hairy/manual.txt) none of this would have happened."
Jon Haddock

*Rhapsody Spray 3*
2000
Screenprint
133.4 x 158.8 cm
Edition of 6
Photograph: D. James Dee

## Carl Fudge

**Place of birth** London, UK
**Representation** Ronald Feldman
Fine Arts, New York
**Courtesy** Ronald Feldman Fine Arts

**Recent exhibitions**
**Solo** Bernard Toale Gallery, Boston (2001) >
Ronald Feldman Fine Arts, New York (2000)
> Ronald Feldman Fine Arts, New York
(1998) > Bernard Toale Gallery, Boston
(1998) > Schmidt Contemporary Art, St
Louis, MI, USA (1997) > **Group** *BitStreams*,
Whitney Museum of American Art, New York
(2001) > *Digital: Printmaking Now*, Brooklyn
Museum of Art, NY, USA (2001) > *Glee:
Painting Now*, Aldrich Museum of
Contemporary Art, Ridgefield, CT, USA,
travelled to Palm Beach Institute of
Contemporary Art, FL, USA (2000-01) >
*2001*, University of the Arts, Philadelphia
(2000) > *PICT*, Banff Center for the Arts,
Walter Phillips Gallery, Canada (2000)

"All of my images are derived from a
representational source that has been
transformed.

"The culture of the copy and the replica
is fascinating within a rubric of the handmade. The prints that are adapted from
contemporary cartoons are executed using
a silkscreen process.

"The starting point for the paintings are
17th-century Ukiyo prints. Here the interest
lies with the hidden images and form. The
theme of veiling and unveiling is explored
both technically and metaphorically.

"The space of the Eastern print is also
of significance as it is modernist in form.
Compositions are flat, graphic, and de-
emphasise the illusionism so emphasised
in Western art.

"Inspiration comes from a wide variety of
sources. Art historical influences range from
Albrecht Dürer to Warhol. Within popular
culture, the colour and graphics of
animation are a current fascination."
Carl Fudge

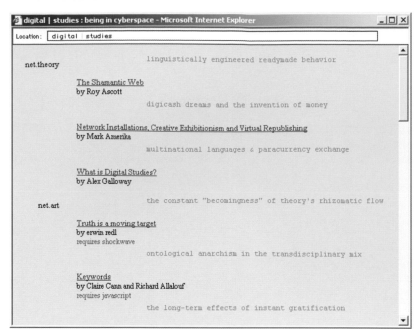

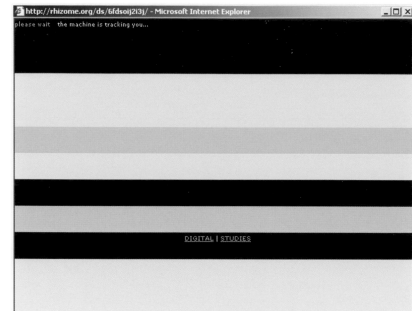

*Digital Studies: Being in Cyberspace*
1997

## Mark Amerika

**Courtesy** Mark Amerika; Alex Galloway; Anne Burdick; Jay Dillemuth

Mark Amerika, who was has just been named a '*Time* magazine 100 Innovator', as part of its continuing series of features on the most influential artists, scientists, entertainers, and philosophers into the 21st century, is the author of two novels, *The Kafka Chronicles* and *Sexual Blood*. He is also the director of Alt-X (www.altx.com), which he founded in 1993. His web art projects have been exhibited in various museums including the Whitney Biennial in New York (2000), and the Centre Georges Pompidou in Paris. There are two large-scale retrospectives of his work in 2001, at the ACA Media Arts Plaza in Tokyo and the ICA in London.

### On Being Retro in the Zeroes

"And yet, and yet… denying temporal succession, denying the self, denying the astronomical universe are apparent desparations and secret consolations. Our destiny is not frightful by being unreal; it is frightful because it is irreversible and iron-clad. Time is the substance I am made of. Time is a river which sweeps me along, but I am the river; it is a tiger which destroys me, but I am the tiger; it is a fire which consumes me, but I am the fire." Jorge Luis Borges, from *A New Refutation of Time*.

To paraphrase Barbara Kruger, "every-time I hear the word 'retrospective', I reach for my cheque book." What could an internet art retrospective possibly mean when the work already co-exists with everything else that is easily accessible on the web? Does viewing *GRAMMATRON*, my large-scale digital narrative created between 1993-1997, take on a different meaning, different value, when it appears (virtually re-appears) on a Japanese museum website that contextualises its presentation as a retrospective?

On the net, space is cheap, ever-expandable, ready for mark-up. Compared to major museum shows, the resources needed to produce a full-on internet art retrospective are relatively minimal. What is most important is that there exists the will, and maybe the power. Will power. And the passage of a certain amount of time to justify its retroness. In our accelerated blur culture, the Eighties were retro in the Nineties. So the mid-Nineties can be retro in early Zeroes, no? It's a fine feeling to be retro in the Zeroes, to be a real, commodified 'thing-in-itself' even as 'the work itself' still, somehow, seems unreal.

You still cannot touch it. You still cannot sequester it. You still cannot stop it from generating the audience it will inevitably generate. You can associate yourself with it. You can network with it. You can link to it. You can even purchase it and say that it's part of your collection as long as it remains accessible to the distributed net community that gives it its ultimate value. For that matter, you can co-market your own historical persona with its aura.

Which reminds me: what would have happened if Benjamin had seen the emergence of the net? Would it have reaffirmed his position on art objects losing their aura in lieu of an increased network-value for the avant-pop celebrity that composed the work? The fact is, works of net art maintain their aura in ways beyond mere objecthood. Their so-called 'immateriality' confers upon them a radically different kind of marketplace value, one that grows with every new person that visits the site (over a million served). The value of net art plays with the notion of scarcity in a serious way, essentially saying to the mainstream art institution and/or adventurous collector, "the more attention I get, the higher my market value, and the more time I put into the work's creation, the more you will have to pay to have the privilege of calling me yours, of collecting me the way you would collect the rarest of Dead Sea Scrolls."

A work like my *GRAMMATRON* has, after four long years of web notoriety, recently been referred to as 'ancient' and 'a relic', and looks every bit like 1993-1997. As new media art curator Christiane Paul might say, that's a kind of aura in and of itself. The truth is, *GRAMMATRON* is now part of art history, not just net art history. All one has to do is experience it, see it for what it is, and become educated about its historical and cultural context as well as its position in the attention economy.

New media curator Steve Dietz, who nurtured my second major net art work, *PHON:E:ME*, into existence, once noted (while remixing the concepts of many others into a succinct phraseology, as he often does): "This new millennium is a zero moment, a moment of profound renewal, when everything we thought we knew is wrong…"

If you thought net art had no major-league market value, you were wrong. If you thought that there was no difference between an internationally-renowned net art work that took four years to develop and a provocative one-liner that took a half a day to put on the web, you were wrong. If you thought that an internet art retrospective was light years away, you were wrong. Speed is a function of time and to be is to blur.

"The world runs on internet time," says Andy Grove, CEO of Intel. This internet art retrospective is, like so many other conceptual net art works, ahead of its time. But for how long? As Baudrillard reminds us, "[t]he image is no longer given the time to become an image." In this regard, it can also be said that net art was never given enough time to become net art."

(Mark Amerika, from *Avant-Pop: The Stories of Mark Amerika, a Retrospective of Internet Art*)

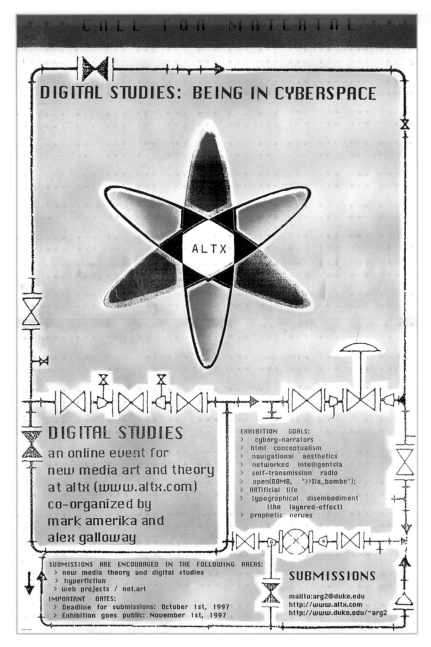

Poster call for *Digital Studies*
1997

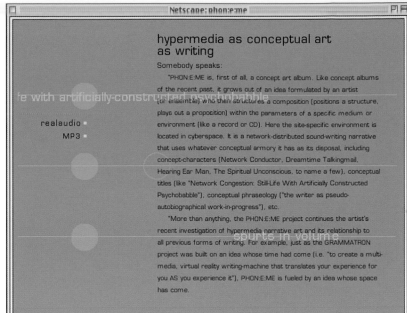

### hypermedia as conceptual art as writing

Somebody speaks:

"PHON:E:ME is, first of all, a concept art album. Like concept albums of the recent past, it grows out of an idea formulated by an artist (or ensemble) who then structures a composition (positions a structure, plays out a proposition) within the parameters of a specific medium or environment (like a record or CD). Here the site-specific environment is located in cyberspace. It is a network-distributed sound-writing narrative that uses whatever conceptual armory it has as its disposal, including concept-characters (Network Conductor, Dreamtime Talkingmail, Hearing Ear Man, The Spiritual Unconscious, to name a few), conceptual titles (like "Network Congestion: Still-Life With Artificially Constructed Psychobabble"), conceptual phraseology ("the writer as pseudo-autobiographical work-in-progress"), etc.

"More than anything, the PHON:E:ME project continues the artist's recent investigation of hypermedia narrative art and its relationship to all previous forms of writing. For example, just as the GRAMMATRON project was built on an idea whose time had come (i.e. "to create a multi-media, virtual reality writing-machine that translates your experience for you AS you experience it"), PHON:E:ME is fueled by an idea whose space has come.

realaudio
MP3

*PHON:E:ME*
1999

*HOLO-X*
1998

McGill & Son Paper and Printing
2001
Plexiglas, powder-coated
aluminium, enamel paint, glue,
and plastic letters
121.9 x 304.8 cm
Edition of 2

Hanoi Travel
2000
Plexiglas, powder-coated
aluminium, enamel paint, glue,
and plastic letters
182.9 x 182.9 cm
Edition of 2

Ebony Eyes Beauty Salon
2000
Plexiglas, powder-coated
aluminium, enamel paint, glue,
and plastic letters
198.1 x 151.8 cm
Edition of 2

## Ken Lum

**Date of birth** 1956
**Place of birth** Vancouver
**Place of residence** Vancouver
**Representation** Andrea Rosen
Gallery, New York
**Courtesy** © Ken Lum;
Andrea Rosen Gallery
**Photography** Oren Slor

**Recent exhibitions**
**Solo** Andrea Rosen Gallery, New York
(2001) > Centre for Contemporary Art,
Kitakyushu, Japan (2001) > Galerie im
Taxispalais, Innsbruck, Austria (2001) > LA
Galerie, Frankfurt (2000) > The Gate
Foundation, Amsterdam (2000) > Plug-In
Gallery, Winnipeg, Canada (1999) > **Group**
Kunsthalle Vienna (2001-02) > *Unpacking
Europe*, Museum Boijmans van Beuningen,
Rotterdam, travelled to House of World
Cultures, Berlin (2001) > *Contemporary
Photography II: Anti-Memory*, Yokohama
Museum of Art, Japan (2000) > Bienal de
Havana (2000)

"[This series contains] stories of possible
shopkeepers, many of whom are immigrants
from a place they cannot return to but a
place that remains active in their hearts and
minds. To suggest this is already to test the
contradictions between public and private
expression, especially as it traverses the
discourse of commerce.

"I want the 'signs' to reveal something of
the persons behind them. I want the viewer
to ask, for example: Who is Amir? Gosh, he
does a lot of different things in his store!
Why in God's name is he going back to
Eritrea? I want the idea of personal desire
and catastrophe to hover not so far from
the surfaces of my signs. The theme of my
work also questions art. I want my works
to look like Pop Art but to express great
discontentment.

"As in almost all of my work, I get my
ideas from walking about and noticing the
surfaces of the city. In my case, many of my
works relate to the environment of East
Vancouver, a lower-middle class neighbourhood where I grew up. I like the idea of
trying to tell personal stories that often
intersect politics, private and otherwise.
Most of my ideas just come to me as I am

walking about finding myself asking basic
questions when I see something interesting.
For example, when I see someone yelling at
someone, I try to think what could be the
intricacies involved in such a scene and
how can I express some of these intricacies
in the form of art. I also like very much the
idea of art that really touches on the look
of non-art without it ever expressing a
dissatisfaction with art.

"I think there is a lot of potential content
for art out there and it amazes me that so
much of it never gets dealt with as art. Or
worse, it gets dealt with but the work also
has the agenda of rejecting art, which is
preposterous in my view.

"For this latest series, the materials
are plexiglas and powder-coated aluminum
because they are a medium specific to a
certain standard sign form. Having said this,
I am not interested in simply remaking a
piece like a readymade – these are all
'fake' signs of fake businesses. Also, they
are framed in a depth of only two inches –
basically the depth of a painting. I do this
so that the lessons of painterly exigetic
analysis can be applied to the reading
of my works, even though my works are

not strictly paintings.

"In art, I was inspired, like a lot of other
artists, by artists such as Dan Graham and
Ed Ruscha. I like the clarity of their work,
but the more clear they are, the more
complex their meanings. I like a lot of
American avant-garde art of the 1960s –
from Warhol to the Minimalists to various
Conceptualists. I think Sixties American art
opened up so many possibilities for an artist
such as myself, from a different background.
Also, all of that art tested the question of
politics. I don't necessarily mean in the
restricted sense but the wider Aristotelian
sense. I like a lot of contemporary artists
today, from Tony Oursler to Yinka Shonibare
to Gillian Wearing. Their works speak
content, they challenge the viewer, but also
their works function as interesting art. I am
also influenced by a lot of English text art
of the Seventies such as Conrad Atkinson,
Victor Burgen, and Yves Lomax, but I
never liked the 'look' of their art – too
instructional, too dry, too dismissive of the
potential of art to do what art does best,
to animate the viewer." Ken Lum

# Ebony Eyes
## BEAUTY SALON

### UNISEX HAIR, NAIL & SKIN CARE

THIS WEEK ONLY
BONUS MANICURE
WITH FACIAL
WALK INS WELCOME
ALL POWER
TO THE PEOPLE !

*Panda and Bamboo*
2001
Enamel paint and glitter
on canvas
248.9 x 182.9 cm

*Pa*
2001
Enamel paint and glitter
on canvas
243.8 x 182.9 cm

## Rob Pruitt

**Date of birth** 1964
**Place of birth** Washington, DC, USA
**Place of residence** New York
**Representation** Gavin Brown's
Enterprise, New York
**Courtesy** Gavin Brown's Enterprise

**Recent exhibitions**
**Solo** *Pandas and Bamboo*, Gavin Brown's
Enterprise, New York (2001) >

Contemporary Art Center, Cincinnati, OH,
USA (2001) > *Flea Market*, Gavin Brown's
Enterprise, New York (2000) > *Psychic
Predictions for the New Millennium & Things
to do with Lemons*, Cabinet Gallery, London
(2000) > *101 Art Ideas You Can Do Yourself*,
Gavin Brown's Enterprise, New York (1999)
> **Group** *Vantage Point*, Irish Museum of
Modern Art, Dublin (2001) > *The Silk Purse
Procedure*, Arnolfini and Spike Island, Bristol,
UK (2001) > *Salon*, Delfina Project Space,
London (2000) > *New York Projects*, Delfina,
London (2000) > *Protest and Survive*,
Whitechapel Art Gallery, London (2000)

*Winter*
2001
Enamel paint and glitter on
canvas
248.9 x 182.9 cm

*Villa Savoye: Le Corbusier*
2001
Oil on canvas
45.5 x 90.5 cm

*Falling Water: F. L. Wright*
2001
Oil on canvas
50.2 x 61 cm

## Satoshi Watanabe

**Date of birth** 1967
**Place of birth** Hyogo, Japan
**Place of residence** Osaka, Japan
**Representation** Taro Nasu Gallery,
Tokyo
**Courtesy** Satoshi Watanabe;
Taro Nasu Gallery, Tokyo

### Recent exhibitions
**Solo** Mackintosh Gallery, Glasgow School of
Art (2001) > Mitaka City Arts Center, Tokyo
(2001) > Taro Nasu Gallery, Tokyo (2001) >
Kohji Ogura Gallery, Nagoya, Japan (2000)
> **Group** *Systemic Painting 2000*, Bunpodo
Gallery, Tokyo (2000) > *Philip Morris Art
Award 2000*, Ebis Garden Place, Tokyo
(2000) > *VOCA 2000*, Ueno Royal Museum,
Tokyo (2000) > *Compact Disc V.A*, Kobe Art

Village Center, Hyogo, Japan (1999) > *The
Field of Vision*, Kyoto Shijyo Gallery,
Japan (1998)

"In my expression, there is an oscillation
inside of me between extrovert and
introvert. So I have been taking a sort of
neutral style. As a result, I confess, this style
seems a bit addictive.

"People in Glasgow [inspire me],
because living abroad gives you an
opportunity to think a lot about yourself.
My main inspirations come from TV and the
idea of tourism. Now and then I wonder how
cultural exchanges are made.

"I use oil paints and vinyl adhesive
stickers. The former is supposed to be a
long-standing material, and the latter is
the opposite. This contrast is interesting to
me. But unfortunately, viewers don't seem
to feel cosy when they see the weakness
of the stickers..." Satoshi Watanabe

## Francesco Spampinato

**Date of birth** 1978
**Place of birth** Catania, Sicily
**Place of residence** Bologna
**Representation** Galleria Marabini,
Bologna
**Courtesy** Galleria Marabini

**Recent exhibitions**
**Solo** Galleria Marabini, Bologna (2001) >
Galleria Mars'Sala, Bologna (2000) > XY
Arte Con Artista, Bologna (1999) > Galleria

Catus, Bologna (1999) > *Working in
Progress,* Bologna (1999) > **Group**
*Emporio,* Via Farini, Milan (2000) > XY
Arte Con Artista, Bologna (1999) > Galleria
Cactus, Bologna (1999) > *Exit,* Campo
delle Fragole, Bologna (1999) > *Space,*
Ravenna, Italy (1999)

**Description of work** "I represent states of
mind, stream-of-consciousness. My subjects
are universal types, man-machines. They are
unconscious, busy within their own fear, vain
expectations and common mitigations. I
want people to use my works as a proof of
identity, caught in the trap of the brands,

stars, pop, the again-and-again in the history
of the human being. But at the end which is
the subliminal message? Which is the
product for sale?"

**Materials used** "I use acrylic colours which
are spread with the help of a brush or a
roller. This technique allows me to obtain
uniform areas of colour, which can cover
even big spaces. I am not interested in
brush work, in the dirtiness of painting, or
the technique of dripping. What I want is
to obtain clean way of painting as if it were
a printed surface done by a machine. I want
to be accurate."

**Creative inspiration** "I would say everything
concerning my childhood, which I spent
during the Eighties, starting with the birth
of video games and Manga, things that were
running parallel with those up-fluctuating
surfaces, fired by the sun belonging to my
memories from Sicily. The graphic advertise-
ment of the Seventies. The infinitive space
given by the Baroque style present in Italy
and during the fifteenth century. The music
of Kraftwerk together with Air."
Francesco Spampinato

*Ages*
2001
Forty-five panel piece
355 x 760 cm

## Gilbert & George

**Representation** Jay Jopling/
White Cube, London
**Courtesy** Jay Jopling/White Cube

Gilbert & George began working together in
1967 when they met on the advanced
sculpture course at Central Saint Martin's
School of Art in London. Since then, they
have had major exhibitions at Musée d'Art
Moderne de la Ville de Paris; Solomon R.
Guggenheim Museum, New York; Central
House of the Artists, New Tretyakov Gallery,
Moscow; National Art Gallery, Beijing; Art
Museum, Shanghai; Sezon Museum, Tokyo;
Stedelijk Museum, Amsterdam; and the
Hayward Gallery, London. In 2001 they will
have solo exhibitions at the School of Art,
Athens and Château d'Arenthon, France and
in 2002 at Centro Cultural de Belém, Lisbon.

*Thirteen*
2001
Twelve panel piece
338 x 213 cm

*Untitled (They seem to display...)*
2001
Acrylic on canvas
200 x 250 cm

Installation: Maureen Paley Interim Art, London

THERE'S NOTHING, NOTHING TO BE SUSPICIOUS OF, NOTHING TO THINK ABOUT, NOTHING TO HOLD ME HERE ANOTHER SECOND.

*Untitled (There's nothing...)*
2001
Acrylic on canvas
120 x 75 cm

## Muntean/Rosenblum

**Date of birth** In collaboration since 1992
**Place of residence** Vienna
**Representation** Maureen Paley Interim Art, London
**Courtesy** Maureen Paley Interim Art

### Recent exhibitions
**Solo** Maureen Paley Interim Art, London (2001) > Art: Concept, Paris (2001) > Chicagoprojectroom, Los Angeles (2001) > Susanna Kulli, St. Gallen, Switzerland (2000) > *Where Else*, Secession, Vienna (2000) > Georg Kargl, Vienna (1999) > **Group** *The*

*City of Tomorrow and the Exhibition Year One*, Bo01, Malmö (2001) > Fondazione Sandretto Re Rebaudengo, Turin, Italy (2001) > Berlin Biennale (2001) > *Melodrama*, Tate Gallery Liverpool, UK (2001) > *City Racing 1988-1998*, ICA, London (2001)

"The paintings showing young people in various urban surroundings are entirely constructed and artificial. They combine different and disparate material to form a new entity, which produces no linear narrative, but has narrative gestures.

"Photographs taken out of magazines are sampled, cut, segmented, and put together to make new compositions. Classical iconographic elements of the old masters are used together with the quality

of painting to transform any reference to fashion. This simultaneous mix results in a whole set of tensions and connotations that contributes to our concept of 'Precise Ambiguity'.

"The work focuses on various issues like the difficulty of coming up with a contemporary notion of the subject, the incoherent structure of the self, and the need to construct different identities at the same time. Sometimes the structure is enlarged and the paintings become part of a whole installation. A sort of tableau displaying a wide range of mediums like sculpture, photography and performative elements.

"Major influences are: Nicolo dell'Arca, Giovanni Battista Piazzetta and the music of Johannes Ockeghem." Muntean/Rosenblum

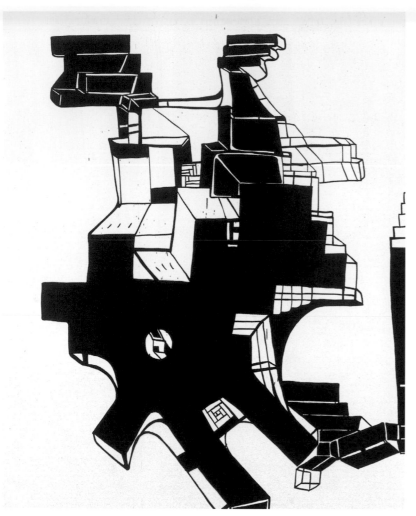

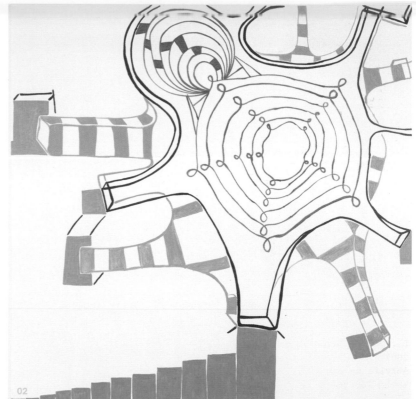

## Joanne Greenbaum

**Representation** greengrassi,
London; D'Amelio Terras,
New York
**Courtesy** greengrassi

### Recent exhibitions
**Solo** D'Amelio Terras, New York (2001) >
greengrassi, London (1999) > D'Amelio
Terras, New York (1998) > D'Amelio Terras,
New York (1997) > Arena Gallery, Brooklyn,
NY, USA (1996) > **Group** greengrassi,
London (2001) > *Warped, Painting and the
Feminine*, Angel Row Gallery, Nottingham
travelled to Middlesbrough Art Gallery,
Rugby Art Gallery and Museum, UK (2001) >
*Mapping, Territory, Connexions*, Anne de
Villepoix, Paris (2000) > *Points, Lignes,
Plans*, Galerie des Filles du Calvaire, Paris
(2000) > D'Amelio Terras, New York (2000)

"A current theme [of my work] is a fictional
presence in undetermined architecture.
Impossible structures that could be seen
as a type of over-conceptualised still-life.
The story I am telling is my journey through
each painting, not particularly edited on the
canvas. Themes emerge without my knowing
exactly what the theme will turn out to be,
but once it does emerge, I work with that
theme until the new one presents itself.

s"I usually prepare a group of canvases
together, but then work slowly on one
painting at a time. This way, each work in
the series becomes a reference point for
the next. When they are all done, it is a
cumulative group that has taken on a
character of its own. It is always a delight
and surprise to see how they are relating
and interacting with each other as a
coherent series.

"I love and use traditional materials –
oil paint right out of the tube, watercolour,
gouache. The hardest thing to do and the
most challenging as a painter is to create
something fresh using these traditional
limitations in the year 2001. That said,
my favourite drawing tool is a cheap
ballpoint pen.

"As of right now some influences/
inspirations could be Eva Zeisel's industrial
designs and Lee Bontecou's paintings of
the Sixties for their physical and psychic
aggressiveness. Matisse and Picasso remain,
as always, a continual source of inspiration,
as they tried to reinvent what a painting
could be each time they set out."
Joanne Greenbaum

**01**
*Untitled*
2001
Oil on canvas
152.4 x 122 cm

**02**
*Untitled*
2000
Oil on canvas
152.4 x 152.4 cm

**03**
*Untitled*
1999
Oil on canvas
127 x 127 cm

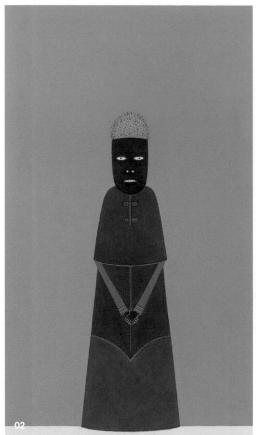

01
*Untitled*
2000
Gouache on paper
48.3 x 33 cm

02
*Untitled*
2001
Gouache on paper
20.3 x 11.4 cm

03
*Untitled*
2000
Gouache on paper

# Laylah Ali

**Date of birth** 1968
**Place of birth** Buffalo, NY, USA
**Representation** 303 Gallery,
New York
**Courtesy** 303 Gallery

**Recent exhibitions**
**Solo** Institute of Contemporary Art, Boston (2001) > Yerba Buena Center for the Arts, San Francisco (2001) > 303 Gallery, New York (2000) > MassMOCA, North Adams, MA, USA (2000) > Museum of Contemporary Art, Chicago (1999) > **Group** *Freestyle*, Studio Museum in Harlem, New York (2001) > *FRESH: The Altoids Curiously Strong Collection 1998-2000*, New Museum, New York (2001) > *Art on Paper 2000*, Weatherspoon Art Gallery, The University of North Carolina at Greensboro, USA (2000) >

*Collectors Collect Contemporary*, Institute of Contemporary Art, Boston (1999) > *No Place Rather Than Here*, 303 Gallery, New York (1999)

**Description of work** "The challenge has been to devise a particular story that functions as many particular stories. When I started the *Greenheads*, I was interested in creating a figure that I hadn't seen before – one that acted as a figurative question mark. A figure that prompted both me and the viewer to ask: Who is it? What is it? Why does it exist? Rather than a figure that comes with historical associations that immediately reveal themselves. And then, when this question mark was placed in certain situations, the narrative options started to do unpredictable and predictable things, depending on who was doing the looking.

"I start [a series of work] with notes – some written, some visual. I make drawings,

usually on scraps of paper, that I collect in a notebook. For about a two-month period, I usually hash out the ideas and details right down to what kind of socks they should be wearing. I then make meticulous pencil drawings based on the relationships that I have worked out through the previous body of sketches. When all of the final drawings are done, I work out the colour, and then, finally, I begin painting. I work on a group simultaneously. It all sounds faster and more efficient than it actually is."

**Materials used** "For this series, I've used gouache on paper. I like the immediacy of paper. It's flexible and portable, though it can have a mind and character of its own at times. Gouache is great for small detailed work and the colour is vibrant and rich, and it's not a flashy medium, which I like. It does what I need it to do without stealing the show."

**Creative inspiration** "Inspiration is a tough concept for me – it's a little optimistic about what spurs the creative process. What motivates me to make work is not necessarily from something inspired; it feels more prosaic, almost like a kind of service that has exalted moments. I have questions and ideas about the world that I live in and I need a place to chart that mental interaction. It's a selfish act that, perhaps, reaches out. Certainly, there are people I admire and work that makes me think and respond. Jacob Lawrence's paintings and lifelong process interests me, and I love Joe Sacco's work, and Lydia Davis's writing. I try to keep connected with what other people are thinking about. But ultimately, it's my own electrical loose ends, and the depressive socialist in me, that gets me in the studio."
Laylah Ali

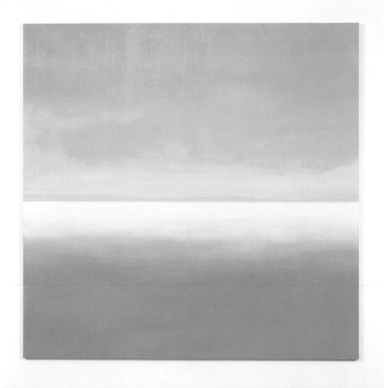

*Grunion Run*
2001
Oil on Canvas
90 x 92 inches

*Sunday Painting*
2001
Oil on Canvas
90 x 90 inches

## Byron Kim

**Date of birth** 1961
**Place of birth** La Jolla, CA, USA
**Representation** Max Protetch
Gallery, New York
**Courtesy** Max Protetch Gallery

### Recent exhibitions
**Solo** Max Protetch Gallery, New York (2001)
> *Whitney Philip Morris: Wall Drawings by
Byron Kim,* Whitney Museum of American
Art at Philip Morris, New York (1999) >
*Roche's Point Studies,* Max Protetch Gallery,
New York (1999) > Museum of
Contemporary Art, Chicago (1998) > *Byron
Kim: Process,* Hatton Gallery, Colorado
State University, Fort Collins, CO, USA

(1998) > **Group** *Here and Now,* Zacheta
National Gallery, Warsaw, travelling to
Arsenal Gallery, Bialystok, Poland (2001) >
*It's Not What You See: Perverting
Minimalism,* Museo Nacional Centro de Arte
Reina Sofia, Madrid (2001) > *Here and Now,*
National Gallery, Warsaw (2001) > Kwangju
Biennale, Korea (2000) > Sonje Art Center,
Seoul (2000)

### Description of work
"I simply wanted to
make some paintings in which I could get
lost. I wanted to make paintings that were
more about nothing than a blank canvas
would be. In order to achieve this I made
paintings that hover between abstraction
and representation. They are big. They are
about the sky and they are about nothing. I
want you to lose yourself, too.

"In this particular series I departed

somewhat from my usual process. That is, I
found my subject matter through the painting. Like a real painter I found content
through the paint. Usually, however, I start
with an idea. The work, then, becomes the
manifestation of this idea."

**Materials used** "So far, I've made paintings.
Despite this, I feel I have no particular
allegiance to any particular mediums or
techniques. I like to think that the medium or
technique is what's required by the idea. I'd
like to try video and photography now."

**Creative inspiration** "My main influences
have been Ad Reinhardt and Robert
Smithson because they were the real
polemicists of their respective times in New
York. They are masters of deadpan."
Byron Kim

*Dark Water*
1998
Acrylic and glitter on canvas
183 x 183 cm

## Kate Bright

**Place of birth** Suffolk, UK
**Place of residence** London
**Representation** Emily Tsingou
Gallery, London
**Courtesy** Emily Tsingou Gallery

**Recent exhibitions**
**Solo** Emily Tsingou Gallery, London (2001) >
Emily Tsingou Gallery, London (1999) >

**Group** *All of My Heart*, Arte e Personae,
Florence (2001) > *Surface Tension – New
British Painting*, Holly Snapp Gallery, Venice
(2001) > *Exploration of the Environment-
Landscape Redefined*, Barbara Gillman
Gallery, Miami (2000-01) > *Salon*, Delfina
Project Space, London (2000) > *There is No
Spirit in Painting*, Le Consortium, Dijon,
France (2000) > *Wooden Heart*, avco,
London (2000) > *Another Country: The
Constructed Landscape*, Lawrence Rubin
Greenberg Van Doren Gallery, New York
(1999) > Taro Nasu Gallery, Tokyo (1999)

"I have always made work concerned in
some way or another with landscape, trying
to find new ways of depicting the natural.
  "The glitter for the highlights on a
painting of water was a literally brilliant
substitution for depicting the natural in
paint, whilst also referring to the illusory
aspects of straight painting. I continue to
use it for pragmatic reasons. All the different
materials I use – polystyrene, glitter and
glass pieces – stand in very successfully
for the phenomena that they represent."
Kate Bright

All images:
*Untitled*
1996-98
From the series *End of an Age*
C-Print (Fuji longlife colour print)
184 x 143 cm

## Paul Graham

**Date of birth** 1956
**Place of birth** UK
**Place of residence** London and New York
**Representation** Galleria Marabini, Bologna
**Courtesy** Galleria Marabini

### Recent exhibitions
**Solo** *End of an Age*, Galleria Marabini, Bologna (2001) > *Paintings*, Lawrence Rubin Greenberg Van Doren Fine Art, New York (2000) > *Paintings*, Bob Van Orsouw Gallery, Zurich (2000) > *Paintings*, Anthony Reynolds Gallery, London (2000) > *End of an Age*, Scalo, New York (1999) > **Group** Venice Biennale (2001) > *British Art Show*, Fruitmarket Gallery, Edinburgh (2000, travelling) > *Some Parts of the World*, Finnish Museum of Photography, Helsinki (2000) > *Invitation to the City*, Centre Bruxelles 2000, Brussels (2000) > *Unhoused*, Antiguo Colegio de San Ildefenso, Mexico City (2000)

Paul Graham's latest series, *End of an Age*, consists of 49 large colour photographs of 20-somethings hanging out in clubs somewhere in Western Europe or the US. Most of these images are portraits that catch the singular subject unaware and unposed, usually in profile, often leaning against a wall. No one looks directly into the lens. Harsh, stark, sharply-defined flash pictures alternate with moodier available-light images that contain more saturated colour. These are silent images made in a loud place, still images in a fast place.

# AARDMAN

The name Aardman usually conjures up images of *Wallace and Gromit*, criminal penguins, wrong trousers, and escaping chickens. However, besides the Oscar-winning directors, there is much more to this extraordinary animation company, set up almost 30 years ago in the provincial city of Bristol, UK. Since its inception the company has been joined by a host of talented commercials directors, each with their own unique style, who have created award-winning work from their own fertile imaginations. Its client list covers top brands on an international basis.

Aardman was set up in 1972 when a BBC children's TV producer offered the company's founders, Dave Sproxton and Peter Lord, a chance to make short animated films for his programme *Vision On*. The first professional character created was the plasticine man Morph, who soon became a national children's favourite and is remembered by several generations of British adults. Following the success of Morph, Aardman began to get requests to create animated commercials for TV and cinema. Their very first commercial in 1984 was for Enterprise Computers in which various competing computers were shown as rickety fossils. Since then Aardman has given life to all manner of

inanimate objects and edible products, and currently produces about 25 commercials each year. Some of the most memorable commercial work has been based on the directors own already-existing characters. For example, the Heat Electric campaign was based on a short film *Creature Comforts*.

Although best known for clay animation, Aardman has now broken into several other fields including computer animation which was used in a recent national campaign for the Co-op, showcased in this feature. The most recent innovation has been the latest campaign for Comfort Fabric Softener where new ground was broken by creating a set and Cloth Family made entirely out of different fabrics (shown in ZOO 9). A total of 80 metres of fabric was used to create the set and the characters, which included over 30 different kinds of materials and trims.

The following is just a small sample of work by three Aardman directors: Darren Walsh, Will Byles and Luis Cook. Each has his own unique style, and the eclectic mix of media and animation types gives an overview of the depth of the commercial and individual work produced by the company.

Darren Walsh: Pringles *Couch*

**Agency** Grey Advertising, New York

Darren Walsh: *Happiness Bear*

Commissioned by the BBC for the programme *Happiness*

Darren Walsh first became acquainted with animation while studying art and design in 1989. Particularly interested in the work of Norman McLaren, whose pioneering films (made for the National Film Board of Canada) *Neighbours* and *Chairy Tale*, explored pixillation techniques and the manipulation of optical sound. Darren was encouraged to use a Standard 8 mm camera, to make a collection of 'old' movies and the result won him a place on the animation degree course in Farnham, UK. He graduated from Farnham with his first film *Oozat* which used a mixture of pixillation and mask animation. This film won the Best European Short Film at The Cork International Film Festival, and the Jury Prize at Hiroshima Film Festival. From there Darren went on to direct for two years at the bolexbrothers studio, who are well known for their use of pixillation and stop motion. Having refined the mask/pixillation technique, Darren then freelanced for a further two years, making commercials and short experimental films. His short pilot *Angry Kid* sparked interest at Aardman, who offered to develop it into a series. Darren has been there ever since.

Will Byles: Test film

Will Byles: Co-op *Food Glorious Food*

Will Byles: Test film

## Will Byles

While in his early twenties Will set up a small illustration business working in photo-realistic airbrushing. After joining a repertory theatre in Norwich called the Maddermarket and appearing in over 60 plays. From here he went on to design and direct (and also wrote a novel). This led to a desire to become involved in the film industry and he started as a runner on a commercial animation shoot in London. He worked his way up through the ranks of model maker, assistant animator, animator, and then director, working with several animation companies including Aardman, on over 100 commercials and short films. During this time he wrote, animated, directed, acted, edited, post produced, and produced a couple of short films including *The Epilogue with Mr Bedspread*.

He went on to set up his own successful film company with his wife, Emma: HarumScarum Films Ltd allowed him the time and resources to experiment with computers, and with his background in the sciences, love of the arts and knowledge of film, he was able to unlock the potential of CGI in a way that allowed him a great deal of creative freedom. He made a couple of live action-shorts, *The Wedding* and *Promo*. and HarumScarum lasted for three years until Will went back to being a freelance director and CGI animator. He started working again at Aardman where they asked him to take over their budding CGI department, and has been working there for just over a year.

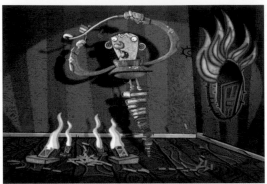

Luis Cook: Prevacid *Great Balls of Fire*

## Luis Cook

In 1985 Luis Cook started a degree in graphic design in London, during which he travelled in Asia, painting, drawing and taking photos for development organisations. After graduating and working as an illustrator in London he was taken on to direct graphics sequences for the BBC. At the same time he continued studying at the Royal College of Art. In the following two years he produced two short animated films, both screened on television in the UK. After teaching and printmaking in Mexico City, Luis ended up back at the BBC in Bristol, working on documentaries, titles sequences, animation, and live-action material.

Six years ago he was taken on by Aardman as a director. He has since worked on several prestigious ad compaigns for Smarties, Polos, Special K, and Daewoo cars. He also recently directed a short film for the World Wildlife Fund, which is featured in the ZOO 10 showcase.

**Directors** Luis Cook, Steve Harding-Hill
**Agency** Bates, New York
**Photography** Tony Hepburn

## Luis Cook

**01** Daewoo *Clay* **Agency** Duckworth Finn Grubb Waters, London
**02** Polo Classics **Agency** J Walter Thompson, London
**03** Smarties *Smartipants* **Agency** J Walter Thompson, London
**04** Idents commissioned by Channel 4
**05** Terrence Higgins Trust *Nobs in Space* **Agency** Abbott Mead Vickers·BBDO, London
**06** The Telegraph *Snail* **Agency** J Walter Thompson, London
**07** Aardman moving logo
**08** Special K *Fatal Flaws* **Agency** Leo Burnett, Chicago
**09** Comfort *Leaving* **Agency** Ogilvy & Mather, London

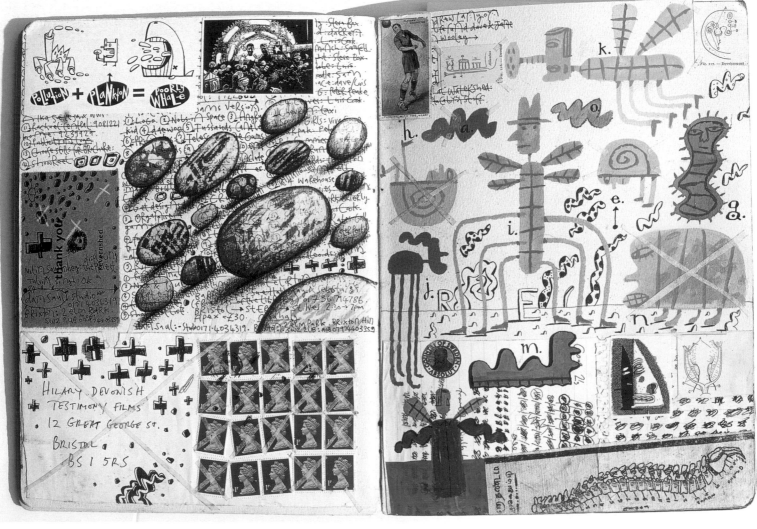

Luis Cook's Scrapbook
and Artwork

**Photography** Tony Hepburn

 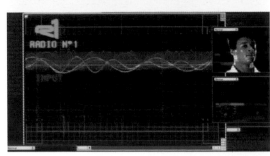 

## Alex & Martin: Air *Radio #1* promo  ↘ ⦿

**Directors** Alex & Martin
**Production** Partizan, Paris
**Producer** Charlotte LePot
**Director of photography** David
Ungaro

**Offline** Olivier Gajan
**Online** Buf, Paris
**Record company** Source, Paris

Set in an endless landscape of identical futuristic tower blocks, the action follows the comically synchronised domestic routine of a robotic-looking couple. Their breakfast preparations are choreographed with split-second timing, but as they sit down to eat, a malfunction brings things to an explosive – and messy – conclusion.

## Dawn Shadforth: Backyard Dog *Baddest Ruffest* promo  ↘ ⦿

**Director** Dawn Shadforth
**Production** Black Dog/RSA, London
**Producer** Cindy Burnay
**Director of photography** Fredrik
Callinggard
**Art director** Roger Swanborough
**Stylists** Christian Hutter,
Lucy Manning
**Telecine** Marcus Timpson;
The Mill, London

**Offline** Dawn Shadforth
**Online** The Mill, London
**Record company** East West, London
**Commissioner** Nisha Parti

The name of the band and the name of the production company may have gone some way to suggesting the setting for this video: most of the action takes place inside a dog. The up-tempo track is perfectly suited to the

jaunty gait of the Staffordshire bull terrier which takes the starring role. With band-members Anif and Lloydy at the controls, the dog is powered by the energy of the party going on in its belly. The mood of the revellers is influenced by events in the out-side world: when Backyard Dog spots an attractive bitch in the park, things start to get heavy...

**Kuntz & Maguire: The Avalanches *Frontier Psychiatrist* promo**

**Director** Tom Kuntz, Mike Maguire
**Production** Propaganda, London
**Producer** Richard Weager
**Director of photography** Jake Polonsky
**Art director** Roger Swanborough
**Stylist** Mr Gammon
**Hair and make-up** Kirsten Chalmers

**Telecine** Mark Geffen; Rushes, London
**Offline** Tony Kearns; Swordfish, London
**Online** Rushes, London
**Record company** XL Recordings, London
**Commissioner** Richard Skinner

Australian group The Avalanches have a magpie approach to making music taking the technique of sampling audio clips from other sources to new heights. *Frontier Psychiatrist* is an entertaining patchwork of dialogue and sountrack samples filched from vintage movies. Inspired by the creative process behind recording the track, directors Tom Kuntz and Mike Maguire approached the video in a similar spirit, assembling a disparate cast of performers to recreate the key samples live onstage as part of a kind of deranged variety show. The ensemble includes elderly twin psychiatrists, a turtle with the head of an old man, a contortionist, a ventriloquist, a ghostly choir, an ageing cross-dressing drummer, and none other than Tom Kuntz himself disguised in a monkey suit.

Mint Royale

"show me"

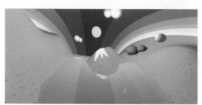

Mint Royale's STAR ISLAND

50

**MINISAURUS**
H: 21"   W: 40kg
SPEED: 9 Mph

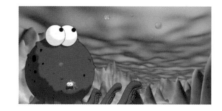

## Unit9: Mint Royale *Show Me* promo, game and microsite

**Concept** Unit9
**Creator and director** Ben Hibon
**Producer** Tom Sacchi
**3D graphics** Roberto Simoni
**Programming** Chris Peck
**Record company** Faith & Hope,
Manchester, UK
**Commissioner** Amul Batra

"The promo is the voyage of a cute little creature in a minimal world that comes into existence from nothing and at the end fades back out of existence. The cute creature, Minty, in his brief life learns to fly and swim, meets other creatures in various environments. He is a sweet, happy, curious creature, perhaps a bit of a troublemaker. There is a melancholic element, however, in the fact that this world is all just a dream, and that Minty and his friends do not really exist except in this dimension.

"In many ways, this is where the story begins. This short dream of a video is then referenced on the cover of the single, which leads to the website; and on the website you find there is more of this dream... You can purchase a piece of the dream through a Minty action figure, play a Shockwave game and if you score high you are then led to a card game that is dependent on the creatures you capture. The creatures become more alive, because there are descriptions of them, and little statues of them, they are advertised, etc.

"The particular thing about this project is that we've created enough material and self-referential marketing that you would almost doubt that the video was made for the song, and think the song was made for the video.

"All in all the whole project took just under a month. It was great to be defining the look for the single as a whole and not just be working on one lonely piece of the puzzle. We saw the opportunity of providing a well-integrated solution and we went for it. Each peace of the puzzle has a precise reason for being and reinforces the project as a whole." Tom Sacchi, Unit9

To visit the Mint Royale microsite go to www.faithandhoperecords.co.uk/mintroyale/

## Ed Gill: The Beta Band *Broke* promo

**Director** Ed Gill
**Production** Academy Films, London
**Producer** Laura Kaufman
**Director of photography** Ivan Bird
**Art director** Patrick Lyndon
Stafford, Adam Zoltowski
**Telecine** Stefan Perry;
FrameStore, London
**Offline** Mark Edinoff; Sam Sneade
Editing, London
**Online** Dan Williams, Tim Rudgard;
Red Post Production, London
**Record company**
Parlophone, London
**Commissioner** Faith Holmes

"The Watermelon Teachings. The band wanted something humorous, different, aggressive, with all of them in it, and with a little R+B influence. I just wanted to capture the natural beauty of watermelons on 35mm film and get some good reflections in the black sump oil. The mask of the 'Watermelon Guru' was based on an ancient Javanese puppet.

"Re: coaxing a good performance from a watermelon: watermelon meditation is an ancient and long forgotten skill. Only a true master can show you the way to airborne fruit combat!" Ed Gill

## Howard Shur: Satellite *Lighten Up the Load* promo and short film ↘ ●

## Howard Shur: *Font Man* short film ↘ ●

**Director** Howard Shur
**Production** Propaganda Films,
Los Angeles
**Producer** Youree Henley
**Director of photography** Roman
Jacobi
**Art director** Mark Snelgrove
**Stylist** Scott Free

**Offline** Steve Rees
**Online** Steve Koker:
Fence Post, Los Angeles
**Record company** Mercury Records,
London
**Commissioners** John Hassay,
Richard Skinner

**Production** Propaganda Films,
Los Angeles
**Producer** Paige Hamilton
**Director of photography** Lance Bangs
**Art director** Mark Snelgrove
**Offline** Howard Shur

Recently quitting his job as assistant to
Spike Jonze, Howard Shur is now

concentrating on his own directing career.
The germ of the idea for *Font Man* had been
in the back of his mind for some time.
"I had always thought it was funny that
people don't realise that fonts have been
around for much longer than computers.
I think I overheard someone say they were
going to call Apple and complain about
Helvetica." *Lighten Up the Load*, on the
other hand was dreamt up on the spur of
the moment, and cut as both a short film
and a promo on the theme 'what goes
around comes around'.

 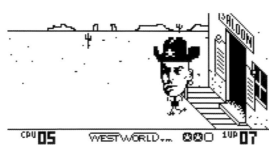 

## Shynola: Stephen Malkmus *Jo Jo's Jacket* promo ↘ ●

**Director** Shynola
**Production** Oil Factory
**Record company** Domino Recording
Company, London
**Commissioner** Laurence Bell

Directing team Shynola has, until now, been
content to specialise in animation, but their
video for musical hero Stephen Malkmus
marks their live-action debut. All ardent
music fans, the four-strong group took on
the job partly as a favour to pioneering
independent record label Domino
Recordings, and partly for the thrill of
working with one of their favourite artists.

"We basically got a copy of the album, and
then got to say which track we'd like to do,
and Domino said whether or not they'd
consider releasing it as a single!" explains
Shynola's Gideon Baws. "*Jo Jo's Jacket* had
obvious comedy appeal," (the singer
imagines himself as Hollywood legend Yul
Brynner) "and we just sat around talking
crap until the early hours, saying things like

'wouldn't it be stupid if Steve had a really
big head/was in an arcade machine/jumped
off a cliff...' Then we went away and did it,
and damn the consqeuences."

## Philippe André: Roger Sanchez *Another Chance* promo ↘ ●

**Director** Philippe André
**Production** Harry Nash, London
**Producer** Dominic Wilcox
**Director of photography**
Robert Papais
**Art director** Dania Saragovia
**Telecine** Jean Clement;
MPC, London

**Offline** Nicolas Wyman-Harris
**Online/Flame**
Christophe; MPC, London
**Record company**
Sony Music, London
**Commissioner** Marisa Hine

The promo for this track from American DJ Roger Sanchez is presented more like a short film than a conventional music video. The setting is nighttime NYC: a young woman carrying a large, cumbersome red heart tries to strike up conversation with passers-by. Put off by her over-familiarity and the awkwardly large heart, they studiously avoid her, and with each rejection, her heart shrinks a little smaller. By the time it has been reduced to the size of a small handbag, she is dejected and

vulnerable: when a good-looking young man asks if she wants help, she reluctantly accepts, and as they talk her confidence and optimism begin to return. The inclusion of background noise and over a minute of dialogue in the middle of the track adds to the atmosphere of this unusually emotive video.

## Philippe André: Morcheeba *World Looking In* promo ↘ ●

**Director** Philippe André
**Production** Harry Nash, London
**Director of photography** Tim
Maurice-Jones
**Art director** Careen Hertzog
**Telecine** Frank: MPC, London

**Offline** Richard Orrick; NWH,
London
**Online** Stephane Allander; MPC,
London
**Record company** East West
Records, London
**Commissioner** Nisha Parti

This track from British band Morcheeba recieved widespread publicity when it was used in a car commercial, but André's video undoubtedly does more to capture the mood of the song. Travelling in a vintage BMW, the band and their car emerge from a tunnel shrunk down to the size of toys. Their vehicle is the plaything of twin boys who take turns to 'drive' it around their sprawling country home, along carpeted corridors, down bannisters, before

unceremoniously dunking it in a fishbowl. The band and car were shot against a bluescreen, acting out their imagined reactions to the various scenes, and the background footage was filmed using a DV camera turned upside down to get more of a floor-level perspective.

## H5: Super Furry Animals *Juxtaposed Wit' U* promo

**Director** H5
**Production** Partizan, Paris
**Editor** Sophie Fordrinoy;
Duran, Paris
**Record company** Sony, London
**Commissioner** Adam Dunlop

Set in New York this computer-animated video tells the story of a yuppie couple on a lavish night out. The directors have recreated the effect of a thermo-imaging camera, with all the charcters represented by the pattern and colour suggested by their body heat. The lyrics of the song have a disaffected, misogynistic edge – "You've got to tolerate all the people that you hate, I'm not in love with you, but I won't hold that against you..." – that's reflected in the final fate of the two main characters. As they peer down on the city streets from the roof of a skyscraper, a helicopter crashes down on it, obliterating them in a gigantic orange fireball.

## Numéro 6: Supermen Lovers *Starlight* promo

**Director** Numéro 6
**Production** Partizan, Paris
**Online** Duran, Paris
**Record company** BMG, Paris

A lonely young boy records a remix of the Supermen Lovers track in his bedroom and runs downstairs to show his parents what he has done. Totally ignoring their son they stare at the TV where a singing skeleton is performing the song. Fed up, the boy returns to his room where he discovers that his musical aspirations are shared by a rat which also occupies his room. They tear off to the big city to find a producer to work with. They appear on TV, but their performance still fails to attract the attention of the the boy's mother and father. Up in space, however, some aliens have picked up the broadcast and like what they see...

Tereza Stehlikova: *The Flight of Bazelon* short film

**Director** Tereza Stehlikova
**Production** The Royal College of Art, London
**Animation** Tereza Stehlikova
**Sound** Touch Music, AER, Ryoji Ikeda, Scala & Chris Watson

Synopsis: Two glass children cut off from the rest of the world and their history are spending their time inside a kind of vacuum within a crystal tower. But something unexpected happens which forever disturbs the artificial equilibrium of the place. And so the boy leaves in search of a new

experience and finds himself in a land of strange creatures, forms and colours. He returns home changed. While he has been away the girl too has changed, transformed into a glass city.

"I made my film using Softimage 3D software, starting with drawings and sketches of each character. The two glass characters were inspired by the shapes and stuctures of crystals. The 2D creatures were all designed on paper and afterwards I rebuilt their shapes in the computer using flat grids. Using Photoshop I scanned drawings and photographs and attached those to the surfaces of objects built in Softimage. This enabled me to create a more textured look and richness and variety of colours (which is otherwise almost impossible).

"The whole film from beginning to end took about nine months to complete. Two months of story development (I wrote it myself) and storyboarding.

"The character design and building of skeletons and later the models took about five months of non-stop work, from 9 am to midnight, or similar, every day (no life but animation in the world of strange creatures!). There was also a lot to think about in terms of lighting, materials (glass, etc). Then there was rendering over nights, outputting all the files onto Beta tape, which took at least two weeks: one week of editing; the sound was created by Touch Music, based on original sound recordings of birds and environmental atmospheres."
Tereza Stehlikova

The Brothers Quay: *In Absentia* short film; Nic Roeg: *Sound* short film

*In Absentia*
**Director** The Brothers Quay
**Music** Karlheinz Stockhausen
A Koninck production for BBC and
Pipeline Films.
**Executive producers** Christian
Seidel, Rodney Wilson.

*Sound*
**Director** Nic Roeg
**Music** Adrian Utley
A Sunreset production for BBC
and Pipeline Films.
**Executive producers** Christian
Seidel, Rodney Wilson.

These collaborations between composers and film-makers of international repute are part of the BBC Two series 'Sound on Film', and were jointly commissioned by the network and Pipeline Films in association with NPS Television. A study of obsession and loneliness, *In Absentia* is a haunting, dream-like interpretation of Stockhausen's original score, which the composer describes as "a landscape that people have abandoned".

Alone in a bleak room, a woman compulsively writes the words 'darling come' using fragments of pencil lead. There is no resolution to her isolation. *Sound* is described as "a meditation on celebrity, the nature of memory, and an exploration of how the way people see is changed by what they hear." Starring supermodel Claudia Schiffer, the film intertwines different languages, music, and digital effects with beautiful imagery.

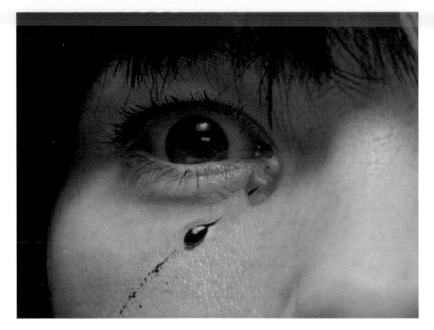

Inez van Lamsweerde, Vinoodh Matadin: Björk *Hidden Place* promo

**Directors** Inez van Lamsweerde,
Vinoodh Matadin
**Art director** Michael Amzalag,
Mathias Augustyniak;
M.M, Paris
**Production** Academy Films, London
**Producer** Mark Whittow-Williams
**Director of photography** Dan Landin
**Special effects** Andrew Walsh, Nigel
Swift, Roger Wotton
**Telecine** Tareq Kubaisi,
VTR, London
**Online** Rachel Mills,
Glassworks, London

**Record company** One Little
Indian, London
**Commissioner** Paul McKee

The video for this first track from Björk's
latest and most introspective album is a
unique and hypnotic collaboration between
photographer Inez van Lamsweerde and her
partner Vinoodh Matadin. The video opens
with a head and shoulders view of Björk
with her face almost obscured by her heavy
dark hair being blown this way and that. The
rest of the video is shot in one continuous
take. As the camera closes in or her face, a

pearly purple tear forms in the corner of
Björk's eye, trickling down her cheek and
disappearing into her mouth. Almost
immediately another gravity-defying rivulet
flows from her mouth up into her nostril.
As this process repeats, more delicate
black illustrations trace the path of the
tears and disappear again. The artists began
working with the singer even before the
song was completed, making the
production a collaboration in the truest
sense – the track was even altered to
incorporate extra sounds which would
enhance the video. *Hidden Place* is the
first of five videos from Björk's new album
*Vespertine*, each of which is shot by artists
or photographers rather than regular
video directors.

*Me Kissing Vinoodh (Passionately)*
1999
C-print on plexiglas
6.2 x 11.2 m

## Inez van Lamsweerde and Vinoodh Matadin

**Date of birth** 1963; 1961
**Place of birth** Amsterdam
**Representation** Art + Commerce, New York
**Courtesy** Inez van Lamsweerde and Vinoodh Matadin; Matthew Marks Gallery, New York; Art + Commerce;

Inez van Lamsweerde and Vinoodh Matadin met in Amsterdam where they started their career as a photography team. Both artists have a strong profile as young, innovative fashion photographers making strong, unique images for magazines including Paris *Vogue*, *Visionaire*, Harper's Bazaar, and W

*W Magazine* and their clients: Louis Vuitton, Yohji Yamamoto, Helmut Lang, Balanciaga and Gucci.

Using elements from the fashion world in their artwork, van Lamsweerde and Matadin have exhibited in galleries and museums worldwide, including Matthew Marks Gallery and Guggenheim Museum in New York, the Venice Biennale, and the Stedelijk Museum in Stockholm.

*Me Kissing Vinoodh (Passionately)* is an enormous photograph comprising of four panels. The image originally depicted van Lamsweerde and Matadin in a passionate embrace on the street but van Lamsweerde has later removed Vinoodh's presence, leaving a symbolic gap. In the resultant image, of the artist alone, van Lamsweerde's face seems torn into a new physiognomy, that of one violently without the other.

*Amfar Benefit, Cannes, 2000*
2000
C-Print
50.8 x 69.9 cm
Edition of 5

## Jessica Craig Martin

**Representation** Artemis Greenberg
Van Doren Fine Art, New York
**Courtesy** Artemis Greenberg Van
Doren Fine Art

**Recent exhibitions**
**Solo** Museo Nacional Centro de Arte Reina

Sofia, Madrid (2002) > Galleria Maze, Turin,
Italy (2001) > Dorothée de Pauw Gallery,
Brussels (2001) > Fiction Inc., Tokyo (2000)
> Colette, Paris (2000) > Maureen Paley
Interim Art, London (1999) > **Group** *I Am A
Camera*, Saatchi Gallery, London (2001) >
*Party Pictures: From Studio 54 to Cannes
2000*, Lawrence Rubin Greenberg Van Doren
Fine Art, New York (2000) > *Greater New
York*, P.S.1 Contemporary Art Center, New
York (2000)

*Alzheimer's Benefit, The Waldorf-Astoria*
*Hotel, New York, 1999*
1999
C-Print
50.8 x 76.2 cm
Edition of 5

*Dia Benefit Party, NY, 1999*
1999
C-Print
50.8 x 61 cm
Edition of 5

*The Red Coat* series
2001

## Sophie Dubosc

**Date of birth** 1974
**Place of residence** Paris
**Major awards** Special prize,
Hyères Festival, France (2001)
**Courtesy** Sophie Dubosc

"*The Red Coat* series is a fictional work in progress. It is about a feminine character walking alone at night, whose face we never see. There is no story, no narrative, but themes of loneliness and anxiety. The red coat is an image of the collective imagination. The idea first came from a visual interest and pleasure by seeing a woman in a red coat. The subject was formal from the very beginning. Then the themes appeared but I am still following her and trying to understand what is going on. I will continue this in Autumn and Winter (it is a subject for these seasons).

"The materials I use are the format 4.5 x 6, a tripod and flash, and an electric torch or carlights for the light. So the lights can be white or yellow, which creates different atmospheres."

**Creative inspiration** "Regarding staged photography, I look at Duane Michels, Tracey Moffatt, and mostly Francesca Woodman." Sophie Dubosc

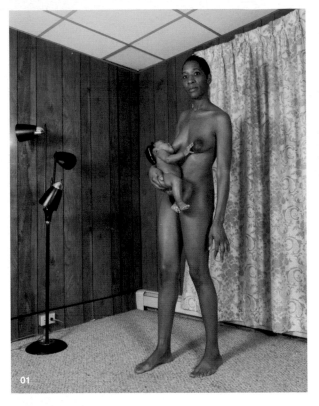

01

02

03

04

01
*Mother and Child, Poughkeepsie, NY*
2000
C-Print
114.3 x 90.2 cm
Edition of 6

02
*Rhinebeck, New York*
2000
C-Print
114.3 x 90.2 cm
Edition of 6

03
*Ghent, NY*
2000
C-Print
114.3 x 90.2 cm
Edition of 6

04
*Middleton, WI*
2000
C-Print
114.3 x 90.2 cm
Edition of 6

05
*Untitled (Poughkeepsie Journal)*
2000
C-Print
114.3 x 90.2 cm
Edition of 6

## Katy Grannan

**Date of birth** 1969
**Place of birth** Arlington, MA, USA
**Place of residence** Brooklyn,
NY, USA
**Representation** Artemis Greenberg
Van Doren Fine Art, New York
**Courtesy** Artemis Greenberg Van
Doren Fine Art

**Recent exhibitions**
**Solo** 51 Fine Art, Antwerp (2001) >
Lawrence Rubin Greenberg Van Doren Fine
Art, New York (2000) > Kohn Turner Gallery,
Los Angeles (2000) > **Group** *Reflections
Through A Glass Eye*, International Center
for Photography, New York (2000) > *Bluer*,
Carrie Secrist Gallery, Chicago (2000) >
Kohn Turner Gallery, Los Angeles (2000) >
*Another Girl, Another Planet*, Lawrence
Rubin Greenberg Van Doren Fine Art, New
York (1999) > *Female*, Wessel + O'Connor
Gallery, New York (1999) > P.S.1
Contemporary Art Center, New York (1999)
> DFN Gallery, New York (1998)

01

# Andres Serrano

**Date of birth** 1950
**Place of birth** New York
**Representation** Paula Cooper Gallery, New York
**Courtesy** Paula Cooper Gallery

**Recent exhibitions**
**Solo** *World Without End*, The Cathedral of Saint John the Divine, New York (2001) > *Objects of Desire*, Andre Simoens Gallery, Knokke-Zoute, Belgium (2001) > *The Interpretation of Dreams*, Paula Cooper Gallery, New York (2001) > *Body and Soul*, Bergen Art Society, Norway, travelled to Rogaland Kunst Museum, Stavanger, Norway; Tromsø Art Society, Norway; Stenersenmusett, Oslo, Helsinki City Art Museum; Ciurlionis National Museum of Art, Kaunas, Lithuania; Ludwig Foundation, Aachen, Germany; Barbican Art Centre, London (2000-01) > Galerie Edition Kunsthandel/20.21, Essen, Germany (2000) > **Group** *Because Sex Sells: Part II*, Nikolai Fine Art, New York (2001) > *Give & Take*, Serpentine Gallery and Victoria & Albert

Museum, London (2001) > *Full Frontal, Photographic Portraits*, Jan Weiner Gallery, Kansas, MO, USA (2001) > *The Reality-Effect: Contemporary American Photography*, Guild Hall of East Hampton, New York (2001) > *Red*, Julie Saul Gallery, New York (2000)

"I start with an idea. In this case, it was the title of the show, *The Interpretation of Dreams*. From there the images flowed. I knew that with such a title I was free to explore a number of possibilities, some psychological, some radical and some sexual. After all, who's to say that my 'dreams', which are not really dreams, are incorrect? Although the title of the show is misleading because I don't pretend to interpret these 'dreams', I just record them.
   "I use a camera because I can't paint, nor do I want to. My equipment is basic, almost minimal. I am more interested in the execution of ideas than I am in technical ability.
   "Bob Dylan has been one of my biggest influences. Also, Marcel Duchamp and Luis Buñuel. And in this case, Freud, although I didn't read the book." Andres Serrano

All images:
2001
Cibachrome, silicone, plexiglas, wood frame
152.4 x 125.7 cm
Edition of 3

01
*The Interpretation of Dreams (Daddy's Little Girl)*

02
*The Interpretation of Dreams (Lori and Dori)*

03
*The Interpretation of Dreams (White Man's Burden)*

04
*The Interpretation of Dreams (White Nigger)*

05
*The Interpretation of Dreams (Killer)*

02

03

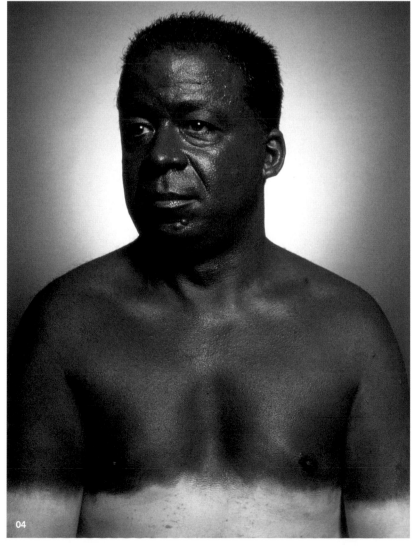

04

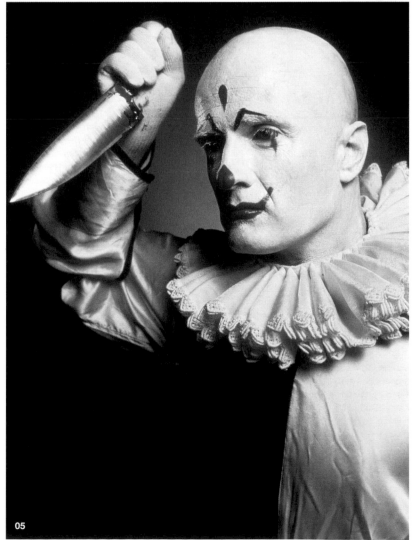

05

*A New Dawn Fades*
Diptych, 2000
(Seaworld shark tank)
Fujiflex
27.9 x 35.6 cm
Edition of 3

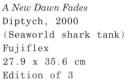

## Dean Sameshima

**Representation** Low, Los Angeles
**Courtesy** Low

### Recent exhibitions
**Solo** Taka Ishii Gallery, Tokyo (2002) > *Too Young to Reason, Too Grown-up to Dream*, Low, Los Angeles (2001) > Galerie Hohenlohe and Kalb, Vienna (2001) > *Display*, Costume National, Los Angeles (2000) > *Wonderland*, Gavlak Projects, Los Angeles (1997) > *A Cute Dilemma*, Re: Solution Gallery, Los Angeles Center for Photographic Studies, Hollywood (1994) > **Group** *Scenes*, Henry Urbach Architecture, New York (2001) > *Artificial Real*, Low, Los Angeles (2000) > *Good Vibrations*, Tomio Koyama Gallery, Tokyo (1999) > *Flaming June, Works on Paper*, Gavlak Projects, Los Angeles (1999)

**Description of work** "In an element of my recent exhibition, *Too Young to Reason, Too Grown-up to Dream*, I displayed a series of guys in clubs dancing. I was spending a lot of time in Brit-Pop/Mod clubs in Los Angeles, partly because I'm obssesed with the music, especially Suede and Pulp, and also because of the array of devastatingly cute boys and aesthetics that don't appear at the usual 'gay clubs'. I started the series by accident. I would go to these clubs and wait till people started to get a bit drunk (including myself) and started 'focusing', therefore photographing, the cutest guy that caught my fancy first that night, photographing him till he either noticed he was being photographed (fear of homophobic confrontation) or till he left the dance floor. The dance floor was the perfect place for me to pop out my point-and-shoot, with all the lights and crowd, just so entranced with the music. In fact the music (sometimes romantically inclined) itself helped me in the actions. Not looking in the viewfinder (that took too much time), I would just shoot away, not having really any concern for the composition, focus, etc... I just wanted a 'good' image of the boy, dancing, smiling, singing along, like me.

"Once the photos were developed I would hope that I got the perfect picture of the 'guy of the night'. Over time, spending time with the images, I thought it would be interesting if I printed out every image, in the order they were taken. I'm always curious when I see photographs/images in magazines and books and wonder about people's editing choices. I wanted to expose my process of 'shooting' and not edit anything. Also, I print my own photographs so I can have complete control over the entire process as well as experiment with print size, colour, cropping, etc. I then presented the images, be it one or ten, in the order they were shot, exposing the action of shooting."

**Materials used** "It depends on the situation. I have my 35 mm point-and-shoot with me at all times. Otherwise I use a Fuji 6 x 9 for landscapes, Hasselblad 2 1/4 for portraits, or a simple Canon Rebel for my re-photography."

**Creative inspiration** "I recently 'discovered' Erna Lendvai-Dircksen while working at the Getty Research Center – she photographed some of the most sexy images of men I have seen in a while, especially her book *Reichsautobahn*, where she juxtaposed shirtless men working on the Autobahn, with landscapes/construction shots of the Autobahn in progress. I don't read German so there are elements in the book I have been left to figure out myself, but there are, I believe, poems below some images. In the end, the images are enough for me.

Also Christopher Williams, for his amazingly sumptuous 'documentary' and 'staged' photographs and his puzzling installations that explore many narratives and eventually come together for me the longer I spend time with the work. The images really stick with me, haunt me."
Dean Sameshima

*Bang (July 3, 2000),* Detail
2000
Fujiflex prints
Set of 5
10.2 x 15.2 on 27.9 x 35.6 cm
Edition of 3

*Cafe Bleu (March 24, 2000),* Detail
2000
Fujiflex prints
Set of 7
10.2 x 15.2 on 27.9 x 35.6 cm
Edition of 3

*Cafe Bleu, (November 5, 1999),* Detail
2000
Fujiflex prints
Set of 5
10.2 x 15.2 on 27.9 x 35.6 cm
Edition of 3

*Pier*

## Garry Simpson

**Place of residence** London
**Representation** Carolyn Trayler Agency, London
**Courtesy** Garry Simpson

"My pictures lie somewhere between the picturesque and the benign. I look for a sense of order in my work, this tends to be man-made and functional.

"A lot of what I do is the product of hours or days of searching. I like the feeling of exploration. By wanting to explore I find that work naturally develops.

I find the fascination of photography inspiring: I disllike monotony and routine. I suppose it reverts back to that sense of exploration. It gives me the reason to go out and look." Garry Simpson

*Grand Isle*

*JJ's Hut*

*Motel Marion*

*Bus Compound*

Alex Porter kisses Michael Jordan
Melrose Avenue, Los Angeles, 5 November 1999

To him, he represented everything perfect

*Alex + Michael*
*LA Pictures*
2000
Lambda print
80 x 80 cm

## Melanie Manchot

**Date of birth** 1966
**Place of birth** Germany
**Place of residence** London
**Representation** Rhodes + Mann
Gallery, London
**Courtesy** Melanie Manchot; Rhodes
+ Mann Gallery

### Recent exhibitions

**Solo** Portland Institute for Contemporary Art,
Oregon (2002) > Cornerhouse Manchester,
UK (2002) > Fotogalerie, Mannheim,
Germany (2001) > Rhodes + Mann Gallery,

London (2001) > Ffotogallery, Cardiff (2000)
> Bucknell Art Gallery, PN, USA (1999) >
**Group** *Something Happened*, Hasselblad
Centre, Gothenburg, Sweden (2001) >
*Fusion*, Rhodes + Mann Gallery, London
(2000) > *Mommy Dearest*, Gimpel Fils,
London (2000) > *The Century of the Body*,
Culturgest, Lisbon, Portugal, travelled to
Musée de l' Elysée, Lausanne, Switzerland
(1999-2000)

Melanie Manchot's work investigates notions
of intimacy, gesture and desire. All the work
is located at the intersection of the public
and the private, of reality and fantasy,
attempting to locate slippages between
these – such as at moments when intensely

private gestures occur in public.

In the series *LA Pictures* (2000), Manchot
approaches strangers, often couples, on the
streets of Los Angeles and asks them for
their brief participation in a project that
aims to chart a space between reality and
fantasy – the space where a lot of our
desires reside. She invites both partners to
be photographed kissing each other and to
then, afterwards, write down who in their
wildest fantasy they would like to kiss and
why. Standing with their backs towards the
camera, each of the images records a brief
moment of intimacy – a kiss – while the
quote underneath challenges what we
assume to be seeing.

*The Fontainebleau Series* is based on

the famous Louvre painting from the School
of Fontainebleau in which two women share
the narrow confines of a bath, one holding
the other's nipple. This series investigates
both the mystery of this painting, and the
ambiguity of touch, of a gesture's
motivation. In the resulting series the artist
has worked with four sets of two women in
various bathrooms on creating potential
narratives carried through minimal moments
of touch.

Melanie Manchot's book, *Love is a
Stranger* (Prestel Verlag) will be published
in October

**01**
*Emma and Charlie I and III*
*Fontainebleau Series*
2001
100 x 125 cm
C-Prints

**02**
*Namita and Zena II and III*
*Fontainebleau Series*
2001
100 x 125 cm
C-Prints

## Shirana Shahbazi

**Date of birth** 1974
**Place of birth** Tehran, Iran
**Place of residence** Zurich
**Representation** Bob van Orsouw
Gallery, Zurich
**Courtesy** Shirana Shahbazi; Bob
van Orsouw Gallery

### Recent exhibitions
**Solo** Photographers' Gallery, London (2001)
> Kunstverein Freiburg, Germany (2001) >
**Group** PHotoEspaña 2001, Madrid (2001) >
*Das Versprechen der Fotografie,* Schirn

Kunsthalle, Frankfurt (2001) > *Heimaten,*
Galerie für zeitgenössische Kunst, Leipzig,
Germany (2001) > *Zurich – Urban Diary,*
Galerie Bob van Orsouw, Zurich (2001) >
*It Takes Two to Tango,* Schedhalle, Zurich
(2001) > *Diplomausstellung,* Hochschule für
Gestaltung und Kunst, Zurich (2000) > *The
World We Grow Into,* AVRO Keizersgracht,
Amsterdam (1999) > *143312 m,* Schöller
Areal, Zurich (1998)

"For this series I travelled two or three times
to Tehran. Back in Europe I worked with the
photographs, so each time it was more
and more clear how I could work in Tehran.
I made the majority of the images during my
trip in 2000 to Tehran with a quite clear idea

of which images I needed to finish the work.
  "I use very conventional photographic
materials and the work is presented as
colour prints in three different sizes. I ask
street poster painters in Tehran to make
large-scale paintings from some of the
photographs. Sometimes these paintings
appear in an installation as they are, and
sometimes they are re-photographed and
returned to the series as colour prints.
  "One of the qualities of photography that
I am interested in is that it can't tell one
straight story. You can let a story keep its
complexity using simple photographs –
this is much closer to any story."
Shirana Shahbazi

*Goftare Nik* series
2000

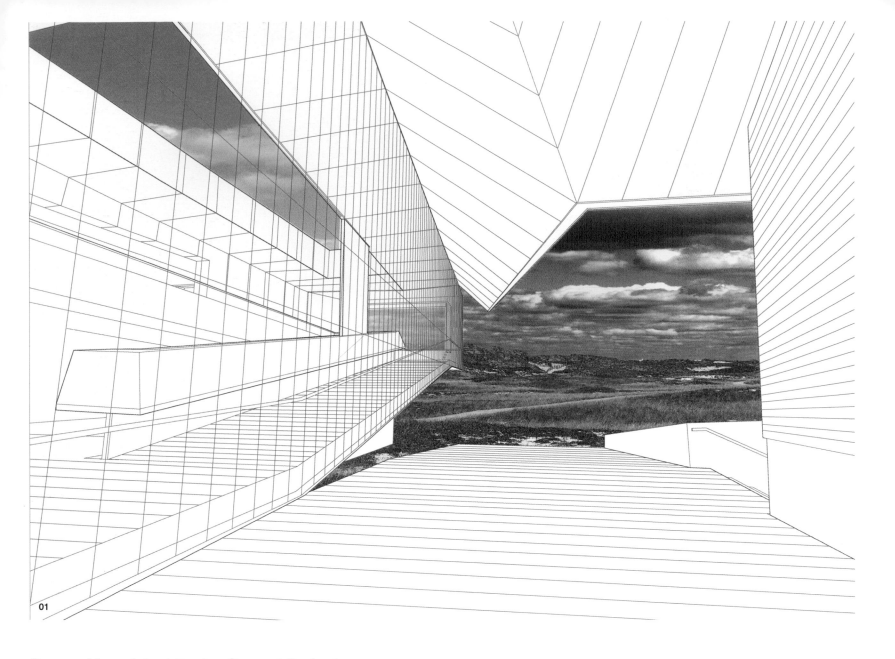

01

## Rogers Marvel Architects: Current Projects

**Architect** Rogers Marvel
Architects, New York
**Structural consultants** Robert
Silman Associates (Studio
Museum); Buro Happold Consulting
Engineers (South Fork); ARUP
(Eyebeam Competition)
**Mechanical consultants**
Mariano D. Molina Consulting
Engineers (Studio Museum);
Mottola-Rini Consulting Engineers
(South Fork); ARUP (Eyebeam)
**Landscape architects** Quennell
Rothschild + Partners
(South Fork)

"While the fabulous and fashionable are
becoming the focus of museums and
museum design, we have been steadily
developing a practice focusing on museums
as institutions. Three current projects begin
to describe our approach. Our fundamental
goal is the operative museum, a building
that engages its cultural community and

converts its mission into architectural
presence. Each of these projects has a
focused content, though none has a fixed
type of exhibition. Our work begins by
exploring the content and situation – history,
site, audience, constraints. From there we
identify and catalogue opportunities, looking
specifically for hidden and unexpected
terrain. Each of these projects represents
intense design and analysis efforts. Each
extracts fundamental spatial concepts from
program and site: each is a product of the
same critical approach to the 'operative'
museum. Each is technically and visually a
product of the process. No material or
shaping presumption is pre-determined.

"The museum as institution is identified
by its relationship with the participant – at
individual, community and global scales."
Rogers Marvel Architects, June 2001

### 01 South Fork Natural History Museum
The South Fork Natural History Society has
operated a programme of wetland
education for over twenty years. We
became involved when they explored
multiple sites of preserved land, resulting
in the purchase of an abandoned winery

near Bridgehampton, New York. Our project
embraced the site's existing structures,
adapting the division between two buildings
to reflect the programmatic split between
childrens' and adult areas. The morphology
of the existing barns with their great shed
roofs is exaggerated and extended to
connect the building back to the surrounding landforms. An interpretation of the
wetlands is displayed in the ramp that
ascends from a pool of groundwater and
leads to exhibition, library and archive
areas. The ramp cantilevers over the wetlands to accentuate its preservation and
to remind the visitor of the removed state
of their observation.

### 02 The Studio Museum in Harlem
Harlem is enjoying a tremendous burst of
energy and attention. The Studio Museum
is on 125th Street, one of the most vibrant
pedestrian strips in the world. The museum's
mission is to discover and display the work
of the African Diaspora. As such, although
rooted in a specific neighbourhood, its
audience is worldwide. Our approach was
to confront these two scales of community.
The new façade grounds the museum in the

global span of international modernism;
while the entry itself transforms an adjacent
vacant lot into a space that recalls the
proportion and public stature of the
neighbourhood streets. This becomes both
sculpture court and entry to the galleries
and auditorium buried below. The simple
glass channel and shadowbox façade
contrast the surrounding retail cacophony;
a long, long clear window interrupts the
façade to erase the boundary between
pedestrian and visitor.

### 03 Eyebeam Atelier Museum of Art
and Technology
The 'Eyebeam' is an invited competition
for a project that seeks to redefine the
museum paradigm for new media art. Our
efforts began by collecting and researching
evidence of 'new media work'. We found
only absolute unpredictability: of content,
technique, size, audience, and duration.
However the museum's goal to foster
interaction between exhibition, production
and education provided a basis that made
'interleaving' of programs, circulation,
structure and services the constant of
the design.

02

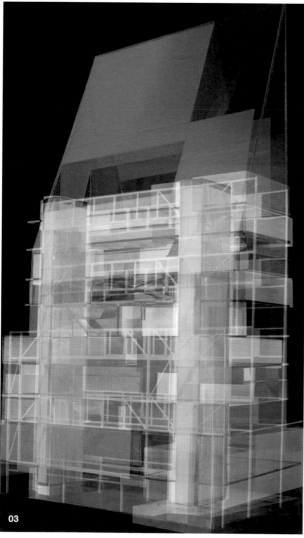

03

02

02

03

## Behnisch, Behnisch and Partner: Museum der Phantasie

**Project** Museum der Phantasie, Bernried, Germany
**Architect** Behnisch, Behnisch and Partner (Prof. Günter Behnisch, Stefan Behnisch, Günther Schaller), Stuttgart
**Creative team** Martin Werminghausen, Roland Stölzle
**Structural engineer** Büro Pfefferkorn & Partner
**Competition** 1996
**Completion** 2001
**Key dimensions** 6,450 m²
**Client** Freistaat Bayern, represented by the Staatliches Hochbauamt München 1
**Photography** Christian Kandzia

The Museum der Phantasie in Bernried on Starnberger See houses the entire collection of Lothar-Günther Buchheim, best known as the author of *Das Boot*. This collection comprises, along with numerous important Expressionist paintings, folk objects, all kinds of curiosities and personal mementos. The museum's setting in the beautiful Bavarian landscape, its orientation and also its intrinsic order have lent themselves to a design that stretches like a spine along which the various building elements are located. Each element has been developed freely according to its function, its own order and shape. From almost every interior space, the visitor is able to view and enter the landscape.

Compartmentalism and 'ideal' viewing conditions, hallmarks of a conventional museum, take second place to connections to the surroundings, low-tech flexibility, and a casual but evocative juxtaposition of 'high' and 'low' art. Folk art and academic art-works are placed beside each other exactly as the Expressionists themselves had done in their studios.

Fluid transitions lead from one part of the museum to another; shorter and longer round tours can be chosen via the two-storey 'spine' and also via the return route through the park. The building elements have been kept lean; the trees, the lake and spatial variety, as well as the play of light and shadow, provide the appropriate setting for the exhibited works.

## MBM Architectes: Pompeu Fabra University

**Project** Law Faculty, Pompeu Fabra University, Barcelona
**Architect** MBM Architectes, Barcelona
**Creative team** Josep Martorell, Oriol Bohigas, David Mackay, Oriol Capdevila, Francesc Gual
**Structural engineer** CBiJM
**Budget** 3,300,000,000 Pesetas
**Key dimensions** 30,000 m²
**Client** Universitat Pompeu Fabra
**Photography** © Duccio Malagamba
**Relevant awards** City of Barcelona Prize for Architecture and Urbanism 2000, awarded February 2001

The Roger de Llúria Barracks, when in military use, occupied a whole street block of the 'Ensanche' area of central Barcelona. The barracks was a building with a perimetrical body 14 metres wide and two transversal volumes that divided the interior open space of the block into three independent patios. Rows of forged iron columns divided them into 7-metre bays. The building comprised ground floor, two more storeys and a vaulted basement.

The initial brief called for some 20 lecture rooms for 120 students in each. To accomplish this the demolition of the two central volumes was necessary in order to create a large interior patio in which a linear building could be situated. In 1999, the consolidation of the Ciutadella Campus of the UPF called for the addition of around 100 individual offices for teachers, in order

for the Law Faculty to move in. For this purpose, another linear building was added on the opposite side of the interior patio, leaving a 20-metre wide space between the two volumes. The level of this patio is lowered to the same level as the original basement, so that the previous bays are now revealed. Furthermore, this patio has been covered at the same level as the original roofing at a height of 17 metres – by a transparent skylight, thus converting it into a covered interior space.

The architectonic intention of the project is that the architectural language of the barracks is not lost with the refurbishment. So, the outer façades and the roofing remain as they were; interior stonework and brick elements are left visible wherever possible, as well as the metallic structure of the stairwell roofing.

The new wings of classrooms and offices, however, have been designed using a contemporary language. The classroom building is rectangular with a concrete structure and a very smooth and straight curtain-wall façade that faces onto the patio. By contrast, the teachers' office building is a floating prism, finished with a wooden planked façade, that has continuous horizontal windows, interrupted by white metal protruding folds.

The finishing of the basement walls is bare brickwork, making the interior patio plinth a unitary element.

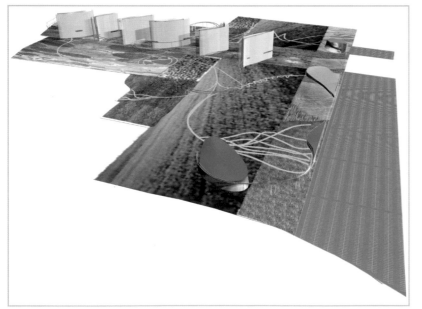

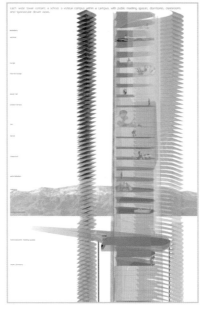

## kOnyk architecture: Towers in the Desert

**Project** Towers in the Desert: Nevada State College Masterplan, outside of Las Vegas, NV, USA
**Architect** kOnyk architecture, New York City

Suspended in the sky between views east to the Black Mountains and west towards the city of Las Vegas above an exquisitely changing native landscape, this proposal for a new Nevada State College at Henderson is a rethinking of the American college campus. In the environmental/technological culture of America in the year 2001 we are proposing a new way to make the campus 'green' and make the college 'urban'.

The entire site is to be planted with flowering species native to Nevada, transforming each month into a different texture and colour, creating an ever-changing 'painted landscape'. This native botanical garden is a public space, open for the use and enjoyment of the citizens of Henderson and the surrounding communities, as well as for NSC students. The college is composed of separate 'pavilions' arrayed within this landscape, connected by an elevated monorail system. This monorail not only moves students but also services each of the buildings, thus preserving the botanical garden below.

Each of the six schools of the college is contained in single individual 24-storey 'slipping' towers, with all classrooms, laboratories, lounges, study halls, dormitories, café and local administration located within. Like airfoils, these 'slipping' towers have wrapping satin aluminium louvred skins, which screen the interior body and reflect the colours of the ever-changing botanical garden below. The undersides of these louvres are anodised, giving off an aura of colour, effectively coding each tower and illuminating the garden by night. These towers are vertical campuses within a campus, where a single building the size of an urban block represents each school. As such, these towers become orientation landmarks, which announce the college's presence to Las Vegas seven miles away.

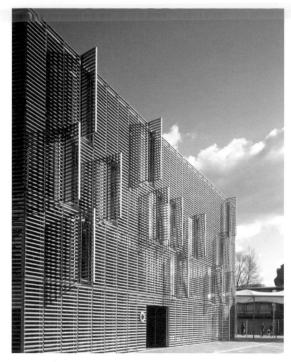

## VIIVA: Finnish Embassy

**Project** Finnish Embassy, Berlin
**Architect**
VIIVA arkkitehtuuri Oy, Helsinki
**Associate architect** Pysall Ruge
Architekten, Berlin
**Structural engineer** IGH
Ingenieurgesellschaft
Höpfner GmbH, Berlin
**Project management**
Drees & Sommer GmbH, Berlin
**Client** Ministry for
Foreign Affairs, Finland
**Awards** ARUP/*World Architecture*
Building of the Year 2001

The Finnish Embassy in Berlin has been built
in a joint embassy centre of the Nordic

countries, in the heart of the reunified Berlin
on the southern side of Tiergarten park. It is
a combination of simplicity and clarity,
which creates both Finnish national identity
and prominent and timeless surroundings
for the activities of the embassy.

The building does not try to impose itself
on an area that is already sharply defined
by the volumes of the buildings, the voids
between buildings and the copper band wall
which surrounds the site. Rather than scar it
with an over-emphasised individuality, the
Finnish Embassy takes its place in the building complex with simplicity and clarity. The
façades follow the line of the plot and the
given height of the buildings. The wooden
treatment of the façades emphasises the
sculptural form of the building.

The transparent glass façades are
entirely covered with larch slats. This lattice-
work acts as a venetian blind, protecting the

interior and filtering incoming light. Direct
views are provided by opening parts of the
lattice. The variety of different positions of
the openable elements gives animation to
the façades during the daytime. The basic
form is regained as the open elements are
closed for the night.

The interior is dominated by a sequence
of spaces which traverse the building. It
starts from the entrance, goes through a
central hall and ends in a small external
courtyard. The circulating aluminium stair-
case and the birch-covered conference
room, suspended above the skylit central
hall, contribute to the complexity of these
spaces. The offices close the central hall on
three sides.

The building materials are Finnish wood
– larch and birch – in various uses,
concrete, steel and glass.

## Naoto Yaegashi + NOrm null OFFice: The Centre of Creative Engineering

**Project** Tohoku University, The Centre of Creative Engineering, Sendai City, Miyagi Prefecture, Japan
**Architect** Naoto Yaegashi + NOrm null OFFice, Sendai, Japan
**Associate architect** Michinoku Architectural Office, Tohoku University Campus Planning Office
**Main contractor** Japan Road Engineering Firm
**Commencement** August 2000
**Completion** May 2001
**Budget** 309,100,000 Yen
**Key dimensions** 697 m²
**Client** Tohoku University
**Photography** © Shinkenchiku-sha

"We have started this project from no-idea, no-image, no-program. We were searching for a key concept through researching the extensive site area of the campus of Tohoku University. From our research, we derived the analysing process and the method of constructing the new Centre of Creative Engineering. And we discovered two very important key concepts: 'disposition' and 'framing'. First, we proposed a square, approximately 40 x 40 metres, and arranged this frame close to the existing library and the artificial pond. Second, by the fieldwork of the whole campus, we thought the existing trees – cherries and zelkovas – as very important objects which were interpenetrated into the new building. We made the surface around this new centre from a stainless skeleton mesh and transparent glass. The overlay of these two materials created some appearances and effects: 'reflection', 'moire', 'transparency'.

"These simple devices reflected the sky, the crowd, the trees, the sunshine, the shade, and so on. And they swayed with the wind and always changed their expression."
Naoto Yaegashi

## Sean Godsell Architects: Future Shack

**Project** Future Shack,
'no fixed address'
**Architect** Sean Godsell
Architects, Melbourne
**Main contractor** RD McGowan
**Building Steel Fabricator** Shush
Metal Products
**Design period** 1985-2001
**Key dimensions** 15 m²
**Photography** Earl Carter
Photography

A mass-produced relocatable house for emergency and relief housing. Recycled shipping containers are used to form the main volume of the building. A parasol roof packs inside the container. When erected, the roof shades the container and reduces heat load on the building. Legs telescope from the container enabling it to be sited without excavation on uneven terrain. The house has applications for a number of needs – post flood, fire, earthquake or similar natural disasters; temporary housing, third-world housing, and so on. The universal nature of the container means that the houses can be stockpiled and easily transported throughout the world. Future Shack can be fully erected in 24 hours.

As architects in stable democracies our responsibilities are reasonably clear-cut. Our role in those societies – where freedom has been ripped away by force, or where nature has devastated whole cities, or when generations of minority groups have been forced into a life of poverty because of a political philosophy – is hazy by comparison. The need to 'house' born out of the adversity of war offers for architects the opportunity to provide shelter for fellow human beings in need. To that end our building is:

– a mass-produced and inexpensive universal module.
– flexible: the base module can be stockpiled for use on an 'as required' basis, with all the infrastructure for the handling of the module available worldwide.
– easily sited.
– self-contained.
– provided with the capacity to be fitted with a bathroom and kitchen, depending on local requirements.
– provided with a parasol roof, the universal symbol of home, which shelters the roof of the module, providing a thermal cushion as well as a contained and protected outdoor space. Roof panels can be interchanged with indigenous materials such as thatch, mud and stick, palm leaves, and so on.
– mobile and reusable.

## McAllister Co: Boat House

**Project** Battersea Park Boat House, London
**Architect** McAllister Co, London
**Creative team** Rod McAllister, Ian Leader
**Structural engineer** Halcrow
**Quantity surveyor** AYH Partnership
**Client** Wandsworth Borough Council
**Photography** © Dennis Gilbert, View Pictures, London

The boat house was constructed as part of a larger restoration project in Battersea Park funded by the Heritage Lottery Fund. The new boat house is designed to accommodate a rescue craft, a small workshop, boat parts storage and a sound-proofed chamber for a lake aerator compressor. It has replaced an earlier blockwork garage which had major structural problems and was considered unsuitable for such an important setting. The building is located so that it appears to float on the water from many aspects and is positioned so as to terminate the new balau boardwalk which sweeps around the lake from the park café.

The large sliding doors at each end of the boat house are of the same width and material as the deck so they become an integral (and moveable) part of the landscape; opening and closing like an in-out sign and allowing views through the building. The design of the new structure was to follow from a rationale established very early on. This is a building which should be robust, withstand vandalism but must also be rather timeless, well proportioned, contribute to its picturesque environment and have an integrity which comes from honesty of construction and materials. It was decided that, wherever possible, materials should be unfinished. The structure, which sits on piles, is a simple three-bay steel box frame supporting twelve greenheart triangles. These in turn support a treated softwood pitched roof clad in unpatinated copper. Rainwater runs off this roof straight into the lake.

Almost hidden within is another building constructed in-situ of concrete. This compressor chamber reflects the original concrete kiosk situated at the far end of the board-walk.

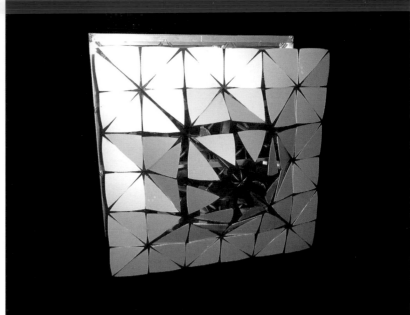

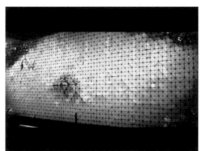 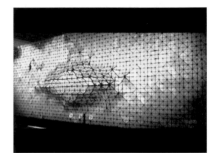

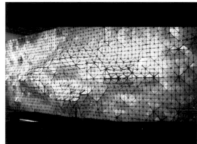 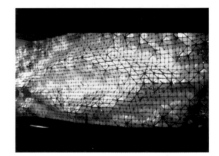

## dECOi: Aegis Hyposurface

**Project** Aegis Hyposurface, Birmingham
**Architect** dECOi, Paris
**Creative team** Mark Goulthorpe, Mark Burry, Oliver Dering, Arnaud Descombes, Gabriele Evangelisti
**Technical Design and implementation** Prof. Mark Burry of Deakin University, Australia with Grant Dunlop
**Programming** Peter Wood, University of Wellington, NZ, Xavier Robitaille, University of Montreal, Canada
**System engineering and design** Prof. Saeid Navahandi, Dr Abbas Kouzani, Deakin University, Australia
**Mathematics** Dr Alex Scott, Prof. Keith Ball, University College London
**Engineering** David Glover, Group IV, ARUP, London

**Façade consultant** Sean Billings, Billings Design Associates, Ireland
**Rubber research** RAPRA, UK; Burton Rubber, UK
**Pneumatic systems/Fabrication** Univer Ltd, Bradford, UK
**Facet manufacture** Spanwall Ltd, Ireland
**Commencement** 1999
**Dimensions** Depth: 0.85–1.35 m; Length: 10 m; Height: 3.5 m;
**Actuators** 576 pneumatic actuators, 2,304 rubber 'squids', 4,608 aluminium facets
**Client** Birmingham Hippodrome Theatre

The Aegis project was created by dECOi architects for a public art competition for the foyer of the Birmingham Hippodrome, UK; the CEBIT Aegis is the fifh prototype for this project, sponsored by CoCreate.

The basic idea of the project is the creation of a dynamically reconfigurable surface that responds interactively to the activity of people, captured by a variety of electronic inputs (movement, sound, etc). The potential this prototype suggests is for an 'architecture of reciprocity', Aegis being a latent surface that is nothing until activated by the presence of people. It suggests possibilities of a dynamic formal universe continually re-calibrated 'real-time' through an electronic sampling of the surrounding environment.

Conceptually the project merely takes the calculating speed of the computer into three-dimensional space, where a matrix of actuators deform a pliable surface in response to 'real-time' events. This might find application as an entertainment/information surface, as at CEBIT, but the principle of co-ordinated three-dimensional variability evidently extends to a wide range of possible applications.

Currently the operating system is pneumatic, chosen for its reliability, low cost, and speed, but one can imagine all manner of other possibilities, extending to the latest developments in 'electronic muscle'. As such the project is a crude precursor to the idea of nanotechnology where many millions of informatically-controlled mechanisms might operate coherently at a molecular level.

The development of the project has demanded a collaboration between different areas of technical expertise, and we have had to search internationally for the appropriate skills needed. Architects, mathematicians, programmers, robotic engineers, pneumatic engineers and rubber researchers have combined in development of such a unique operating system. It is difficult to imagine how such a project could have happened except through an electronic medium, and it suggests to us new patterns of creativity that are emerging. Much of the research work has been done by various Universities (Deakin, Australia; UCL, London; University of Montreal, Canada), reflecting a new relationship between academy and business in a developing electronic environment.

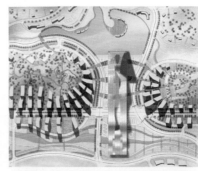

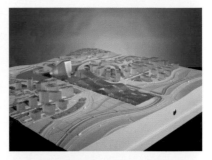

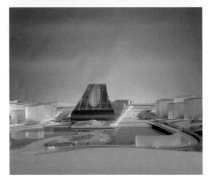

## Architecture Studio: Science City of Guangzhou

**Project** Science City of
Guangzhou, China
**Architect** Architecture
Studio, Paris
**Creative team** Martin Robain, Rodo
Tisnado, Jean-François Bonne,
Alain Bretagnolle, René-Henri
Arnaud, Laurent-Marc Fischer,
Marc Lehmann, Roueïda Ayache
**Urban planner** Christine Moisignac
**Ecological specialist** Marc Barré
**Landscape painter** Régis Guignard
**Landscape consultant** Méristème
**Competition** May 2001
**Key dimensions** 600,000 m²
**Client** Urban Bureau, Guangzhou
**Model maker** Newtone
**CAD images** Architecture Studio
**Photography** Gaston

Cities have always been places for
commercial, cultural and economic
exchanges between people. The wealth
and reputation of a city are measured by
the size of its market and cultural radius.
The experience of the last 50 years in
Europe has shown us that urban thinking
might not just be founded on technical,
economical and functional data.

We have learned that a city is a
complex structure where topography,
history and time are data as important
to apprehend and integrate as the
circulation of automobiles. The design of
the new 'Science City' cannot be considered
without paying attention to what science
has contributed to mankind – that is, precise
and far-reaching knowledge.

We focused on developing our proposal
on the basis of a knowledge of the place
the new city will be built in and developing
our project on the basis of the knowledge
of the constraints. We believe that this
foundation, respect for the environment
and history of the place is a prerequisite
to ensure that the new city can take into
account the constraints of the contemporary
world and offer a harmonious and pleasant
living environment.

The new city will be simultaneously
high-tech and ecological, and similarly
respectful of the agricultural history of
the location and techniques of the future.
Our project is a symbolic act of modernity,
translating the emergence of a city-
company. However these mostly functional
requirements do not necessitate an
abandonment of urban poetry. This is the
goal for a city of the 21st century: to
create an osmosis between construction
and the environment.

## Architecture Studio: Council Building

**Project** New Regional Council
Building, Turin
**Architect** Architecture
Studio, Paris
**Creative team** Martin Robain, Rodo
Tisnado, Jean-François Bonne,
Alain Bretagnolle, René-Henri
Arnaud, Laurent-Marc Fischer,
Marc Lehmann, Roueïda Ayache
**Budget** 77 million Euro
**Client** Council of Piedmont
**Model maker** Newtone
**Photography** Gaston

The construction of a building designed for
a regional institution raises a question about
the position of secular power in the city.
How does one build, in the 21st century, a
regional heart? What sort of architecture
does one apply to this type of government?
How does one flag the importance of this
institution in this global era? Towns throughout Europe are defined by the architecture
of these regional institutions. Since the
middle ages, European towns have boasted
centrally placed town halls and palaces
which have shaped secular power.

Today, this question is fundamental.
When national governments adopt a
European outlook, local and regional
government must present themselves in a
legible and logical way as one fundamental
element of civic life.

Regions are without doubt the basis of
cultural identity in Europe: they predate
nations, and are expressions of local
culture. Today, of course, culture is
international, democratised.

The Piedmont town hall is an important
element in the local cityscape so we
propose a very simple building, easy to
identify that will establish itself in the
collective imagination of the inhabitants
as the place of regional power.

The architecture that we propose for
the Piedmont regional town hall addresses
contemporary contradictions, summarised
as: 'think global, act local'.

The elements from which the
Piedmont town hall is composed have a
universal dimension: a modular plan that
allows great flexibility in terms of growth
around the central structure; glazed
elevations, the use of climatic technology,
and full communications capabilities.
All these elements are part of the global
system – common to new buildings around
the world. To this structure, we propose
adding a new, local, dimension. It is this
local dimension that makes the building
so specific, so special, that supplies its
own poetry and gives the town hall its true
standing in relation to the region of Turin.

## Zaha Hadid: Terminus Hoenheim-Nord

**Project** Terminus Hoenheim-Nord, Strasbourg, France
**Architect** Zaha Hadid Ltd, London
**Creative team** Architectural design: Zaha Hadid; Project architect: Stéphane Hof; Sketch design team: Stéphane Hof, Sara Klomps, Woody K.T. Yao, Sonia Villaseca; Project team: Silvia Forlati, Patrik Schumacher, Markus Dochantschi, David Salazar, Caroline Voet, Eddie Can, Stanley Lau, David Gerber, Chris Dopheide
**Structural engineer** Dr Ing. Luigi Martino
**Project consultants** Mayer Bährle, Roland Mayer
**Commencement** 1999
**Completion** 2001
**Key dimensions**
Site area: 25,000 m²; bus and tram station: 3,000 m²
**Client** C.T.S. [Compagnie des Transports Strasbourgeois]
**Photography** © Hélène Binet

The city of Strasbourg has been developing a new tram-line service to combat increasing congestion and pollution in the city centre. It encourages people to leave their cars outside the city in specially designed car parks, and then take a tram to the inner parts of the city. The first part of this initiative was the development of Line 'A' that ran east to west across Strasbourg. A parallel initiative to the design of the transport system was the inclusion of a number of artists, such as Barbara Kruger and Mario Merz, to make specific installations at key points of the line. Currently, Strasbourg is planning the second line, 'B', that will run north to south. Zaha Hadid has been invited, as part of the new artists' interventions, to design the tram station and a car park for 700 cars at the northern apex of the line.

The overall concept towards the planning of the car park and the station is one of overlapping fields and lines that knit together to form a constantly shifting whole. Those 'fields' are the patterns of movement engendered by cars, trams, bicycles and pedestrians. Each has a trajectory and a trace, as well as a static fixture. It is as though the transition between transport types (car to tram, train

to tram) is rendered as the material and spatial transitions of the station, the landscaping and the context.

The station contains a basic program of waiting space, bicycle storage, toilets, and shop. This sense of three-dimensional vectors is enhanced in the treatment of space: the play of lines continues as light lines in the floor, or furniture pieces or strip-lights in the ceiling. Viewed in plan, all the 'lines' coalesce to create a synchronous whole. The idea is to create an energetic and attractive space that is clearly defined in terms of function and circulation, which is made possible through three-dimensional graphics of light and openings.

As an ensemble, the tram station and car park create a synthesis between floor, light and space. By articulating the moments of transition between open landscape space and public interior space, it is hoped that a new notion of an 'artificial nature' is offered, one that blurs the boundaries between the natural and artificial environments towards the improving of civic life for Strasbourg.

Steve Cochran/Toby Talbot: Casio *Dead Dog*; Auckland Memorial Park *The Thompsons*

**Agency** Colenso BBDO, Auckland, New Zealand
**Creative director** Mike O'Sullivan
**Art director** Steve Cochran
**Copywriter** Toby Talbot
**Photography** Alister Guthrie (*Dead Dog*); Spid (*The Thompsons*)
**Typography** Jacko Van Deventer, Linds Redding
**Medium** Press

# AUSTRALASIAN
# ADVERTISING

Calvin Soh has worked throughout Asia and is currently creative director at Fallon, New York. He started his career as a traffic assistant at O&M Singapore, and then switched to the creative side of advertising. So far he has won Gold Pencils in New York's One Show, Lions in Cannes, and has been accepted into London's D&AD. ZOO asked him to comment on the differences between work from the East and the West, his introduction is then followed by the work of four outstanding creative teams working within the Australasian region.

"What I learnt was the discipline of producing ideas that must transcend language, and cultural and national boundaries. In Singapore alone, there are four different cultures with four main languages, and hundreds of dialects. If it's a Pan-Asian campaign, multiply that by a hundred.

"As a result, the ideas tend to be carried visually. And because there's no wordplay or puns, the idea is intact even after translation. (Do not trifle with translation. Coca-Cola in Mandarin

could mean 'Taste the bitter toad'.) But more than that, the idea has to be universal. Simple emotional truths that binds us all, like love, hate, your first bike, playground bullies, breaking up, etc. So is that a phenomenon unique to Asia? I think not. For proof, just look around you. Your neighbourhood. Your city. Your country. Increasingly, the world is becoming a huge colourful, simmering pariah pot of people.

"The one real difference is the advertising budget. They're considerably smaller in Asia. So agencies are forced to think creatively to utilise other communication tools. It also makes you rely on the simplicity and strength of an idea rather than the execution. It doesn't mean execution suffers, it just means you take the risk and use someone fresh, and not established names. Not a bad thing in my opinion.

"So is there a difference between East and West ideas? Let me answer that with a question. Is the Walkman an idea that works best in the East or West?" Calvin Soh

Josh Robbins/Natalie Knight: G-Shock *Tank*

**Agency** Colenso BBDO, Auckland, New Zealand
**Creative director** Mike O'Sullivan
**Art director** Josh Robbins
**Copywriters** Natalie Knight,
Leo Premutico
**Photography** Alister Guthrie

Josh Robbins/Natalie Knight: MPA *Read*

**Agency** Colenso BBDO, Auckland, New Zealand
**Creative director** Mike O'Sullivan
**Art directors** Josh Robbins, Darren Wongkam
**Copywriters** Natalie Knight, Josh Robbins
**Photography** Alister Guthrie
**Medium** Press

So you've read all the pages in the magazine so far and then you come across this one. And you think, 'that looks interesting' so you start to read. You're reading and reading and then it suddenly dawns on you. This isn't interesting at all. Not one little bit. Well, maybe a tiny bit, but not enough to have kept you reading this long. And then you realise that in fact, you are, still reading. Just reading away, without a care in the world. Reading, reading, reading. And reading nothing in particular to boot. Which is why you should advertise in magazines. Because if it's in a magazine you'll read it. MPA. Advertise in magazines

## Maurice Wee/Renee Lim: Campaign Brief Asia *Toilet*

**Agency** Saatchi & Saatchi,
Hong Kong
**Creative director** Craig Davis
**Art director** Maurice Wee
**Copywriter** Renee Lim
**Photography** Stanley Wong
**Illustration** Phenomenon Digital Art

**Typography** Maurice Wee
**Client** *Campaign Brief* Pty
**Agency** *Campaign Brief*
**Medium** Press, poster
**Exposure** Australasia
**Date** July 2001

Maurice Wee/Renee Lim:
Daisy.U Underwear
*Spirals*

**Agency** Saatchi & Saatchi,
Hong Kong
**Creative director** Craig Davis
**Art director** Maurice Wee
**Copywriter** Renee Lim
**Client** Guangzhou Daisy.U
Underwear Company
**Agency** Discovery Asia
**Medium** Press, poster
**Exposure** China
**Date** July 2001

Maurice Wee/Renee Lim:
Discovery Asia *Danny;
Stuart*

**Agency** Saatchi & Saatchi,
Singapore
**Creative director** Ragdish
Ramakrishnan
**Art director** Maurice Wee
**Copywriter** Renee Lim
**Photography** Bruce Allen
**Client** Discovery Asia Inc
**Agency** Discovery Asia
**Medium** Poster
**Exposure** Singapore
**Date** July 2001

AIR MAIL

CHANGI AIRPORT WELCOMES
EVERGREEN INTERNATIONAL AIRLINES,
THE FIFTH LARGEST CARGO
CARRIER IN THE U.S.

CAAS
Civil Aviation Authority of Singapore

MOVIE THEATRE at SINGAPORE CHANGI AIRPORT

Farrokh Madon/Ng Tian It: Changi Airport *Cargo Box; Movie Theatre*

**Client** CAAS
**Agency** Saatchi & Saatchi, Singapore
**Product** Changi Airport
**Medium** Poster
**Exposure** Singapore
**Art director** Ng Tian It
**Copywriter** Farrokh Madon
**Photography** Eric Seow

**David Hughes**

**Date of birth** 1967
**Place of birth** Liverpool, UK
**Place of residence** London
**Representation** The Garden, London
**Courtesy** David Hughes; The Garden

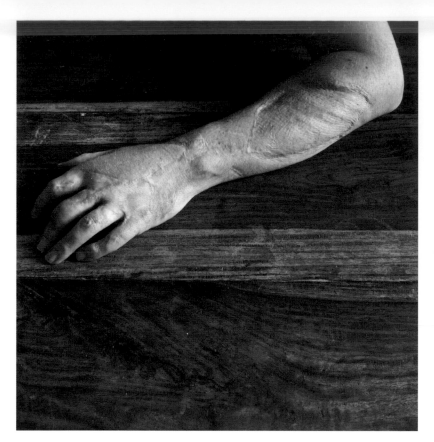

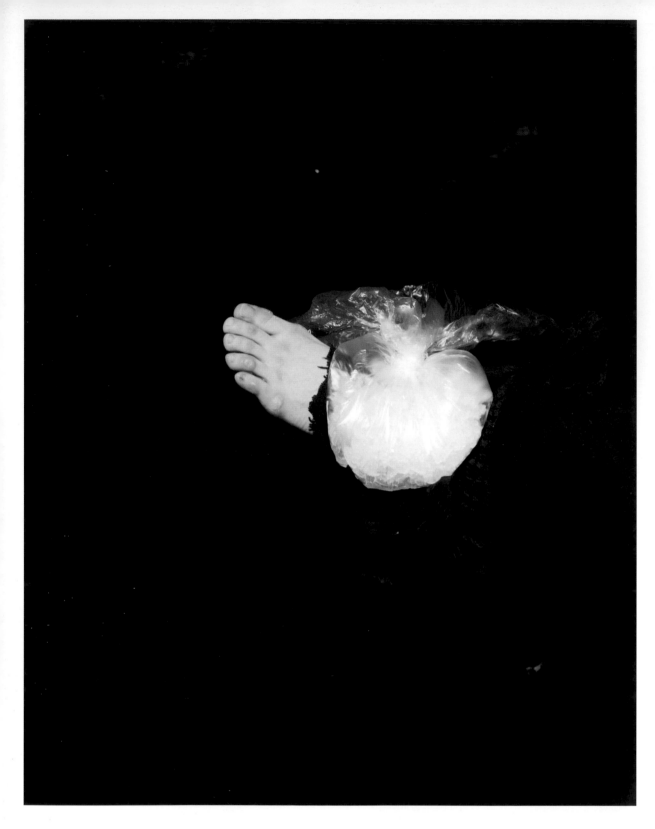

From a book commissioned on the occasion of the 40th anniversary of the National Ballet, Amsterdam, published in August 2001.

## Dana Lixenberg

**Place of birth** Amsterdam
**Place of residence** New York
**Representation** Z Photographic, London and New York
**Courtesy** Z Photographic

**Recent exhibitions** *United States*, Kunsthal, Rotterdam (2001) > *Portraits of Imperial*

*Courts and Eight Women in Jeffersonville, Indiana*, LACPS/knowtribe, Los Angeles (1999)

Dana Lixenberg's work has been published in many magazines, including *The New York Times Magazine, The New Yorker, Newsweek, Vibe, The Sunday Telegraph, Rolling Stone, Max Modes, GQ* and *Flaunt*. She was also recently the subject of a television documentary shown in the Netherlands called *Thru Dutch Eyes*.

01

02

03

04

## Christopher Pillitz

**Representation** Network
Photographers, London
**Courtesy** Network Photographers

"The 41-year old Chevrolet Impala about to drive from Havana to Santiago has been patched up many times over. The driver says this is no problem and a road movie through Cuban daily life begins.

"Matanzas is hot, and shortly after high noon from the shaded roadside Mario is changing another tyre, the fourth time since Havana. Is it such a good idea wanting to cruise across Cuba aboard this old-timer? Of course, it was love on first sight. 'La Nina', Mario's 1959 Chevrolet is the car that came to Havana three months before Fidel Castro, and appeared irresistible. Che Guevara had one just like it. Mario is proud.

"With its bare teeth radiator grill, the stern swung like a Manta ray, the golden brown and chrome shark slid through the sluggish stream of the Malecón. 'Che's has long been in the museum,' Mario says. 'La Nina is still going on its first engine.' But would the 'Little Girl' hold out till Santiago on the other side of the island? Almost 1,000 kilometres away, not counting the detours, Mario's imitation Ray Bans led the way.

"A lot of sweat seeps into the uncomfortable Skai seats of La Nina. It is impossible to cool off even though all the windows are down letting in the breeze. On the motorway from Havana to Matanzas, Mario drove at full throttle – 60 km/h... The needle of the speedometer is always stuck on zero as convoys of lorries overtake, as do Ladas, Volgas and Bulgarian buses. Only a moped tries in vain.

"You cannot complain. It is a car that fits Cuba, a country whose past has been ahead of the rest of the world. Something doesn't seem to be right with its present, and one feels tempted to prolong those yesterdays through nostalgia trips. Mario and La Nina live to do just this."
Christopher Pillitz

05

06

07

08

01
The streets of Trinidad, Cuba,
July 2000

02
Clouds gather over Trinidad,
Cuba, July 2000

03
Clave de Son, a well-known band,
play at Casa de las Tradiciones,
Santiago, July 2000

04
Palero – Pedro Spengler
(Christian/Pagan) conducts a
ritual sacrifice to the Gods
of Orixas

05
The eccentric Billy Benny (38),
a friendly street musician known
to everyone, Santiago

06
Choreographed dancing on the
roof of a building at dusk in
Santiago, July 2000

07
Children from broken families at
a dance rehearsal at the grand
yet faded Casa del Estudiante

08
The 1959 Chevrolet Impala ends
the journey in the Santiago
night, July 2000

01

01
Tetovo, March 2001

02
Liposh above Tetovo, March 2001
Ethnic Albanians in the NLA-
controlled village. Waiting for
the end of the ultimatum.

03
Slupcane, May 2001
Ethnic Albanian civilians during
a break in the shelling.

04
Tetovo, March 2001

05
Gaijre above Tetovo, March 2001
Ethnic Albanian trying to save
his house after the Macedonian
Army took the village, formerly
controlled by the NLA.

## Thomas Dworzak: Macedonia

**Representation** Magnum Photos,
London
**Courtesy** © Thomas Dworzak;
Magnum Photos

In February 2001, fighting between ethnic Albanian militants and Macedonian forces near Macedonia's border with Kosovo raised concerns that this former Yugoslavian republic could be an incubator for the next round of Balkan bloodshed.

Since then, fighting has spread to other parts of the country, first to the mountainous outskirts of Tetovo, the main ethnic Albanian town in Macedonia, and to the region around Kumanovo in the north.

02

03

04

05

Tehran, 2001
The Ayatollah is watching you!  Khomeini's eyes on
a billboard watch over passers-by.

A female supporter of President Mohammad Khatami
in the throes of ecstasy as he addresses
supporters in the Shiroudi stadium, Tehran, 2001.

Female supporters of President Mohammad Khatami
during an election rally, Tehran, 2001.

A young couple relax in the Jamshidiye park,
Tehran, 2001.

## Abbas

**Representation**
Magnum Photos, London
**Courtesy** © Abbas; Magnum Photos

These photographs were taken before the
Presidential election of June 2001, when
Khatami's Iran was torn between
reformists and conservatives. Reformists,
the great majority of the youth, woman
and artists, want to break free of the carcan
of the Iranian Republic.Conservatives cling
to the old values by relentlessly exploiting
the myth of the revolution and the cult
of martyrdom.

*I Am As I Am*, Benares Ashram, India
An older devotee of Anadamayee Ma, who decided to stay in the ashram and renounce the world.

Across the central courtyard, the girls at morning prayer.

Girls washing themselves. Often the younger ones play hide-and-seek amongst the drying saris.

On the Ganges below, the tourists' boats go by. Some of the girls shyly wave.

## Dayanita Singh

**Representation** Network
Photographers, London
**Courtesy** Network Photographers

"These images are from a girls ashram in Benares, full of life and light, not morbid and gritty as Benares often can be in black-and-white. I was extremely lucky to get access into this ashram, where no one has shot before and I doubt anyone else will, as I was supposed to study there as a child. It is the ashram of probably the most important female guru of the 20th century in India. I waited many years to find something of my own to say about Benares, all the time getting more and more frustrated with the imagery I saw, and I think I found my Benares voice." Dayanita Singh

Lise Sarfati
*Backstage of the legendary cabaret,*
*Moulin Rouge*

# MAGNUM: PARIS XVIIIE

The three colours, like a flag of victory are flapping. The one who will conquer the summit of the XVIII district town hall, will win the first step to the road of Paris Town Hall. Philippe Seguin, main figure of the RPR and candidate for Paris Town Hall, dreams today of getting hold of the XVII district, which has been left wing since 1995. His opponents are Daniel Vaillant, mayor of the XVII district and Minister for the Interior, and the favourite and uncompromising opponent, Bertrand Delanoe, second on the list in the run for the town hall. During the battle, the agency

Magnum sent 16 of its photographers to this highly-considered quarter. They found nostalgia and trendiness, tradition and a melting-pot.

"The XVII district remains for me the only true quarter of Paris. A quarter of the future, with a strong past. A multi-racial and tolerant quarter. A quarter where I feel safe."
Raymond Depardon

All images courtesy of Magnum Photos, London.

Bruno Barbey
*Café Le progrès, rue Yvonne Le Tac.*

Alex Majoli
*At cabaret Michou*

Abbas
*Muslims in a mosque, rue Polonceau*

01
Raymond Depardon
*View from the roof of the city hall of the*
*18th arrondissement*

02
Josef Koudelka
*Area of the SNCF, the French railroads.*

03
Thomas Dworzak
*Smoking crack in the Metro*

04, 05
Bruce Gilden
*Coming out of Metro station at Barbès*
*Rochechouart*

01

02

01
Richard Kalvar
*Dancing at Café Le Colibri*

02
Gueorgui Pinkhassov
*Montmartre, the funicular going up to the Sacré Coeur.*

03
Martin Parr
*Tourists at the Sacré Coeur.*

04
Gueorgui Pinkhassov
*Swedish painter Katarina Axelsson paints a series of the Place de Clichy.*

05
Gueorgui Pinkhassov
*Metro station at Place des Abbesses*

## ADVERTISING

**Aardman**
Gas Ferry Road
Bristol BS1 6UN
UK
T: [44 117] 984 8485 F: 984 8486
W: www.aardman.com

**Abbott Mead Vickers·BBDO**
151 Marylebone Road
London NW1 5QE
UK
T: [44 20] 7616 3500 F: 7616 3600
W: www.amvbbdo.co.uk

**Academy Commercials**
16 West Central Street
London WC1A 1JJ
UK
T: [44 20] 7395 4155 F: 7494 0348
E: post@academyfilms.com

**Aimaq-Rapp-Stolle**
Münzstrasse 15
10178 Berlin
Germany
T: [49 30] 308 8710 F: 3088 7171
W: www.ars-berlin.com

**Arden Sutherland-Dodd**
6 D'Arblay Street
London W1V 3FD
UK
T: [44 20] 7437 3898 F: 7287 2150

**Arnold Worldwide**
101 Huntington Avenue
Boston
MA 02199-7603
USA
T: [1 617] 587 8000 F: 587 8004
W: www.arn.com

**Bartle Bogle Hegarty**
60 Kingly Street
London W1R 6DS
UK
T: [44 20] 7734 1677 F: 7437 3666
W: www.bbh.co.uk

**Bartle Bogle Hegarty Ltd**
28 Duxton Hill
Singapore 089610
Singapore
T: [65 ] 221 0811 F: 221 0911

**BBDO Chicago**
410 North Michigan Avenue
8th Floor
Chicago
IL 60611
USA
T: [1 312] 337 7860 F: 337 6871
W: www.bbdo.com

**BMP DDB**
12 Bishops Bridge Road
London W2 6AA
UK
T: [44 20] 7258 3979 F: 7258 4153
W: www.bmpddb.com

**Bob Industries**
250 Mercer Street #B306
New York NY 10012
USA
T: [1 212] 677 2775 F: 533 4084

**BRW & Partners S.R.L.**
via Savona 97
20144 Milano
Italy
T: [39 02] 424121 F: 424 1270
W: www.brwpartners.com

**Cliff Freeman & Partners**
375 Hudson Street 8th Floor
New York NY 10014
USA
T: [1 212] 463 3200 F: 463 3225
W: www.clifffreeman.com

**Colenso Communications**
100 College Road
Ponsonby, Auckland
New Zealand
T: [64 9] 360 3777 F: 360 3756

**Dentsu Inc**
1-11 Tsukiji
Chuo-ku
Tokyo 104-8426
Japan
T: [81 3] 5551 5111 F: 5551 2220
W: http://www.dentsu.co.jp

**Deutsch Inc**
111 Eighth Avenue
14th Floor
New York NY 10011
USA
T: [1 212] 981 7600 F: 353 9852
W: www.deutschinc.com

**Euro RSCG Works**
84 rue de Villiers
92683 Levallois-Perret
France
T: [33 1] 41 34 34 34
F: 41 34 34 32

**Fallon**
79 Fifth Avenue
14th Floor
New York NY 10003
USA
T: [1 212] 367 2300 F: 206 0489

**Fallon Worldwide**
50 South Sixth Street
Minneapolis MN 55402
USA
T: [1 612] 758 2345 F: 758 2346
W: www.fallon.com

**FCB**
79 rue Baudin
92300 Levallois-Perret
France
T: [33 1] 41 06 75 00
F: 41 06 78 41
W: www.bozell.com

**Flying Fish NZ**
60 Sentinel Road
PO Box 47017
Herne Bay, Auckland
New Zealand
T: [64 9] 378 0238 F: 378 0812
W: www.flyingfish.co.nz

**Forsman & Bodenfors**
Kyrkogatan 48
411 08 Göteborg
Sweden
T: [46 31] 176730 F: 138353

**Gorgeous Enterprises Limited**
23-24 Greek Street
London W1V 5LG
UK
T: [44 20] 7287 4060 F: 7287 4994

**Harry Nash Productions**
27-29 Beak Street
London W1F 9RU
UK
T: [44 20] 7025 7500 F: 7025 7501
E: kateelson@harrynash.co.uk

**HSI Productions**
3630 Eastham Drive
Los Angeles CA 90232
USA
T: [1 310] 558 7100 F: 558 7101
W: www.hsiproductions.com

**HSI Productions**
7 West 18th Street
New York NY 10011
USA
T: [1 212] 627 3600 F: 627 5947

**Hungry Man**
2nd Floor
39-43 Brewer Street,
London W1R 3FD
UK
T: [44 20] 7287 8750 F: 7287 8751

**Industry Films**
260 King Street East, #200
Toronto ON M5A 4LF
Canada
T: [1 416] 815 1717 F: 815 0147
E: shoot@industryfilms.com
W: www.industryfilms.com

**Itinerant Films**
58-59 Great Marlborough Street
London W1V 1DD
UK
T: [44 20] 7287 7881 F: 7287 7882
E: it@dircon.co.uk

**J. Walter Thompson**
484 St Kilda Road
Melbourne VIC 3004
Australia
T: [61 3] 9868 9111 F: 9867 7568

**J. Walter Thompson Publicidade Ltda**
Rua Mário Amaral, 50
Paraiso
CEP 04002-020
São Paulo
Brazil
T: [55 11] 3888 8000
F: 884 5209

**John Doe**
Tussen de Bogen 22
1013 JB Amsterdam
Netherlands
T: [31 20] 528 9000
F: 528 9777
E: john@john-doe.nl
W: www.john-doe.nl

**Jung von Matt**
Glashttenstrasse 38
20357 Hamburg
Germany
T: [49 40] 431210
F: 4321 1113
W: www.jvm.de

**Jung von Matt an der Isar**
Schwere-Reiter Strasse 35
80797 München
Germany
T: [49 89] 3063 2616 F: 3063 2613
W: www.jvm.de

**Leo Burnett**
60 Sloane Avenue
London SW3 3XB
UK
T: [44 20] 7591 9111 F: 7591 9126
W: www.leoburnett.com

**Lowe Lintas & Partners**
Bowater House
68-114 Knightsbridge
London SW1X 7LT
UK
T: [44 20] 7584 5033 F: 7584 9557
W: www.lowelintas.co.uk

**Mad Dogs & Englishmen**
126 Fifth Avenue
12th Floor
New York NY 10011
USA
T: [1 212] 675 6116 F: 505 1494
W:www.maddogsandenglishmen.com

**Malcolm Moore Deakin Blayze Ltd**
24 Store Street
London WC1E 7BA
UK
T: [44 20] 7692 3993 F: 7813 0753
W: www.malcolmmoore.com

**Markenfilm GmbH & Co.**
Schulauer Moorweg 25
22880 Wedel
Germany
T: [49 4103] 123165 F: 15243
W: www.markenfilm.de

**McCann-Erickson Europe**
30 Howland Street
London W1A 1AT
UK
T: [44 20] 7580 6690 F: 7323 2883

**Melle, Pufe, GmbH**
Katharina-Heinroth-Ufer 1
10785 Berlin
Germany
T: [49 30] 2540 3600 F: 2840 4544
W: www.melle-pufe.de

**Merkley Newman Harty**
200 Varick Street
New York
NY 10014-4810
USA
T: [1 212] 366 3500 F: 366 3637
W: www.mnh.com

**Modernista!**
109 Kingston Street
2nd Floor
Boston MA 02111
USA
T: [1 617] 451 1110 F: 451 8680
W: www.modernista.com

**Mother**
200 St Johns Street
London EC1V 4RN
UK
T: [44 20] 7689 0689
F: 7689 1689
W: www.motherlondon.com

**Nexus Network**
Akasaka Heim 3F, 8-8-7
Akasaka, Minato-ku
Tokyo
Japan
T: [81 3] 5412 7001 F: 5412 7002
E: prod@nexnet.com

**Ogilvy & Mather**
10 Cabot Square, Canary Wharf
London E14 4QB
UK
T: [44 20] 7345 3000 F: 7345 9022
W: www.ogilvy.com

**Ogilvy & Mather**
33 Yonge Street 11th Floor
Toronto
ON M5E 1X6
Canada
T: [1 416] 367 3573 F: 363 2088
W: www.ogilvy.com

**Outsider**
2nd Floor
41-42 Foley Street
London W1P 7LD
UK
T: [44 20] 7636 6666 F: 7323 0242
E: outsider@outsider-ltd.co.uk

**Partizan LA**
8330 West 3rd Street
Los Angeles CA 90035
USA
T: [1 323] 653 6660 F: 653 6661

**Passion Pictures Ltd**
25-27 Riding House Street
London W1P 7PB
UK
T: [44 20] 7323 9933 F: 7323 9030
E: info@passion-pictures.com

**Rogue Films**
10 Mortimer Street
London W1N 7DF
UK
T: [44 20] 7907 1000 F: 7907 1001
W: www.roguefilms.com

**Saatchi & Saatchi Advertising**
80 Charlotte Street
London W1A 1AQ
UK
T: [44 20] 7636 5060 F: 7637 8489
W: www.saatchi.com

**Saatchi & Saatchi Advertising**
101-103 Courtenay Place
PO Box 6540
Wellington
New Zealand
T: [64 4] 385 6524 F: 385 9678

**Saatchi & Saatchi Advertisng (China)**
51/F Sun Huang Kai Centre
30 Harbour Road
Wanchai
Hong Kong
China SAR Hong Kong
T: [852 ] 2582 3333 F: 2802 8213

**Saatchi & Saatchi Singapore**
3D River Valley Road #03-01
Clarke Quay
Singapore 179023
Singapore
T: [65 ] 339 4733 F: 339 3916

**Satellite Films**
1741 Ivar Avenue
Hollywood
Los Angeles CA 90028
USA
T: [1 323] 802 6600 F: 802 6601

**Scholz & Friends**
Chaussee Strasse 5
10115 Berlin
Germany
T: [49 30] 2853 5300 F: 2853 5599

**St. Luke's**
22 Duke's Road
London WC1H 9AB
UK
T: [44 20] 7380 8930 F: 7380 8899
W: www.stlukes.co.uk

**Studio AKA**
30 Berwick Street
London W1V 3RF
UK
T: [44 20] 7434 3581 F: 7437 2309

**SVC**
142 Wardour Street
London W1V 3AU
UK
T: [44 20] 7734 1600 F: 7437 1854
W: www.svc.co.uk

**Taxi Advertising & Design**
495 Wellington Street West
Toronto ON M5V 1E9
Canada
T: [1 416] 979 7001 F: 979 7626

**TBWA Werbeagentur GmbH**
Saarbrücker Strasse 20-21
10405 Berlin
Germany
T: [49 30] 4432 9332 F: 44 32 93 11

**Töchter + Söhne**
Hardenbergstraße 88
Berlin
Germany
T: [49 30] 3150 8310 F: 3150 8340
E: kontakt@toechterundsoehne.com

**Verba DDB**
via Solari 11
20144 Milano
Italy
T: [39 02] 581931 F: 8940 1445

**Wanda Productions**
50 avenue du President Wilson
Batiment 122
92214 Saint Denis la Plaine
France
T: [33 1] 49 46 63 63 F: 49 46 63 64

**Wieden + Kennedy**
224 NW 13 Avenue
Portland OR 97209
USA
T: [1 503] 937 7000 F: 937 8000
W: www.wk.com

**Wild Brain**
2650 18th Street
San Francisco
CA 94110
USA
T: [1 415] 553 8000 F: 553 8009
W: www.wildbrain.com

# ARCHITECTURE

**Archimation**
Bleibtreustrasse 47
10623 Berlin
Germany
T: [49 30] 8867 9555 F: 8867 9558
E: alex@archimation.com
W: www.archimation.com

**Architecture Studio**
10 rue Lacuée
75012 Paris
France
T: [33 1] 43 45 18 00
F: 43 43 81 43
E: as@architecture-studio.fr
W: www.architecture-studio.fr

**Barkow Leibinger Architekten**
Schillerstrasse 94
10625 Berlin
Germany
T: [49 30] 315 7120 F: 3157 1229
E: info@barkowleibinger.com
W: www.barkowleibinger.com

**Behnisch, Behnisch and Partner**
Christophstraße 6
70178 Stuttgart
Germany
T: [49 711] 607720 F: 607 7299
E: buero@behnisch.com
W: www.behnisch.com

**Camenzind Gräfensteiner**
Samariterstrasse 5, Postfach
8030 Zürich
Switzerland
T: [41 1] 253 9500 F: 253 9510
E: info@camenzindgrafensteiner.com
W: www.CamenzindGrafensteiner.com

**dECOi**
Atelier 81
65 rue du Faubourg St Denis
75010 Paris
France
T: [33 1] 40 22 07 03 F: 40 22 07 03
E: dECOi@easynet.fr

**Didier Fiuza Faustino**
62 rue Tiquetonne
75002 Paris
France
T: [33 1] 40 33 93 96 F: 48 89 32 22
E: faust@mesarchitecture.com
W: www.mesarchitecture.com

**Erskine Tovatt Arkitektkontor AB**
Gustav III's väg 4
PO Box 156
178 02 Drottningholm
Sweden
T: [46 8] 759 0050 F: 759 0106
E: albert@erskine.se
W: www.erskine.se

**Foster and Partners**
Riverside Three
22 Hester Road
London SW11 4AN
UK
T: [44 20] 7738 0455
F: 7738 1107
E: enquiries@fosterandpartners.com
W: www.fosterandpartners.com

**Geoffrey Reid Associates**
West End House
11 Hill's Place
London W1F 7SE
UK
T: [44 20] 7297 5600 F: 7297 5601
E: gra@gra-l.co.uk
W: www.geoffreyreidassociates.com

**Gewers Kühn & Kühn Architects**
Carnotstrasse 7
(Gemini Quay)
10587 Berlin
Germany
T: [49 30] 283 0820 F: 2830 8253
E: info@gkk-architekten.de
W: www.gkk-architekten.de

**Grüntuch Ernst Architekten BDA**
Hackescher Markt 2-3
10178 Berlin
Germany
T: [49 30] 308 7788 F: 308 7787
E: info@gea-berlin.de
W: www.gea-berlin.de

**Judah Ltd**
Linton House
39-51 Highgate Road
London NW5 1RT
UK
T: [44 20] 7284 1101 F: 7267 0661
E: gerry@judah.co.uk
W: www.judah.co.uk

**Karmebäck und Krüger**
Nollendorfstrasse 11-12
10777 Berlin
Germany
T: [49 30] 215 4515 F: 215 4543
E: k.k@snafu.de

**Kim Dalgaard & Tue Trærup Madsen Arkitekter M.A.A.**
Rosenvængets Hovedvej 27, 1

2100 København Ø
Denmark
T: [45 ] 35 38 35 51
F: 35 26 23 31
E: kim@dalgaard.com
W: www.dalgaard.com

**kOnyk architecture pc**
61 Pearl Street
#590
Brooklyn
New York City
NY 11201-8339
USA
T: [1 718] 852 5381 F: 852 1890
E: konyk@konyk.net
W: www.konyk.net

**Lifschutz Davidson Ltd**
Thames Wharf Studios
Rainville Road
London W6 9HA
UK
T: [44 20] 7381 8120 F: 7385 3118
E: mail@lifschutzdavidson.com
W: www.lifschutzdavidson.com

**Llewelyn-Davies**
Brook House
Torrington Place
London WC1E 7HN
UK
T: [44 20] 7637 0181
F: 7637 8740
E: info@llewelyn-davies-ltd.com

**Mario Campi Architect & Partners**
via Cassarinetta 28
6900 Lugano
Switzerland
T: [41 91] 993 1477 F: 993 1329
E: studio@mariocampi.ch

**Mark Braun Architekten BDA RIBA**
Mommsenstrasse 59
10629 Berlin
Germany
T: [49 30] 327 7830 F: 3277 8329
E: mbraun@braunarchitekten.com

**MBM Architectes**
Plaça Reial 18, Pral
08002 Barcelona
Spain
T: [34 93] 317 0061 F: 317 7266
E: publicacions@mbmarquitectes.com
W: www.mbmarquitectes.com

**McAllister Co**
220a Queenstown Road
London SW8 4LP
UK
T: [44 20] 7720 0458 F: 7720 0958
E: mail@mcallister.co.uk
W: www.mcallister.co.uk

**Melon Studio**
26 North Street
Clapham Old Town
London SW4 0HB
UK
T: [44 20] 7720 9281 F: 7720 8531
E: chris.c@melonstudio.co.uk

**Nicholas Grimshaw & Partners Limited**
1 Conway Street
Fitzroy Square
London W1T 6LR
UK
T: [44 20] 7291 4141 F: 7291 4194

E: donnatheacampbell@ngrimshaw.co.uk
W: www.ngrimshaw.co.uk

**Naoto Yaegashi + NOrm null OFFice**
2F-4 Atsumi Building
1-23 Futsuka-machi
Aoba-ku
Sendai 980-0802
Japan
T: [81 22] 716 3111 F: 716 3444
E: nno@lily.ocn.ne.jp

**Nyréns Arkitektkontor ab**
Ferkensgränd 3
PO Box 1250
111 82 Stockholm
Sweden
T: [46 8] 698 4300 F: 202981
E: tomas.lewan@nyrens.se
W: www.nyrens.se

**OMA/Rem Koolhaas**
Heer Bokelweg 149
3032 AD Rotterdam
Netherlands
T: [31 10] 243 8200 F: 243 8202
E: oma@euronet.nl

**Oman & Videcnik-OFIS Architects**
Beethovnova 9
1000 Ljubljana
Slovenia
T: [386 1] 426 4531 F: 426 4531
E: spelavid@hotmail.com
E: rok.oman@guest.arnes.si

**Peter Ebner + Franziska Ullmann**
Windmühlgasse 9/26
1060 Wien
Austria
T: [43 1] 586 8522 F: 587 7887
E: ebner-ullmann@aon.at

**Raumlabor**
Almstadtstrasse 48-50
10119 Berlin
Germany
T: [49 30] 2758 0882 F: 247 6319
E: post@raumlabor-berlin.de
W: www.raumlabor-berlin.de

**Rogers Marvel Architects**
145 Hudson Street
Third Floor
New York NY 10013
USA
T: [1 212] 941 6718 F: 941 7573
E: rrogers@rogersmarvel.com
W: www.rogersmarvel.com

**Sandellsandberg**
Riddargatan 17D II
114 57 Stockholm
Sweden
T: [46 8] 5062 1700 F: 5062 1707
E: matilda.s@sandellsandberg.se
W: www.sandellsandberg.se

**sauerbruch hutton architects**
Lehter Strasse 57
10557 Berlin
Germany
T: [49 30] 397 8210 F: 3978 2130
E: office@sauerbruchhutton.de
W: www.sauerbruchhutton.de

**Sean Godsell Architects**
8A Daly Street
South Yarra VIC 3141
Australia

T: [61 3] 9824 1444 F: 9824 1477
E: godsell@netspace.net.au

**Sheppard Robson**
77 Parkway
Camden Town
London NW1 7PU
UK
T: [44 20] 7485 4161 F: 7267 3861
E: tim.evans@sheppardrobson.com
W: www.sheppardrobson.com

**Shigeru Ban Architects**
5-2-4 Matsubara Ban Building
1st Floor
Setagaya
Tokyo 156
Japan
T: [81 3] 3324 6760 F: 3324 6789
E: sba@tokyo.email.ne.jp
W: www.dnp.co.jp/millennium/sb/van.html

**Softroom**
34 Lexington Street
London W1F 0LH
UK
T: [44 20] 7437 1550 F: 7437 1566
E: softroom@softroom.com
W: www.softroom.com

**Studio Libeskind**
Windscheidstrasse 18 D
10627 Berlin
Germany
T: [49 30] 327 7820 F: 327 78299
E: info@daniel-libeskind.com

**T.R. Hamzah & Yeang Sdn Bhd**
8 Jalan Satu
Taman Sri Ukay
Ampang Selangor 680 00
Malaysia
T: [60 3] 4257 1966 F: 4256 1005
E: trhy@tm.net.my
W: www.trhamzah-yeang.com

**Terry Farrell & Partners**
7 Hatton Street
London NW8 8PL UK
T: [44 20] 7258 3433 F: 7723 7059
E: bthompson@terryfarrell.co.uk
W: www.terryfarrell.com

**VIIVA arkkitehtuuri Oy**
Laivurinkatu 37
00150 Helsinki
Finland
T: [358 9] 2709 1720 F: 2709 1729
E: viiva@kolumbus.fi

**West 8**
**Landscape Architects & Urban Planners bv**
PO Box 24 326
3007 DH Rotterdam
Netherlands
T: [31 10] 485 5801 F: 485 6323
E: west8@west8.nl

**Zaha Hadid Ltd**
Studio 9, 10 Bowling Green Lane
London EC1R 0BQ
UK
T: [44 20] 7253 5147 F: 7251 8322
E: press@zaha-hadid.com

**Zvi Hecker**
Oranienburgerstrasse 41
10117 Berlin
Germany
T: [49 30] 282 6914 F: 282 7322

E: hutterer@zvihecker.com
W: www.zvihecker.com

# ART & PHOTOGRAPHY

**303 Gallery**
525 West 22nd Street
New York NY 10011
USA
T: [1 212] 255 1121 F: 255 0024

**Ace Gallery**
275 Hudson Street
New York NY 10013
USA
T: [1 212] 255 5599 F: 255 5799

**Andrea Rosen Gallery**
525 West 24th Street
New York NY 10011
USA
T: [1 212] 627 6000 F: 627 5450
E: andrea@rosengallery.com

**Anthony d'Offay Gallery**
9-23-24 Dering Street
London W1S 1AJ
UK
T: [44 20] 7499 4100 F: 7493 4443
E: gallery@doffay.com
W: www.doffay.com

**Arndt & Partner**
Auguststraße 35
10119 Berlin
Germany
T: [49 30] 280 8123 F: 283 3738
E: arndt@arndt-partner.de
W: www.arndt-partner.de

**Art + Commerce**
755 Washington Street
2nd Floor
New York NY 10014
USA
T: [1 212] 206 0737 F: 463 7267
E: agents@artandcommerce.com
W: www.artandcommerce.com

**Art Partner**
145 Hudson Street, 2nd Floor
New York NY 10013
USA
T: [1 212] 343 9889 F: 343 9891
W: www.artpartner.com

**Artemis Greenberg Van Doren Fine Art**
730 Fifth Avenue
7th Floor
New York NY 10019
USA
T: [1 212] 445 0444 F: 445 0442
E: lrgart@aol.com

**Birgit Meixner**
Simon-Dach-Straße 32
10245 Berlin
Germany
T: [49 30] 292 19 68

**Bob van Orsouw**
Limmatstrasse 270
8005 Zürich Switzerland
T: [41 1] 273 1100 F: 273 1102
E: bobvanorsouw@access.ch

**carlier | gebauer**
Torstraße 220
10115 Berlin
Germany
T: [49 30] 280 8110 F: 280 8109
E: bthumm@is.in-berlin.de

**Carolyn Trayler Agency**
30 Percy Street
London W1T 2DB
UK
T: [44 20] 7636 1100 F: 7636 1190
E: cathy@trayler.co.uk
W: www.trayler.co.uk

**Chantal Hoogvliet**
60 rue Vieille du Temple
75003 Paris
France
T/F: [33 1] 42 72 78 99
E: RepChant@wanadoo.fr

**Cokkie Snoei Gallery**
Mauritsweg 55
3012 JX Rotterdam
Netherlands
T: [31 10] 412 9274

**Contemporary Fine Arts**
Sophienstraße 21
10178 Berlin
Germany
T: [49 30] 283 6580
F: 283 6582
W: www.cfa-berlin.com

**D'Amelio Terras**
525 West 22nd Street
New York NY 10011
USA
T: [1 212] 352 9460 F: 352 9464
W: www.damelioterras.com

**Emily Tsingou Gallery**
10 Charles II Street
London SW1Y 4AA
UK
T: [44 20] 7839 5320 F: 7839 5321
E: emily@emilytsingougallery.com
W: www.emilytsingougallery.com

**Erik Göngrich**
goengrich@gmx.net

**Florian Zeyfang**
fz@thing.de

**Galerie Art: Concept**
16 rue Duchefdelaville
75013 Paris
France
T: [33 1] 53 60 90 30 F: 53 60 90 31
W: www.galerieartconcept.com

**Galerie Barbara Thumm**
Auguststraße 22
10117 Berlin
Germany
T: [49 30] 283 4223 F: 283 4231

**Galerie Barbara Weiss**
Zimmerstraße 88-91
10117 Berlin Germany
T: [49 30] 262 4284 F: 881 7677
W: www.galeriebarbaraweiss.de

**Galerie Daniel Buchholz**
Neven-DuMont Straße 17
50667 Köln
Germany

T: [49 221] 257 4946 F: 253 351
E: galeriebuchholz@t-online.de

**Galerie Giti Nourbakhsch**
Rosenthaler Straße 72
10119 Berlin Germany
T: [49 30] 4404 6781 F: 4404 6782
W: www.nourbakhsch.de

**Galerie Kamm**
Almstadtstraße 5
10119 Berlin
Germany
T: [49 30] 2838 6464 F: 2838 6464
E: galeriekamm@snafu.de
W: www.art-exchange-berlin.de/kamm

**Galerie M + R Fricke**
Linienstraße 109
10115 Berlin
Germany
T: [49 30] 283 5345 F: 285 8919
E: mandrfricke@compuserve.com

**Galerie Neu**
Phillip Straße 13
10115 Berlin
Germany
T: [49 30] 285 7550 F: 281 0085
E: galerie.neu@snafu.da

**Galerie Peter Kilchmann**
Limmatstrasse 270
8005 Zürich
Switzerland
T: [41 1] 440 3931 F: 440 3932

**Galerie Seitz & Partner**
Wielandstraße 34
10629 Berlin
Germany
T: [49 30] 8867 9041 F: 8867 9042

**Galerie Wohnmaschine**
Gipsstraße 3
10119 Berlin
Germany
T: [49 30] 3087 2015 F: 3087 2016
E: Wohnmasc@aol.com

**Galerie Zürcher**
56 rue Chapon
75003 Paris
France
T: [33 1] 42 72 82 20 F: 42 72 58 07
E: zurchergal@easynet.fr

**Galleria Marabini**
via Nosadella 45
40123 Bologna
Italy
T: [39 051] 6447 482 F: 6440 029
E: info@galleriamarabini.it
W: www.galleriamarabini.it

**Garry Simpson**
W: www.garrysimpson.com

**Gavin Brown's Enterprise**
436 West 15th Street
New York NY 10011
USA
T: [1 212] 627 5258 F: 627 5261
E: passerby@bway.net

**greengrassi**
39c Fitzroy Street
London W1T 6DY UK
T: [44 20] 7387 8747 F: 7388 3555

**Griedervonputtkamer Galerie**
Sophienstraße 88
10178 Berlin
Germany
T: [49 30] 2887 9380 F: 2887 9381
E: griedervonputtkamer@gmx.net

**h.a.l.**
Unit 5, Fourth Floor
11-13 Hatton Wall
London EC1N 8HX
UK
T: [44 20] 7831 5454 F: 7831 6441
W: www.hal-photography.co.uk

**Howard House**
2017 Second Avenue
Seattle WA 98121
USA
T: [1 206] 256 6399 F: 256 6392
E: billy@howardhouse.net

**Jack Tilton / Anna Kustera Gallery**
49 Greene Street
New York NY 10013
USA
T: [1 212] 941 1775 F: 941 1812
E: jtiltong@earthlink.net

**Jay Jopling / White Cube**
44 Duke Street
St. James's
London SW1Y 6DD
UK
T: [44 20] 7930 5373 F: 7930 9973
E: info@whitecube.com
W: www.whitecube.com

**Karyn Lovegrove Gallery**
6150 Wilshire Boulevard
Space 8
Los Angeles CA 90048
USA
T: [1 323] 525 1755 F: 525 1245
E: karyn@karynlovegrove.com
W: www.karynlovegrovegallery.com

**klosslondon.com**
T: [44 20] 7354 8568 F: 7359 2304

**Klosterfelde**
Zimmerstrasse 90/91
10117 Berlin
Germany
T: [49 30] 283 5305 F: 283 5306
E: klosterfelde@snafu.de
W: www.klosterfelde.de

**Kuckei + Kuckei**
Linienstraße 158 (Hof)
10115 Berlin
Germany
T: [49 30] 883 4354 F: 8868 3244

**Leila Méndez**
Aribau 271 6-3
08021 Barcelona
Spain
T: [34 93] 200 7453
E: leila@leilamendez.com
W: www.leilamendez.com

**Low**
9052 Santa Monica Boulevard
Los Angeles
CA 90069
USA
T: [1 310] 281 2691 F: 281 2692
E: low@lowlosangeles.com

**Magnum Photos**
5 Old Street
London EC1V 9HL
UK
T: [44 20] 7490 1771 F: 7608 0020
E: Magnum@magnumphotos.co.uk
W: www.magnumphotos.co.uk

**Mark Amerika**
E: mark.amerika@colorado.edu

**Maureen Paley Interim Art**
21 Herald Street
London E2 6JT
UK
T: [44 20] 7729 4112 F: 7729 4113
E: interim.art@virgin.net

**Max Protetch**
511 West 22nd Street
New York NY 10011
USA
T: [1 212] 633 6999 F: 691 4342
E: info@maxprotetch.com

**Mysterious Al**
E: al@mysteriousal.com
W: www.mysteriousal.com

**NEL Europe**
Ruysdaelstraat 92-94 HS
1071 XH Amsterdam
Netherlands
T: [31 20] 470 2944 F: 470 2945
E: ask@nel.nl
W: www.nel.nl

**NEL USA**
158 Lafayette Street
5th Floor
New York NY 10013
USA
T: [1 212] 925 1450 F: 925 6487
E: ask@nel.nl

**Network Photographers**
4 Nile Street
London N1 7ZZ
UK
T: [44 20] 7490 3633 F: 7490 3643
E: info@networkphotographers.com
W: www.networkphotographers.com

**Nicole Klagsbrun Gallery**
225 Lafayette Street
Room 608
New York NY 10012
USA
T: [1 212] 925 5157 F: 925 0759

**Nora Bibel**
Kopernikusstraße 15
10245 Berlin Germany
T: [49 30] 2966 8244 F: 2966 8244
E: nbibel@gmx.de

**Paschutan Buzari**
buzari@snafu.de

**Patrick Painter Gallery**
2525 Michigan Avenue
Unit B2
Santa Monica CA 90404
USA
T: [1 310] 264 5988 F: 264 5998
E: painterinc@hotmail.com

**Paula Cooper Gallery**
534 West 21st Street
New York NY 10011

USA
T: [1 212] 255 1105 F: 255 5156

**Photography Now Büro für Fotografie**
Invalidenstraße 115
101115 Berlin
Germany
T: [49 30] 615 1421 F: 615 1422
E: photography.now@t-online.de
W: www.photography-now.com

**Rhodes + Mann**
1a Fullwood's Mews
London N1 6BF
UK
T: [44 20] 7233 3074 F: 7233 3076
E: rhomann@dircon.co.uk

**Ronald Feldman Fine Arts**
31 Mercer Street
New York NY 10013
USA
T: [1 212] 226 3232 F: 941 1536

**Sabine Schründer**
Kopernikusstrasse 15
10245 Berlin
Germany
T: [49 172] 287 3507

**Schipper + Krome**
Auguststraße 91
10117 Berlin
Germany
T: [49 30] 2839 0139
F: 2839 0140
E: office@schipper-krome.com

**Sophie Dubosc**
T: [33 1] 42 64 24 29
M: [33 6] 82 39 47 27
E: dubosc@ensba.fr

**Stephen Friedman Gallery**
25-28 Old Burlington Street
London W1S 3AN UK
T: [44 20] 7494 1434 F: 7494 1431
E: info@stephenfriedman.com

**Taro Nasu Gallery**
1-8-13 Saga Koto-ku
Tokyo 135-0031
Japan
T: [81 3] 3630 7759 F: 3630 7759
E: taronasu@tkh.att.ne.jp

**The Garden**
Second Floor
57a Lant Street
London SE1 1QN
UK
T: [44 20] 7403 9400 F: 7357 9222

**White Cube²**
48 Hoxton Square
Shoreditch
London N1
UK
T: [44 20] 7749 7475
W: www.whitecube.com

**Z Photographic**
10 Adela Street
London W10 5BA
UK
T: [44 20] 8968 7700 F: 7968 7722

**Z Photographic**
476 Broome Street
New York NY 10013

USA
T: [1 212] 431 9222 F: 941 1320

**Zinc Gallery**
Skeppargatan 86
114 59 Stockholm
Sweden
T: [46 8] 662 3009 F: 662 3048
E: info@zincgallery.com
W: www.zincgallery.com

# DESIGN

**Åbäke**
Studio 1c/2
18-24 Shacklewell Lane
London E8 2EZ
UK
T & F: [44 20] 7249 2380
E: a.b.a.k.e@free.fr

**alias_gampermartino**
Unit 13c 20-30 Wild Rents
London SE1 4QG
UK
T & F: [44 20] 7407 7302
E: m.gamper@lycos.com

**Archirivolto**
via Martiri della Libertà 46
53034 Colle Val D'Elsa
Italy
T: [39 0577] 922 701 F: 923 025
E: archirivolto@cybermarket.it
W: www.archirivolto.it

**ASYL Design Inc**
#501, 29-17 Sakuragaoka-cho
Shibuya-ku
Tokyo 150-0031
Japan
T: [81 3] 5728 8288
E: info@asyl.co.jp
W: www.asyl.co.jp

**Beezlebug Bit**
1325 Howard Avenue
#524
Burlingame CA 94010
USA
T: [1 650] 615 6700
W: www.beezlebugbit.com

**Belief**
1832 Franklin Street
Santa Monica
CA 90404
USA
T: [1 310] 998 0099 F: 998 0066
E: graphics@belief.com
W: www.belief.com/exp/un02/main.html

**Bonaldo SpA**
via Straelle 3
35010 Villanova di Camposampiero
Italy
T: [39 049] 929 9011 F: 929 9000
E: bonaldo@bonaldo.it
W: www.bonaldo.it

**büro für form**
Hans-Sachs-Strasse 12
80469 München
Germany
T: [49 89] 2694 9000 F: 2694 9002
E: meet@buerofuerform.de
W: www.buerofuerform.de

**Cappellini SpA**
via Marconi 35
22060 Arosio
Italy
T: [39 031] 759 111 F: 763 322
E: info@cappellini.it
W: www.cappellini.it

**Christophe Pillet**
81 rue St. Maur
75011 Paris
France
T: [33 1] 48 06 78 31

**ClassiCon GmbH**
Perchtinger Strasse 8
81379 München
Germany
T: [49 89] 748 1330 F: 780 9996
E: info@classicon.com
W: www.classicon.com

**David design**
Stortorget 25
211 34 Malmö
Sweden
T: [46 40] 300 000 F: 300 050
E: info@david.se
W: www.david.se

**DED Associates**
Workstation
15 Paternoster Row
Sheffield S1 2BX
UK
T: [44 114] 249 3939 F: 249 3940
E: info@dedass.com
W: www.dedass.com

**Delapse**
PO Box 2509
Parklands
2121 Johannesburg
South Africa
T: [27 11] 507 3000
W: www.delapse.com

**Denis Santachiara**
Alzaia Naviglio Grande, 156
20144 Milano
Italy
E: desanta@libero.it

**Designbüro … Adam und Harborth**
Max Beer Strasse 25
10119 Berlin
Germany
T: [49 30] 3087 2074 F: 2838 7205
E: designbuero@snafu.de

**DesignDepot / [kAk) Magazine**
4 Smolensky Boulevard
Office 31
119034 Moscow
Russia

**Droog Design**
Sarphatikade 11
1017 WV Amsterdam
Netherlands
T: [31 20] 626 9809 F: 638 8828
E: info@droogdesign.nl
W: www.droogdesign.nl

**Elixirstudio / Blast Radius**
W: www.elixirstudio.com
E: arnaud@elixirstudio.com

**Fabio Novembre**
via Mecenate 76

20138 Milano
Italy
T: [39 02] 504 104
F: 502 375
E: fabio@novembre.it
W: www.novembre.it

**Fernkopie**
Schönhauser Allee 182
10119 Berlin
Germany
T: [49 30] 4405 3650
F: 4405 3651
E: fernkopie@snafu.de

**Flong**
E: golan@flong.com

**Flos SpA**
via Angelo Faini 2
25073 Bovezzo
Italy
T: [39 030] 24381 F: 271 1578
W: www.flos.it

**For Use**
Canisiusg. 13/16
1090 Wien
Austria
T: [43 1] 310 2572
F: 310 2572

**fork unstable media ost**
Wollinerstrasse 18/19
10435 Berlin
Germany
T: [49 30] 443 5070
F: 4435 0711
E: info@fork.de
W: www.fork.de

**Friendchip**
W: www.friendchip.com

**General Working Group**
3203 Glendale Boulevard
Los Angeles
CA 90039
USA
E: worker@generalworkinggroup.com
W: www.generalworkinggroup.com

**Graphic Thought Facility**
Unit 410
31 Clerkenwell Close
London EC1R 0AT
UK

**Harry & Camila Creators of Signs**
via G. Meda 43
20141 Milano
Italy
T: [39 02] 846 4141 F: 846 4141
E: harry.camila@flashnet.it

**Inflate**
11 Northburgh Street
London EC1V 0AN
UK
T: [44 20] 7251 5453 F: 7250 0311
E: info@inflate.co.uk
W: www.inflate.co.uk

**Ingo Maurer GmbH**
Kaiserstrasse 47
80801 München
Germany
T: [49 89] 381 6060 F: 3816 0620
W: www.ingo-maurer.com

**IMG SRC, INC.**
1F Chisinihouji 6 9 Ohinarutyou
Shibuya-ku
Tokyo 150-0045
Japan
T: [81 3] 5459 6464
E: info@imgsrc.co.jp

**Ippei Gyoubu**
3-40-22-201 Esaka Chou
Suita City
Osaka 564-0063
Japan
F: [81 6] 6821 0710

**Jérôme Olivet**
76 rue Beaubourg
75003 Paris
France
T & F: [33 1] 42 74 43 42
F: 42 74 43 42
E: jerome@jeromeolivet.com
W: www.jeromeolivet.com

**Karim Rashid Inc**
357 West 17th Street
New York NY 10011
USA
T: [1 212] 929 8657 F: 929 0247
E: office@karimrashid.com
W: www.karimrashid.com

**Linge Hansen**
Sankt Hans Gade 22 2.tv.
2200 København N
Denmark
T: [45 ] 35 35 22 68
E: linge@linge.dk
W: www.linge.dk

**Living World**
#501, 29-17 Sakuragaoka-cho
Shibuya-ku
Tokyo 150-0031
Japan
T: [81 3] 3461 6681
W: www.livingworld.net

**MetaDesign**
Bergmann Strasse 102
10961 Berlin
Germany
T: [49 30] 6957 9200
F: 6957 9222
E: mail@metadesign.de
W: www.metadesign.com

**MK12 Studios**
2016 Main Street
Kansas City
MO 64108
USA
T: [1 816] 931 2425
E: info@mk12.com
W: www.mk12.com

**Moccu**
Christburgerstrasse 46
10405 Berlin
Germany
T: [49 30] 4403 2984
F: 4373 9129
E: info@moccu.com
W: www.moccu.com

**Monica Förster**
Kyrkslingan 11
111 49 Stockholm
Sweden

**Moorhead & Moorhead**
00 Oanal Olreet #000
New York 10002
USA
W: www.moorheadandmoorhead.com

**Mori Building**
12-32 Akasaka
1-Chome
Minato-ku
Tokyo 107-6090
Japan
T: [81 3] 5562 8015
E: koho@mori.co.jp
W: www.mori.co.jp

**OFFECCT interiör ab**
Skövdevägen
PO Box 100
543 21 Tibro
Sweden
W: www.offecct.se

**Plan A**
Eskildsgade 34, 3.
1657 København V
Denmark
T: [45 ] 35 55 11 64
F: 35 55 11 64
E: anette@plana.nu
W: www.plana.nu/

**Rinzen**
E: they@rinzen.com
W: www.rmxxx.com.
W: www.rinzen.com

**Shift!**
W: www.shift.de

**Skop**
Gerichtstrasse 12/13
13347 Berlin
Germany
T: [49 30] 4660 4046 F: 4660 4045
E: skop@skop.com
W: www.skop.com

**Slowmotion**
10567 National Boulevard #3
Los Angeles CA 90034
USA
E: jeff_millerkc@hotmail.com

**Ständige Vertretung**
Oranienburger Strasse 87
10178 Berlin
Germany
T: [49 30] 3087 2818 F: 281 1241
E: info@staendige-vertretung.com
W: www.staendige-vertretung.com

**Studio Job**
Willemstraat 29 C
5611 HB Eindhoven
Netherlands
T: [31 40] 252 5458 F: 252 5463
E: info@studiojob.nl

**Studio Werner Aisslinger**
Lückhoffstrasse 24
14129 Berlin
Germany
T: [49 30] 3150 5400 F: 3150 5401
E: aisslinger@berlin.snafu.de
W: www.aisslinger.de

**Styling srl**
via dell'Industria 2
35010 Borgoricco

Italy
T: [00 049] 001 07 111. 901 0700
E: styling@styling.it
W: www.styling.it

**Transform Corporation**
House 201, 6-8-15 Minami Aoyama
Minato-ku
Tokyo 107-0062
Japan
T: [81 3] 3498 8141
E: info@transform.co.jp

**Wanders Wonders**
Jacob Catskade 35
1052 BT Amsterdam
Netherlands
T: [31 20] 422 1339
W: www.marcelwanders.nl

MOVING
IMAGE

**Academy Films**
16 West Central Street
London WC1 1JJ
UK
T: [44 20] 7395 4155 F: 7494 0348
E: sasha@academyfilms.com

**Blue Source Ltd**
The Fish Tank
Saga Centre
326 Kensal Road
London W10 5BZ
UK
T: [44 20] 7460 6020 F: 7460 6021
E: leigh.m@bluesource.com
W: www.bluesource.com

**Department M/
DoRo Produktion**
Leuschnerdamm 13
10999 Berlin
Germany
T: [49 30] 616 9210 F: 614 1877
E: dptm@berlin.doro.net
W: www.doro.net

**Harry Nash Productions**
27-29 Beak Street
London W1F 9RU
UK
T: [44 20] 7287 6700 F: 7287 6800
E: kateelson@harrynash.co.uk

**Marcus Bauer**
Markendorfer Strasse 26
13439 Berlin
Germany
E: agri@hdk-berlin.de

**Oil Factory**
Circus House
26 Little Portland Street
London W1N 5AF
UK
T: [44 20] 7255 6255 F: 7255 6277
E: toby@oilfctry.dircon.co.uk
W: www.oilfactory.com

**Partizan Midi Minuit**
10 rue Vivienne
75002 Paris
France
T: [33 1] 53 45 01 23

F: 53 45 01 24
E: charlotte.tepot@midi•minuit.fr

**Partizan Midi Minuit**
Brunswick Studios
7 Westbourne Grove Mews
London W11 2RU
UK
T: [44 20] 7792 8483 F: 7792 8870
E: dan.dickenson@partizan.com

**Propaganda Films**
16 West Central Street
London WC1A 1JJ
UK
T: [44 20] 7292 8787 F: 7287 1885
E: harriet@propaganda-europe.co.uk

**Propaganda Films**
940 N Mansfield Avenue
Hollywood
Los Angeles CA 90038
USA
T: [1 323] 802 7100
F: 463 7874

**Royal College of Art**
Kensington Gore
London SW7 2EU
UK
T: [44 20] 7590 4444
F: 7584 8217
W: www.rca.ac.uk

**RSA Films**
42-44 Beak Street
London W1R 3DA
UK
T: [44 20] 7437 7426 F: 7734 4978
E: cburnay@rsafilms.co.uk

**Trigger Happy Productions**
Rosenthaler Strasse 38
10178 Berlin
Germany
T: [49 30] 284 8970 F: 2848 9755
E: sandmann@triggerhappyproductions.com

**Unit9 Ltd**
43-44 Hoxton Square
London N1 6PB
UK
T: [44 20] 7613 3330 F: 7613 5085
E: tom@unit9.com
W: www.unit9.com

# SAPPI

Sappi is one of the leading paper producers in the world. Our speciality is making coated papers that are specifically designed for the production of annual reports, calendars, promotional brochures, catalogues, labels, posters, and high-quality books like the one you are reading. Our papers are manufactured in a range of finishes, with glossy, silk and matt surfaces to choose from, and a wide variety of weights, depending on the specific requirements of graphic designers, printers and customers.

In 1997, Sappi became the first global coated-fine-paper company with paper mills on three continents and a sales network covering almost every country in the world. This is a considerable achievement considering that up until the last decade, Sappi was purely a South African-based company that came into being in 1936, making paper from straw.

Today, Sappi is probably better known by the names of the most well-known coated-paper brands on the market, namely Magno, HannoArt, Uni, Royal, Somerset, Lustro, Strobe, and Empress, to name a few.

We are committed to providing the finest possible papers for our paper users. For almost a quarter of a century, we have been rewarding excellence in printing by means of the Sappi Printer of the Year Awards. Printers in every corner of the globe now participate in this contest, proving that they are committed to providing superior print to the market.

Since graphic designers play a decisive role in the specification of papers on which their creative designs are realised, we are dedicated to adding value to the design community by entering into partnership with the leading design website creativebase.com, and by establishing the 'Idea Exchange', a programme of facilitating idea generation, sharing and communication across the design and print community.

We believe that graphic designers are intrinsically designing for a better world. We know that many of them have great ideas that could raise the awareness of, and even funds for, worthy humanitarian causes that they feel strongly about. Too many of these ideas are not being realised due to the lack of funds made available to the organisations dedicated to these causes. With the introduction of the annual 'Ideas that Matter' initiative we are inviting graphic designers from around the world to apply for substantial grants from Sappi to realise these ideas and help society in a way they feel is important. Together with the graphic design community we can make a generous contribution to society.

In addition, we play our part in ensuring a sustainable future for generations to come. In manufacturing our paper and growing our trees, we manage the impact on the local environment by implementing internationally recognised environmental systems and certification. We care about air-emissions, waste-water treatment and water usage as well as noise levels. Our innovation in terms of oxygen bleaching and reduced chlorine usage is world renowned. Sappi contributes substantial funding to the World Wide Fund for Nature each year and has been awarded the Gold Panda Award in this regard. Manufacturing paper with care for its environmental impact is a primary concern within our operational policies.

Sappi will continue to grow as a company and as such will expand its operations and the availability of its papers more widely than ever before. We are ensuring that as we develop we continue to be focused on the technical performance requirements of printers and the ideas of graphic designers. We firmly believe that through a close relationship based on understanding, we can supply coated papers that contribute significantly to the visual appeal of printed ideas.

Two Sappi papers are used in ZOO 10. The Berlin feature is printed on 150 gsm HannoArt Gloss; the remainder of the publication is printed on 150 gsm Magno Matt Classic.

# BACK ISSUES

Each edition of ZOO forms part of a library of outstanding international creative talent. ZOO showcases the developments in the visual arts since the beginning of 1999, and provides an invaluable and permanent resource for research into the current and retrospective work of some of the world's most significant creative talent. Each issue includes over 360 pages of outstanding new creative work and special features.

From issue 03, ZOO also includes an hour-long DVD featuring moving-image work shown in the publication; from issue 07, the running time increases to 90 minutes.

To order back issues, please complete the order form enclosed with the issue, or order online from www.zooworld.net

For further information, please contact:
ZOO
245 Old Marylebone Road
London NW1 5QT, UK
T: [44 20] 7258 6900  F: [44 20] 7258 6901
W: www.zooworld.net
E: office@zooworld.net

**ZOO 01**  March 1999
Ambient Advertising /
Berlin Regeneration / Chris Ofili /
Cranbrook Academy of Art /
World Press Awards

**ZOO 02**  June 1999
Volkswagen / Zaha Hadid /
Walker Art Center /
Droog Design /
Japanese photography

**ZOO 03**  October 1999
DM9DDB / JVC Center, Guadalajara /
Venice Art Biennale /
Hussein Chalayan /
Network Photographers

**ZOO 04**  February 2000
@radical.media / Olympics architecture /
1999 Turner Prize / Stefan Sagmeister /
MoMA dot.jp internet project /
Magnum: *Our Turning World* exhibition

**ZOO 05**  May 2000
Absolut Vodka /
Alsop & Störmer /
William Kentridge /
John Maeda / Mario Testino

**ZOO 06**  August 2000
Cake / EXPO 2000 Hannover /
Whitney Biennial /
P.S.1 *Greater New York* exhibition /
Imaginary Forces / Tracey Moffatt

**ZOO 07**  November 2000
Laforet Harajuku /
Venice Architecture Biennale /
Nordic Art /
Jonathan Barnbrook

**ZOO 08**  April 2001
Los Angeles / Johnny Hardstaff /
*S, C, P, F... / fig-1 /
Me Company & Hussein Chalayan /
Dilly Gent / Cecil Balmond

**ZOO 09**  June 2001
Japanese Graphic Design / Paulo Sutch /
Tribute to Alighiero and Boetti /
Makoto Sei Watanabe / Paolo Roversi /
Spanish Graphic Design / French Directors